PROFIT, PIETY
AND THE PROFESSIONS
IN LATER MEDIEVAL
ENGLAND

LF

9

9

2011

PROFIT, PIETY
AND THE PROFESSIONS
IN LATER MEDIEVAL
ENGLAND

Edited by
MICHAEL HICKS

ALAN SUTTON

First published in the United Kingdom in 1990
Alan Sutton Publishing Limited, Brunswick Road, Gloucester

First published in the United States of America in 1990
Alan Sutton Publishing Inc., Wolfeboro Falls, NH 03896–0848

British Library Cataloguing in Publication Data

Profit, piety and the professions in later medieval England.
  1. England, history
  I. Hicks, M.A. (Michael A.)
  942

  ISBN 0-86299-643-0

Library of Congress Cataloging in Publication Data applied for

Jacket illustration: To Masters of the Bench of the Inner Temple
(*A.C. Cooper Ltd*).

Typesetting and origination by
Alan Sutton Publishing Limited, Gloucester
Printed in Great Britain by
Dotesios Printers Limited

Contents

Abbreviations

BBCS	*Bulletin of the Board of Celtic Studies*
BI	Borthwick Institute, York
BIHR	*Bulletin of the Institute of Historical Research*
BJRL	*Bulletin of the John Rylands Library*
BP	Borthwick Paper
BRCU	A.B. Emden, *Biographical Register of the University of Cambridge to AD 1500* (Cambridge 1963)
BROU	A.B. Emden *Biographical Register of the University of Oxford* (3 vols Oxford 1959–61)
Bristol GRB	*Great Red Book of Bristol* (3 vols Bristol Record Society 1931–51).
Bristol LRB	*Little Red Book of Bristol*, F.B. Bickley (ed.), (2 vols Bristol 1900)
CAD	*Catalogue of Ancient Deeds* (HMSO)
CCR	*Calendar of the Close Rolls* (HMSO)
CFR	*Calendar of the Fine Rolls* (HMSO)
Chaucer's Works	G. Chaucer, *The Canterbury Tales*, F.N. Robinson (ed.), (Oxford 1978)
CIPM	*Calendar of Inquisitions post mortem* (HMSO)
CIPM (RC)	*Calendarium Inquisitionum post mortem sive Escaetarum* (4 vols Record Commission 1806–28)
Clough, Profession	*Profession, Vocation and Culture in Later Medieval England*, C.H. Clough (ed.), (Liverpool 1982)
CPL	*Calendar of Papal Letters* (HMSO)
CPP	*Church, Politics, and Patronage in England and France in the Fifteenth Century*, R.B. Dobson (ed.), (Gloucester 1984)
CPR	*Calendar of the Patent Rolls* (HMSO)
CSPM	*Calendar of State Papers Milanese* (HMSO)
Devon, *Issues*	F. Devon, *Issues of the Exchequer, Henry III to Henry VI* (Record Commission 1835)
DKR	*Reports of the Deputy Keepers of the Public Record Office*
DNB	*Dictionary of National Biography*
EcHR	*Economic History Review*
EHR	*English Historical Review*
Foedera	*Foedera, Conventiones, Literae, et cujuscunque genera Acta*, T. Rymer (ed.), (20 vols 1727–35)

GC	*Great Chronicle of London*, A.H. Thomas and I.D. Thornley (eds), (1938)
GEC	*Complete Peerage of England*, H.V. Gibbs and others (eds), (13 vols 1910–59)
GMR	Guildford Muniment Room
HMC	Historic Manuscripts Commission
HJ	*Historical Journal*
Ives, *Common Lawyers*	E.W. Ives, *The Common Lawyers in Pre-Reformation England* (Cambridge 1983)
JEH	*Journal of Ecclesiastical History*
LQR	*Law Quarterly Review*
McFarlane, *Nobility*	K.B. McFarlane, *Nobility of Later Medieval England* (Oxford 1973)
MS, MSS	Manuscript(s)
NH	*Northern History*
Paston L&P	*Paston Letters and Papers of the Fifteenth Century*, N. Davis (ed.), (2 vols Oxford 1971–6)
Paston Letters	*The Paston Letters*, J. Gairdner (ed.), (6 vols 1904)
POPC	*Proceedings and Ordinances of the Privy Council of England 1386–1542*, N.H. Nicolas (ed.), (7 vols Record Commission 1834–7)
PRO	Public Record Office
RO	Record Office
RP	*Rotuli Parliamentorum* (6 vols Record Commission 1832)
RS	Rolls Series
SJC	St John's College, Cambridge
Steel, *Receipt*	A.B. Steel, *The Receipt of the Exchequer 1377–1485* (Cambridge 1954)
SR	*Statutes of the Realm* (11 vols Record Commission 1810–28)
TBGAS	*Transactions of the Bristol and Gloucestershire Archaeological Society*
TRHS	*Transactions of the Royal Historical Society*
VCH	*Victoria County History*
WAM	Westminster Abbey Manuscript
YAJ	*Yorkshire Archaeological Journal*
YB	*Year Book 20 Edward I; 30 & 31 Edward I; 32 & 33 Edward I*, A.J. Horwood (ed.), (3 vols RS 1861–4); *Les Reportes des cases en les ans des Roys Edward IV, Richard III, etc.*, J. Maynard (ed.), (1879)

Public Record Office Call-Numbers

All documents in the Public Record Office are cited by their PRO call numbers only. These are identified below.

C 1 Early Chancery Proceedings
C 47 Chancery Miscellanea
C 54 Chancery, Close Rolls
C 61 Chancery, Gascon Rolls
C 81 Chancery, Warrants for the Great Seal, Series I
C 82 Chancery, Warrants for the Great Seal, Series II
C 137 Chancery, Inquisitions Post Mortem, Henry IV
C 139 Chancery, Inquisitions Post Mortem, Henry VI
C 141 Chancery, Inquisitions Post Mortem, Richard III
C 142 Chancery, Inquisitions Post Mortem, Series II
C 145 Chancery, Inquisitions Miscellaneous
C 146 Chancery, Ancient Deeds, Series C
C 219 Chancery, Parliamentary Writs
C 237 Chancery, Tower and Rolls Chapel Series, Bails on Special Pardons
C 255 Chancery, Tower and Rolls Chapel Series, Miscellaneous Files and Writs
CP 25(1) Common Pleas, Feet of Fines, Series I
CP 26 Common Pleas, Notes of Fines
CP 40 Common Pleas, De Banco Rolls
DL 28 Duchy of Lancaster, Accounts Various
DL 29 Duchy of Lancaster, Ministers' Accounts
DL 37 Duchy of Lancaster, Chancery Rolls
E 28 Exchequer, T(reasury of) R(eceipt), Council and Privy Seal
E 36 Exchequer, T.R., Miscellaneous Books
E 40 Exchequer, T.R., Deeds, Series A
E 101 Exchequer, K(ing's) R(emembrancer), Accounts Various
E 122 Exchequer, K.R., Customs Accounts
E 136 Exchequer, K.R., Escheators' Accounts
E 149 Exchequer, K.R., Inquisitions Post Mortem, Series I
E 150 Exchequer, K.R., Inquisitions Post Mortem, Series II
E 152 Exchequer, K.R., Enrolled Inquisitions
E 154 Exchequer, K.R., Inventories of Goods and Chattels
E 159 Exchequer, K.R., Memoranda Rolls
E 163 Exchequer, K.R., Miscellanea
E 179 Exchequer, K.R., Subsidy Rolls

E 199 Exchequer, K.R., Sheriffs' Seizures
E 202 Exchequer, K.R., Writs
E 210 Exchequer, K.R., Ancient Deeds, Series D
E 314 Exchequer, A(ugmentations) O(ffice), Miscellanea
E 326 Exchequer, A.O., Ancient Deeds, Series B
E 327 Exchequer, A.O., Ancient Deeds, Series BX
E 328 Exchequer, A.O., Ancient Deeds, Series BB
E 364 Exchequer, L(ord) T(reasurer's) R(emembrancer), Foreign Rolls
E 368 Exchequer, L.T.R., Memoranda Rolls
E 383 Exchequer, L.T.R., Writs
E 401 Exchequer, Exchequer of Receipt, Receipt Rolls
E 403 Exchequer, Exchequer of Receipt, Issue Rolls
E 404 Exchequer, Exchequer of Receipt, Warrants for Issues
E 405 Exchequer, Exchequer of Receipt, Tellers' Rolls
KB 27 King's Bench, Coram Rege Rolls
KB 29 King's Bench, Controlment Rolls
PROB 11 Prerogative Court of Canterbury, Register Copy Wills
PSO 1 Privy Seal Office, Warrants, Series I
PSO 2 Privy Seal Office, Warrants, Series II
REQ 1 Court of Requests, Miscellaneous Books
REQ 2 Court of Requests, Proceedings
SC 1 Special Collections, Ancient Correspondence
SC 2 Special Collections, Court Rolls
SC 6 Special Collections, Ministers' and Receivers' Accounts
SC 8 Special Collections, Ancient Petitions
SC 11 Special Collections, Rentals and Surveys, Rolls
SC 12 Special Collections, Rentals and Surveys, Portfolios
STAC 2 Court of Star Chamber, Proceedings, Henry VIII

Introduction

These papers are the proceedings of the conference on Recent Research in Fifteenth-Century English History that I organized at King Alfred's College, Winchester on 10–12 July 1987. This was the eleventh such conference and the tenth to produce a volume of conference papers. These collections partly compensate for the absence of a late medieval journal. Barring the first, all have been published by Alan Sutton Publishing of Gloucester, [1] which has also served late medievalists well through its work for the Richard III Society, its monographs and its reprints of sources. It is to Suttons that we owe this volume.

The first conference at Cardiff in 1970 inspired others at Bristol (1973), Sheffield (1976), abortively, at Oxford, and regularly since 1978. During the 1980s there evolved two cycles held in alternate years, a 'senior' cycle and a 'junior' one. 'Senior' conferences are for established academics and treat a particular theme, as at York in 1982 (The Church), Nottingham (1984: Gentry), Glasgow (1986: Towns) and Liverpool (1988: The Economy). 'Junior' conferences are opportunities for current and recent research students to meet and give papers. Bristol (1978), Swansea (1979), Reading (1983), Keele (1985), Winchester (1987) and Manchester (1989) are of this type. Although contributors to 'junior' conferences are generally much less experienced and have tended perhaps to overlook the wider context and significance of their work, their assemblies and the resultant volumes are just as valuable. Only postgraduates can now undertake the protracted pioneering research that late medieval history demands and it is therefore they who have most new information and ideas to impart.

Winchester '87 was a 'junior' conference and as such imposed particular constraints on its organizer. First of all, 'junior' conferences are by definition for the inexperienced, for those with limited practice at researching, writing, and public speaking. Hence the low-points on previous occasions. It is hard indeed to select the winners from those without track-records, particularly when a subsidiary aim is to bring together a wide range of interests and to include researchers from less fashionable centres. Research students' primary duty is to present their findings as a thesis and it is therefore unreasonable to impose on them strict word-limits, to direct their choice of subject or approach, or to expect an immediately appropriate lecturing style. Research students are generally hard-up. They depend either on grants or social security or are part-time historians in 9 a.m. to 5 p.m. employment elsewhere. 'Junior' conferences are therefore low-cost and confined to a weekend (Friday evening to Sunday lunch), yet they characteristically contain more papers than the relatively relaxed 'senior' conferences. Inevitably their work needs more editing than those by the more practised senior performers.

Earlier gatherings have set a pattern that overcomes many of these difficulties. First of all, 'junior' conferences focus on seminars about two or more communications on a single theme. These tax only the literary and conversational expertise of the authors and spare them (and hence their audience) any oratorical experiments. At Winchester three seminars featured eight communications: on Piety (Dr Burgess, Mr Wood); on Noble Profit (Dr Vale, Dr Stansfield, Dr Clark); and on the Professions (Mr Beilby, Dr Ramsay, Dr Rawcliffe). Four papers that resisted reduction to a theme by Dr Virgoe, Dr Goldberg, Dr Yates and Mr Griffiths became lectures. They proved a happy selection. Contributors came not just from the universities of Oxford, Cambridge and London, but from York and Swansea, Aberystwyth and Exeter, East Anglia and Keele. The programme attracted sixty delegates, some of them eminent and many of them postgraduates, and went off without an obvious hitch. It was successful as a social reunion, as an academic forum for the exchange of ideas and as an opportunity for relative newcomers to display their wares. All the contributors emerged with great credit.

Collected papers similarly fulfil academic and promotional functions. The expectation of publication helps to shape the programme for the conference. Thirteen papers were commissioned, of which twelve actually materialized – Mr Duthie was the odd man out – and nine were presented for publication. The missing three are: Dr Carole Rawcliffe's 'The Profits of Practice: The Financial and Social Rise of the Medical Profession in the 14th and 15th Centuries'; Dr Martin Yates's 'The Papal Penitentiary as a Source for Late Medieval Ecclesiastical History'; and Mr Robert Wood's 'London and Bury St Edmunds: A Comparative Study in Urban Piety in the 14th and 15th Centuries'. This book would be stronger if they were included. Fortunately the other nine make a worthwhile volume and their departures left space for the inclusion of Miss Margaret Condon's long awaited paper on the profits of office of Reynold Bray. This volume now contains items by three mature historians (Dr Virgoe, Dr Clark, and Miss Condon) and seven by younger scholars, several of whom (Dr Burgess, Dr Goldberg, Mr Griffiths, Dr Ramsay) have also published extensively elsewhere. Sadly only Dr Goldberg has so far secured a permanent appointment appropriate to his talents. Several others have taken employment outside academia and without this outlet their work might have remained relatively inaccessible in their theses.

The quality of the papers is unusually high: there are no lame-ducks here. What invigorating new blood the universities are missing! The topics treated are mainstream concerns for the 1980s. Old-fashioned political history is treated only by Mr Griffiths – superbly, admittedly. The other papers treat five major themes currently preoccupying historians and destined to be the growth areas of the future: pre-Reformation piety; the profits of office, war, and expertise; the rise of the professions; the county community; and women's history. Naturally they contribute substantially to our knowledge in all these areas, for the standard of research is excellent, but they do much more than that. Always precise and technical and hence perhaps not immediately accessible, medieval history is becoming yet more specialist as the statistics, the methodology, and the terminology of the social sciences make themselves felt. These papers register these developments – they are, after all, at the forefront of historical advance – yet all are written clearly and lucidly in language that ordinary people can understand. None are so preoccupied with their minutiae and originality that they lack a sense of proportion or fail to appreciate and *explain* why their work matters. Surely seldom can so many relatively inexperienced historians have sought to generalize about their work? *Apart from* making genuine and important contributions to our knowledge, they also introduce their subjects to the uninitiated reader (not least through their bibliographies), and offer guidance for further reading. In short, these papers and this volume are not just for the specialist researchers, though they will find them essential. They are also invaluable teaching tools, for use by undergraduates and by sixth formers. And they are a pleasure to read.

Although inevitably disparate in contents, this book is thus united by the quality of its components, by the accessible way in which they are addressed, by the relevance of the chosen topics to our modern concerns, and by a shared belief in the value of meticulous research for answering large questions. As we shall see later, there is also a shared search for the ideas, conventions and principles that shaped medieval behaviour.

Dr Virgoe's keynote paper argues that county communities *did* indeed exist in late-medieval England. Against a backcloth of early modern and medieval county studies, he examines the use of the terms 'country', 'county' and 'shire' in the Paston Letters and the composition of attestors to indentures of election. He concludes that 'county-mindedness' *did* exist and that its prime expression, county politics, involved those *below* the rank of gentleman. His conclusions in each case *may* relate only to Norfolk or to East Anglia, for political patterns varied from county to county, and perhaps also over time according to the ebb and flow of magnate power. Rather than moving from noble dominance to county community, Lancashire in the mid-fifteenth century and Norfolk fifty years later may have fallen under the sway of the Stanleys and Howards respectively. Some time, of course, bastard feudal power finally disappeared, but when? 1485, 1570 or 1640? And when did it cease to be possible or to appear desirable to reconstruct it? And how independent were the yeomen and franklins who attested East Anglian indentures in the lifetime of Dr Richmond's politically uncommitted John Hopton?[2]

Dr Burgess' paper is just as wide-ranging, fundamental and provocative. Wills, he points out, are the inevitable source for late-medieval piety, because they are both abundant and individual in content. Often, however, they mislead: because they record only part of the testator's religious activity (and a variable part), ignore religious activity during life (and the most important part of it), and because they depend on *unwritten* rules that are nowhere explained and have to be deduced. His points are convincingly demonstrated from Bristol evidence and explored with reference to concrete examples, such as widows and minors. Wills wholly omit the communal and reciprocal elements in late-medieval piety. His conventions, like those of Dr Fleming for Kent [3] and Virgoe's conclusions mentioned above, *may* be geographically restricted, but his conclusions are not. Peter Heath's depiction of the late-medieval laity of Hull as religiously 'insular, inert, shallow, untouched by new devotions, perfunctory almost in the new ones' is, Burgess points out, 'simply the testamentary impression'; he might have added that it conflicts both with the rich variety of Mrs Kermode's work[4] *and* ignores the chantry deeds and gild accounts that make Hull, like Bristol, a place where the conventions *can* be reconstructed. Yet wills are bound to be used and those who use them may take comfort that they apparently *do* faithfully reflect the religion of testators *in life* as well as at death, albeit only for the narrow range of theological belief that wills portray. By examining the conventions and expanding their scope, Burgess has changed the meaning of conventional piety and shown how it can influence action. That people conformed to convention does not, however, tell us how much they *understood* or how intense was their religious feeling. Were the exceptional figures, such as Margaret Hungerford or William Canynges, exceptional only in degree or in kind? How far can the examples of them or other well-documented individuals be used to generalize for those for whom we have only the wills?

Bar a few exceptional examples, medieval women were subjected to male dominance (fathers, husbands, brothers), omitted from the records, and cannot be studied. So runs the orthodox wisdom. But in today's world of sexual equality people (even men) want to study women and are finding the means to do so. Dr Goldberg's paper examines rural women's employment through the medium of the Ricardian poll-taxes and demonstrates that many women were indeed independently employed after the

Black Death outside the home. More than that, he finds evidence supporting the existence of the West European marriage pattern, correlates variations in servanthood and the sex ratio to the nature of the community and communal change, and demonstrates triumphantly that even such an interim (!) statement ties this understudied 'group' into the mainstream of late-medieval life and developments.

The fourth paper stands somewhat apart and appears despite the author's wishes in response to popular acclaim. W.R.M. Griffiths treats the future Henry V and Wales with a precision (and elegance) never before achieved. What Henry learnt was not so much tactics and strategy as the financial and administrative running of a war: 'not so much the art of war *per se* as the art of war management'. And that, Mr Griffiths argues, surely correctly, helps explain Henry's military success as King. Griffiths' careful and critical paper adds to the burgeoning debate about Henry V, as Dr Allmand's new life is poised to join the recent works of K.B. McFarlane, G.L. Harriss and T.B. Pugh.[5] It does so moreover in a more accessible place, for non-Welshmen at least, than the *Bulletin of the Board of Celtic Studies!*

What is a profession? Taking Dr Ramsay's criteria of 'a clearly defined and delimited membership with a corporate identity and a clear detachment from the laity', there were clearly no professions in the later middle ages. In the early modern period there were some and indeed we have good recent books on the law and the clergy in the late sixteenth and seventeenth centuries.[6] Working on a slightly earlier period and straddling the medieval/early modern divide, J.H. Baker and E.W. Ives have made important contributions, again on the law.[7] For the medieval pre-history of the professions an important stage was marked by the publication of Professor Myers's *festschrift* in 1982, which contained papers on central and local bureaucracy, the civil and common lawyers, and the schoolmasters.[8] An obvious omission was medicine: hence Dr Rawcliffe's paper to the 1987 conference. Several research students are working on the law and three have contributed papers, which dovetail neatly and provide insights to the different stages in its development.

As laymen rather than clerics, the two Scrope chief justices of the early fourteenth century mark a new departure. As Dr Vale shows, it was their indispensable expertise that enabled them to ride out successive political crises. Yet their duties were not purely legal, taking in diplomacy and estate management, and much of their time was spent on (and much of their income derived from) work for other employers. By the early fifteenth century, Dr Ramsay finds that there were more specialist experts in the central courts, but still no legal profession. Many so-called lawyers working at Westminster and elsewhere had not been at the inns of court. The development of the inns as training grounds and communal facilities came later in the century and coincided with a growth in the expertise required for the central courts and the embryonic separation of central and provincial practitioners. Trained lawyers ousted mere clerks from the administrative offices in the courts about the same time as civil lawyers took over the running of the court of Chancery and only a little later than Professor Storey's 'gentlemen-bureaucrats' invaded the royal writing office. Civilians arrived only in the mid-fifteenth century, a hundred years after the origins of Chancery as a court. Their appearance signalled, as Mr Beilby convincingly shows, the transformation of Chancery into a genuine court of equity. Hitherto involving merely 'the subjective ruling of the chancellor based, not on precedent, but on the circumstances of each case', Chancery came to rely on the doctrine of conscience and natural law administered by university-trained civil lawyers, particularly in the growth areas of enfeoffment to use and mercantile contract. Formerly confined to the legal margins, the courts of chivalry and Admiralty, civil lawyers moved onto more lucrative employment in Chancery, took over the archiepiscopal court of arches, organized themselves at Doctors' Commons, and came to represent a genuine alternative to the common law.

The emergence of professional expertise brought changes in the law, as civil lawyers and, somewhat later, common lawyers devised new remedies, but specialization happened initially in response to demand, as clients including the crown increasingly called for knowledge, ingenuity and skill that general bureaucrats could not provide. Legal practice became more exclusive. For the experts themselves it brought monetary gain, a corporate image, pride and coherence, and enhanced status both for the profession and for its members. Whereas under Richard II a lawyer could not be a gentleman, so it was alleged, and the term lawyer carried unattractive connotations to be avoided, by 1500 many people only marginally engaged in legal work adopted the description as a means to financial and social advancement. The experts themselves were not numerous: at the central courts of common law no more than fifty apprentices-at-law in 1518, when only thirty-seven were resident, and only 130 attorneys in 1480, when many scarcely visited the metropolis. That the experts were so few forced not just the crown but private individuals to employ them in many different capacities, so that even the best pleaders, like Thomas Keble, undertook conveyancing and much general business. Inevitably common lawyers and civilians worked together on diplomatic missions, local commissions, baronial councils, and on arbitration panels, on which Mr Beilby contributes significantly to the modern debate.[9] *Perhaps* they self-consciously separated their different functions, but probably they did not. Lawyers did not see their 'other work' as detracting from their 'primary work' in the central courts – what a lot of present-minded assumptions are crammed into this sentence! – but saw it as complementary. People, not institutions, mattered, at least to those within the charmed circle of trained lawyers. To those outside it, notably potential clients, a training to master abstruse technicalities and a professional organization, the obvious marks of merit, restricted the scope for good service (and hence for patronage and employment) to the experts. It also raised the costs, the rewards, and the status of such practitioners.

Then, as now, there was no money in the academic profession and relatively little in medicine, but even mediocre merchants, lawyers and bureaucrats could live very well. Status went with land, however, and the upwardly mobile inevitably invested their profits in it. This is fortunate indeed for the historian, since the evidence of actual earnings (and, indeed, expenses) is always seriously deficient. This is just as true of Dr Vale's two Scrope chief justices, of Miss Condon's Reynold Bray, of Dr Stansfield's John Holland, and even of Dr Clark's Lord Treasurer Bourgchier. Legitimate income can generally be traced, but that was never a source of great profit comparable with the multiple retaining fees, bribes and interest on loans about which we know so little. The lands of the Scropes and Bray, however, are concrete evidence of the profit that *must* have been made. But money alone was not everything: status mattered too, the status of high office and intimacy with the King for Holland and Bourgchier, of local landowning and higher rank for the Scropes and Bray, though the latter, like the Scropes two centuries earlier, found that rank lagged well behind the means to support it.

Generalizations depend on detailed examples and we have not yet sufficient of these to venture confident generalizations about the profits of the law, war and office in the later middle ages, though it is obvious that at all times some (how many?) did very well from each. We have clear warnings enough against speculation in the inconclusive example-swapping of the Gentry Controversy and in the debate on the costs of the Hundred Years War of K.B. McFarlane and M.M. Postan. As always, more case-studies are needed, and here we have four. All follow McFarlane in starting from their subjects' known material and familial background and then analyze what changed. Dr Vale's discussion of her pitifully sparse and miscellaneous information seems superficially most simple of the four, but her strict application of chronology and context and her careful distinction between knowledge and surmise produces an interpretation that we can confidently accept and which outlines where profit lay: evidently as much at the bar and in private service, even in the early fourteenth century, as on the bench. More speculatively, Dr Stansfield contributes directly to the McFarlane–Postan debate with only the second full-scale career study so far attempted. Here the direct evidence is least conclusive, but John Holland's military commitments are made the central theme of his whole career and shape the subsequent fortunes and even the destruction of his family. Public service is also explored in Dr Clark's comprehensive and innovative paper, which not only illuminates the rewards of the treasurership at this date, but contemporary standards of public morality and responsibility as well. Finally, Miss Condon establishes the territorial gains of Henry VII's most trustworthy adviser even without the sources we generally take for granted. Each paper, in short, has much to tell us about *how* to study such topics that future researchers would be wise to take to heart. Moreover, all have added to McFarlane's oversimplified financial calculations a non-monetary balance of account, which makes allowance for the re-ordering of priorities, the political risks, the distractions from family and estate, and the scope for social-climbing that each career structure offered. Quality of life involves more than the cynical pursuit of wealth and other considerations often determined people's activities in the past, just as it does today.

'What this paper has tried to do', Dr Stansfield writes, 'is to set John Holland's career within the context of the French war and to show what a dominating and conditioning factor the war was for him'. This the author achieves. But what does he mean by 'conditioning factor'? Apart from the indirect repercussions of war experienced by everybody, Holland was affected directly by his vicissitudes as a participant. But why did he participate – and why *continue* to participate – at the expense of his financial and other interests? Undoubtedly he was under pressure to serve, but such pressure was not irresistible, for others did not. Why Holland went on fighting, why war was such 'a dominating and conditioning factor' for *him* and not others, is not explicable simply by potential profit or necessity, but by his personal choice. We need an *intellectual* explanation for that choice. What were Holland's motives? Even if, as Dr Stansfield says, 'John Holland was not always so calculating about his commitment', that indicates merely that we should be looking for *unconscious* motives or conditioning factors rather than deliberate and self-conscious decisions. What were they: a commitment to the Lancastrian cause, belief in the just war, personal enthusiasm for war, a military upbringing, the values of chivalry, the desire for personal renown or for prestigious office? And why did they take precedence over such conventional priorities as the integrity of his inheritance, the perpetuation of his lineage, the consolidation and management of his estates, local aggrandisement, and personal profit? We do not know, for the evidence *for Holland* is lacking, but it is these motives that explain the military theme of his career.

For the historian, wrote R.G. Collingwood, 'The cause of the event . . . means the thought in the mind of the person by whose agency the event came about.' 'Historical processes', he wrote, 'are in reality processes of action determined by a thought . . .' [10] Similarly Christopher Hill observed that 'Ideas were all important for the individuals which they impelled into action.'[11] Of course, they cannot be seen in isolation. John Holland could not have pursued his military career (or not *that military career*) had England not been at war with France. But, continues Hill,

> the historian must attach equal importance to the circumstances that gave these ideas their chance. Revolutions are not made without ideas, but they are not made by intellectuals. Steam is essential to driving a railway engine; but neither a locomotive nor a permanent way can be made out of steam.[12]

Late medievalists are not likely to ignore the circumstances, the context in which these ideas operated. That is not the danger. The danger – or rather the reality – is that we exalt the circumstances to the point where the ideas themselves are wholly discounted and where the *intellectual context* is ignored. Seldom, indeed, have we accorded ideas *equal* importance to circumstances, as Hill recommends. Very recently Professor Lander condemned late-medieval politics as not even 'to some extent tempered by principles'.[13] Perhaps. But Hill was not talking of political ideals and principles so much as ideas, not necessarily political in themselves, that affected political behaviour. Such ideas, conscious, unconscious and subconscious, embrace the whole range of values, standards, attitudes, conventions, customs, expectations and assumptions that we all carry around in our heads. This is why historians of past periods need to eschew present-day assumptions and understand the past on its own terms. And this volume shows us in many ways where and how to undertake it.

There are, of course, many precedents for such an approach. Particularly well-known are the efforts of Professor Tillyard and his successors to identify the commonplaces that feature in Shakespeare's plays.[14] Dr Harriss has demonstrated the continuing application of the doctrine of necessity to royal finance.[15] E.P. Thompson's work on eighteenth-century grain riots has been used to explain popular rebellion in the later middle ages too.[16] K.B. McFarlane's own classic paper on 'Bastard Feudalism' laid bare the assumptions on which medieval politics rested.[17] McFarlane again and Dr Keen have demonstrated the relevance to actual warfare of the law of arms.[18] The list is endless.

Religious practice changed little in the late middle ages, writes Dr Burgess. Its

> very stability . . . fostered powerful conventions: for many piety could depend on conventions so well-established that neither prescription nor

explanation were necessary. With the passage of time, these conventions had been dovetailed with perceived duties towards parish, family and associates, and, to labour the point, operated in the absence of written instructions.

Similarly, Dr Goldberg's paper assumes and justifies the existence in late medieval England of the Western European family, with its conventions of the nuclear family, late age of marriage, premarital chastity and life-cycle service, which Professor Laslett and others have demonstrated to be characteristic of early modern England.[19] Re-examining the subject, Dr Alan Macfarlane has shown how these interconnected characteristics are *cultural*, rather than natural or biological. They are distinctive features of our culture, civilization or society, different from what occurs in many other cultures, and are thus a *product* of our society and subject to change, as indeed they have.[20] Many other conventions, assumptions, standards, values and conventions treated in this volume are also *cultural* in this sense. This is true of the the the law, as Mr Beilby reminds us. It is true of the English language, which evolves with use and whose nuances and connotations Dr Virgoe explores to reveal county-mindedness as a source of social cohesion and pride. Dr Ramsay identifies a new-found loyalty to the inns of court and pride in them, which instilled in common lawyers a sense of common purpose, common professional standards and hence practices. Dr Clark explores the distinction contemporaries made between *acceptable* standards of public morality and corruption, a distinction quite different from our own criteria and perhaps also from those of the Elizabethans and Jacobeans.[21] Holland lived above his income at the standard deemed appropriate to an earl and even (if Dr Stansfield's interpretation is correct) sold the marriage of his son rather than curtail the extravagant lifestyle expected of him and on which his port, worship or prestige depended. The Scropes and Bray invested their money in land, not primarily as a source of income or as a secure investment, but to win the status that went with land. However unusual in their expertise and upward mobility, they accepted the conventional equations between land and status, status and display, and sought to emulate them. Most people most of the time accept the conventions of their age and dissent can only be understood in the context of their society.[22] Conduct was conditioned in so many ways by economic, social, political or religious conventions and only afterwards need we consider ideals such as lineage and honour, allegiance, dynasticism or heresy. Political principles *may* have played little part in politics, but contemporary values, standards, expectations and assumptions shaped not just politics, but all other walks of life. Allowing for geographical and social variations – for dominant v plebeian ideology – there is a wealth of non-material influences to consider.

To understand why medieval people act, we now need only to identify the relevant conventions. So to elevate the role of convention, however, brings us close to Jacob Burckhardt's denial of individuality to medieval people, to Peter Heath's inert Hull laity, and to the pre-programmed Hastings retainers ridiculed by Dr Richmond.[23] Only the exceptional appears individual and can be differentiated or discussed. What is missing here is any sense of the strength or intensity of the thoughts and feelings that determined action. Here, perhaps, I may be charged with a concern for events most appropriate to the historian of the élite, politics, or of the biographer, and strictly irrelevant to those concerned with structures, long-term processes or the masses. Yet surely ordinary people have always been confronted with choices every day and it is the sum of such routine decisions that generate long-term change. For change does occur. Population movements, for example, insofar as they depend on shifts in fertility, imply changes in conventions governing marriage and procreation, perhaps themselves (as Dr Goldberg suggests) shaped by alterations in the material world. Why do some conventions prevail over others, so that, for instance, feudalism disappears, county-mindedness grows, and East Anglian yeomen vote in shire elections? Hence there is a continuing role for the context and circumstances that allows us in select cases to deduce what the conventions were, to study their collision, to test (as McFarlane did) their strength in particular circumstances and to chart the evolution of ideas and the structures, institutions and processes that they inform. All of which these papers do. I recommend them wholeheartedly to you and hope that you learn as much from them as I have done.

Michael Hicks

Notes

1. *Fifteenth Century England, 1399–1509: Studies in Politics and Society*, S.B. Chrimes, C.D. Ross and R.A. Griffiths (eds), (Manchester 1972). Those published by Alan Sutton Publishing are: *The Crown and Local Communities in England and France in the Fifteenth Century*, J.R.L. Highfield and R.I. Jeffs (eds), (Gloucester 1981); *Patronage, Pedigree and Power in Later Medieval England*, C.D. Ross (ed.), (Gloucester 1979); *Patronage, The Crown, and the Provinces in Later Medieval England*, R.A.Griffiths (ed.), (Gloucester 1981); *Church, Politics, and Patronage in England and France in the Fifteenth Century*, R.B. Dobson (ed.), (Gloucester 1984), henceforth CPP; *Property and Politics: Essays in Later Medieval English History*, A.J. Pollard (ed.), (Gloucester 1984); *The Gentry and Lesser Nobility of Later Medieval Europe*, M. Jones (ed.), (Gloucester 1986); *People, Politics, and the Community in the Later Middle Ages*, J.T. Rosenthal and C.Richmond (eds), (Gloucester 1987); *Towns and Townspeople in the Fifteenth Century*, J.A.F. Thomson (ed.), (Gloucester 1988).
2. C. Richmond, *John Hopton: A Fifteenth Century Suffolk Gentleman* (Cambridge 1981); 'When did John Hopton become blind?', *Historical Research* lx (1987).

3. P. Fleming, 'Charity, Faith, and the Gentry of Kent 1442–1529', *Property and Politics*, pp. 36–58.

4. J.I. Kermode, 'The Merchants of Three Northern English Towns' in Clough, *Profession*, pp. 7–50.

5. K.B. McFarlane, *Lancastrian Kings and Lollard Knights* (Oxford 1972); G.L. Harriss, *Henry V: The Practice of Kingship* (Oxford 1985); T.B. Pugh, *Henry V and the Southampton Plot of 1415* (Gloucester 1988).

6. See for example, *The Professions in Early Modern England*, W. Prest (ed.), (Beckenham 1987); W. Prest, *The Rise of the Barristers: A Social History of the English Bar 1590–1640* (Oxford 1986); C.W. Brooks, *Pettyfoggers and Vipers of the Commonwealth: The 'Lower Branch' of the Legal Profession in Early Modern England* (Cambridge 1986); R. O'Day, *The English Clergy: The Emergence and Consolidation of a Profession 1558–1642* (Leicester 1979).

7. J.H. Baker, *The Legal Profession and the Common Law: Historical Essays* (1986) ; E.W. Ives, *The Common Lawyers in Pre-Reformation England* (Cambridge 1983).

8. *Profession, Vocation and Culture in Later Medieval England*, C.H. Clough (ed.), (Liverpool 1982).

9. Apart from those cited by Beilby, attention is drawn to the following: M.A. Hicks, 'Restraint, Mediation and Private Justice: George, Duke of Clarence as "Good Lord"', *Journal of Legal History* iv (1983); S. Payling, 'Law and Arbitration in Nottinghamshire 1399 1461', *People, Politics, and the Community*; E. Powell, 'Arbitration and the Law in England in the Later Middle Ages', *TRHS* xxxiii (1983); idem, 'The Settlement of Disputes by Arbitration in Fifteenth Century England', *Law and History Review* ii (1984); C. Rawcliffe, 'The Great Lord as Peacekeeper: Arbitration by English Noblemen and their Councils in the Later Middle Ages', *Law and Social Change in British History*, J.A. Guy and H.G. Beale (eds), (1984); J.T. Rosenthal, 'Feuds and Private Peace-making: A Fifteenth-Century Example', *Nottingham Medieval Studies* xiv (1970); I. Rowney, 'Arbitration in Gentry Disputes in the Later Middle Ages', *History* lxvii (1982); A. Smith, 'Litigation and Politics: Sir John Fastolf's Defence of his English Property', *Property and Politics*.

10. R.G. Collingwood, *The Idea of History* (Oxford 1946), pp. 214–15, 217.

11. C. Hill, *Intellectual Origins of the English Revolution* (Oxford 1965), p. 3.

12. Ibid.

13. J.R. Lander, 'Family, "Friends", and Politics in Fifteenth-century England', *Kings and Nobles in the Later Middle Ages*, R.A. Griffiths and J.W. Sherborne (eds), (Gloucester 1986).

14. E.M.W. Tillyard, *The Elizabethan World Picture* (London 1943); E.W. Talbert, *The Problem of Order: Elizabethan Political Commonplaces and an Example of Shakespeare's Art* (Chapel Hill 1962); R. Eccleshall, *Order and Reason in Politics: Theories of Absolute and Limited Monarchy in Early Modern England* (Oxford 1978).

15. e.g. 'Aids, Loans and Benevolences', *HJ* vi (1963); 'Medieval Doctrines in the Debates on Supply 1616–1629', *Faction and Parliament: Essays in Early Stuart History*, K. Sharpe (ed.), (Oxford 1978).

16. E.P. Thompson, 'The Moral Economy of the English Crowd in the Eighteenth Century', *Past and Present* 50 (1971); *Rebellion, Popular Protest, and the Social Order in Early Modern England*, P. Slack (ed.), (Cambridge 1984); M.A. Hicks, 'The Yorkshire Rebellion of 1489 Reconsidered', *Northern History* xxii (1986).

17. Reprinted in K.B. McFarlane, *England in the Fifteenth Century*, G.L. Harriss (ed.), (1981).

18. Ibid. ch. 3; M. Keen, *The Laws of War in the Later Middle Ages* (Oxford 1965).

19. See for example, P. Laslett, *The World We Have Lost* (1965, 1971); *The World We Have Lost Further Explored* (1984); *Household and Family in Past Time* (Cambridge 1972); *Family Life and Illicit Love* (1977), chs. 1–5.

20. A. Macfarlane, *Modes of Reproduction: Love and Marriage in England 1300–1800* (Oxford 1986).
21. J. Hurstfield, *Freedom, Corruption and Government in Elizabethan England* (1973), chs. 5 and 7.
22. E.H. Carr, *What is History?* (1964 edn), p. 53.
23. J. Burckhardt, *The Civilisation of the Renaissance in Italy*, S.G.C. Middlemore and I. Gordon (eds), (1960), 121sqq.; P. Heath, 'Urban Piety in the Later Middle Ages: The evidence of Hull Wills', *CPP*, pp. 209–34; C. Richmond, 'After McFarlane', *History* lxviiii (1983), p. 58.

1

Aspects of the County Community in the Fifteenth Century

Roger Virgoe
University of East Anglia

During the past thirty years the 'county community' has been a concept primarily employed by historians of early modern England. It is they who have taken the lead in creating profiles of county societies and developing the analytical tools to discuss them. There are now in print substantial studies of the political and social structures and activities of many counties in the sixteenth and seventeenth centuries. Although there has been no consistency in the specific periods studied, the questions asked and the methods employed to answer them, such studies contain not only a great deal of information about early modern society and politics, but also provide a series of models of the 'county community', which can be tested in other periods and other regions.[1]

The concentration of such studies in this period results partly from the continuing desire to explain the breakdown of relations between crown and parliament in the seventeenth century and partly from the proliferation of relevant sources, particularly correspondence. Such studies also reflect the observation of a number of historians that the sixteenth and seventeenth centuries appear to show an intense and growing interest in the county as a focus of sentiment as well as of political and administrative involvement. The development of the importance of government institutions such as quarter sessions is paralleled by intellectual and cultural manifestations of 'county-mindedness'. Some of these have recently been summarized by Dr MacCulloch: the first county histories; genealogical and topographical collections on a county basis; other literary manifestations of county loyalty; and the publication of county maps, which enabled people to visualize their counties in a way previously impossible.[2] Such phenomena were, writes Professor Clark, 'the propaganda myths of a new political and educational elite',[3] but, while admitting that some of them were undoubtedly innovations of the sixteenth century, it is not self-evident that the social and political institutions and sentiments, which lay behind them were equally novel. Professor Everitt does, indeed, admit that the development of county self-consciousness was an evolutionary development and may have begun in some counties before the sixteenth century,[4] while more recently Dr MacCulloch has put forward the interesting suggestion that such sentiments may have fluctuated in intensity and may, for instance, have been stronger in fifteenth-century East Anglia than they were during the early sixteenth century, when the power of the dukes of Norfolk was at its height.[5] The nature of the medieval county is therefore a subject worth investigation. Indeed during the past ten years there have been a number of useful studies of individual counties during the late middle ages, which will be referred to later.

The idea of a 'community of the shire' in the middle ages is, of course, not new. Maitland touched upon it and Helen Cam elaborated his rather legalistic description of the shire as *communitas* in the thirteenth century.[6] She described the community of the shire as 'not so much a social order or estate' as 'an organism . . . a unit held together by proximity, by local feelings, and above all by common living traditions and responsibilities'.[7] These assertions raise a good many questions, of the sort which Dr Clive Holmes has raised in his attack on the 'county-community' school of historians.[8] The county was certainly an administrative unit. Was it also a social unit? How confined by county boundaries were the social relations of its inhabitants? To what extent were smaller regions than counties the real focus of social relations? What was the role of the institutions of the county, largely developed from the pressures of growing crown administration, in making the county a focus for men's actions? How far did the influence of magnates distort the social and political relationships within counties? Were all free men part of this county community, as Cam says, or was it confined to the suitors of the county court, the 'knights of the shire', or later the gentry? How real was the sentiment anyway? Does it dissolve under examination, as some have argued that the 'community of the village' does?[9]

Some years ago Dr Maddicott tried to fill some of the gaps in our knowledge of the county community of the fourteenth century 'between the age of the eyre and the age of the quarter sessions'.[10] More recently a number of studies of individual counties in the later middle ages have explored some of these questions on a smaller scale. As with similar studies of the early modern period, there is no agreement on the precise period to be studied nor on the questions to be asked or methods to be used on such important topics as the definition of the gentry or the leading families of a county. Making allowance both for this and for the different assumptions that the authors inevitably started with, these studies do seem to show wide variations in the social and political structures of different counties and also, sometimes, considerable variations over time. Dr Saul, for instance, concludes that, though seigneurial power was certainly an important factor in fourteenth-century Gloucestershire, it was not all pervasive. His knights and esquires do associate themselves with a shire community and possess some self-consciousness as a territorial and social group.[11] In contrast Christine Carpenter's fifteenth-century Warwickshire appears to be a county dominated for long periods by a single great magnate and she sees not the county but the lord's affinity providing 'the major unifying force among the Warwickshire gentry'. Other county studies, she suggests, tend to underestimate that factor.[12]

Dr Pollard's study of the Richmondshire gentry also emphasizes the importance of lordship as a unifying factor, though here it reinforces the strong social relationships already existing among the elite of that region.[13] For them, the county of Yorkshire hardly seems to exist as a community in which they felt involved. Studies of two much smaller counties, fifteenth-century Derbyshire and fourteenth-century Leicestershire, also emphasize a series of 'small interlinking groups of gentry'.[14] Any county unity was imposed by the crown and does not reflect the social organization of the area. According to Dr Wright, among the Derbyshire gentry there was 'no coherent county social group or community'.[15] On the other hand, Dr Bennett finds considerable evidence of a strong county coherence in both Cheshire and Lancashire in the late fourteenth and early fifteenth centuries – networks of kinship and marriage ties, which are reinforced by frequent meetings for political and social activities.[16] In Cheshire the city of Chester acted as a focus for that unity. It is true that these county societies are seen as part of a wider north-western society and culture and that for lesser gentlemen smaller neighbourhoods are of importance, reinforced institutionally by the much greater vitality of wapentake and hundred, but the reality of a 'county community' is emphasized.[17]

Dr Bennett demonstrates the numerous direct links between the gentry of the north-west and the court in an era where there was no resident dominant magnate. From the 1430s the political society of the two counties was transformed by the rise of the Stanleys to supremacy: the gentlemen of the region now needed Stanley 'brokerage' at court and lordship becomes, perhaps, a more significant force than the county community. Dr MacCulloch suggests the same sort of change in Suffolk society during the sixteenth century.[18] He suggests that the county sentiment evident in East Anglia in the fifteenth-century Paston Letters may have declined during the ascendancy of the Howards during the first part of the sixteenth century. It was only after the fall of the fourth Duke of Norfolk in 1572 that there appeared the full flowering of the county community in this region. This emphasis on the interaction between the county and local magnates responds to one of the criticisms made by Dr

Holmes of the 'county community' school of historians. It is not, of course, a factor which is likely to be played down by historians of the later middle ages.

Dr MacCulloch points out that the fall of the Duke of Norfolk produced quite different reactions in the two counties, where his influence had been so strong. Dr Hassell Smith has graphically described the factionalized society of late-Elizabethan Norfolk. Insofar as the gentry focussed their ambitions upon Norfolk issues and offices, attended meetings together and continued to intermarry, it was a community, but a community riven by personal rivalries and political and religious differences.[19] In Suffolk, on the other hand, Dr MacCulloch shows that comparative harmony reigned among the gentry and a tight grip was kept on possible sources of dissension. The evidence presented shows that these differing county profiles were real and not the result of different observers and sources. Indeed, the two studies demonstrate the particular value of work in this field, when it covers similar enough periods and asks similar enough questions to make meaningful comparisons possible. The differing sources available for different counties at different periods are, of course, inevitably going to influence the way in which such studies are carried out and no uniformity is possible or, perhaps, desirable. If, however, the sorts of questions posed by Dr Holmes and listed earlier in this article were more explicitly put in the writing of such county studies, it might be much easier to distinguish the *real* differences among county communities at any one period as well as changes over time, as distinct from those produced by the varying interests and assumptions of the authors and of the sources available for the areas and counties studied. The remainder of this article will discuss some evidence for two of these questions. How real was the sentiment of a county community in the fifteenth century? And to what extent did that community extend outside the ranks of the gentry?[20]

In the fifteenth-century English-Latin dictionary, the *Promptorium Parvulorum*, the English words 'schyre' and 'cuntre' are each given the Latin equivalent 'comitatus'.[21] These are the two vernacular words that are normally employed to denote the county. The anglicized French word 'countee' does not appear at all in the dictionary and, although it is used in official or semi-official documents such as parliamentary petitions and acts, it rarely appears in more informal writing, such as correspondence.[22] Like 'comitatus' and 'countee', 'shire' has the dual meaning of 'county' and 'county court'. 'Country' does not seem to be used in the later sense, but by the fifteenth century is much the commonest word used to denote both the territory and the inhabitants of the country. A reading of the three main collections of fifteenth-century vernacular correspondence has brought to light only one example of the use of 'countee';[23] 'shire' is used about forty times, often to denote the shire-court or in conventional usages such as 'knight of the shire'; by contrast, nearly 150 examples of the use of the word 'country' were found, the great majority of them clearly meaning the county.[24] Such a usage was not new in the fifteenth century and was to last through to the seventeenth century.[25] To appreciate its implications, a closer look at the contexts in which it appears is necessary. The term 'country' of course has more than one meaning. Very occasionally it is used to denote a rural area: thus Margaret Paston 'purposeyth to go into the contre and ther to soiorn onys a yer'.[26] More commonly it is used to refer to a smaller region or neighbourhood, as in such phrases as 'men of the country there about' (Caister) and 'the contry abowght Walsynham', or Chaucer's description of 'a mershy contree called Holdernesse'.[27] It can also be used to denote a region larger than a county, as when Clement Paston writes from London in 1461 of the hostility felt against the northerners in 'all thys cuntre more than iiii ore v sherys'.[28] There are other places in the correspondence where the meaning is doubtful.[29] But the great majority of uses of the word in correspondence (and, a fairly cursory search would suggest, elsewhere in fifteenth-century English), is to the county.[30] Most of these references are to the physical and administrative territory. When Edward Plumpton writes that 'my lord kepeth a great Cristinmas as ever was in this contre' (Lancashire) or Lord Rivers instructs his servant to find parliamentary seats for three or four 'menne of thys contre' (Norfolk) or Margaret Paston tells her husband that 'here dare noman seyn a gode word for you in this cuntre', the employment of the particular word is of some interest, but throws only a little light on the social and emotional connotations of the county in this period.[31]

More significant is the use of the term 'county' and, occasionally, 'shire' to represent the inhabitants of the county. Although its Latin equivalent or the French or Latin for the 'community of the county' is frequent enough in fourteenth-century or earlier texts,[32] there is no unequivocal pre-fifteenth century example of the use of 'country', 'county' or 'shire' alone with this meaning given in the *Middle English Dictionary*.[33] In the Paston Letters, though not in the other collections of correspondence, it is quite common. When in 1450 William Yelverton writes of 'a marveyllous disposed contree', or in 1461 when Margaret Paston writes of 'the rewylle and demenyng of thys contre', or Sir John Fastolf states that Edmund Blake is to be thanked for 'his friendliness to the country', it is clearly the people rather than the physical territory that is being referred to.[34] Where the 'country' or occasionally 'the shire' is the subject of the sentence, the implication that the country has a personality, has interests and attitudes as a unit, is even clearer. The well-known letter of John Jenney warning that if John Howard is foisted on Norfolk as knight 'the shire shall not be called of seche worshipp as it hathe be', suggests a view of the county as some sort of community, which can have both interests and reputation, an attack on which affects all its members.[35] There are a number of examples of the use of the word 'country' in this context. For instance, in 1447 Edmund Paston wrote that 'meche of all the contre' was ready to take a new master; in 1465 Richard Calle reported that 'all the contre' was glad that the Duke of Norfolk might come to the country; and in 1470 Margaret Paston wrote to her son that 'all the contray wenyth that ye shuld now overcomyn all your trobill'.[36]

Such a usage is clearly colloquial and will normally surface only in informal letters. That is why it would be unwise to infer that the usage and implied sentiments were more prevalent in Norfolk than elsewhere. The fact is that neither the Stonor nor the Plumpton correspondence have enough letters of this kind to allow argument from silence. Nevertheless the Paston references are sufficient to show us that the personification of the county was natural to people of the fifteenth century or at least to those of a certain social class. Evidence for a true county patriotism is more limited. By the sixteenth century it is clear that many did have a sense of belonging to a county as a historical as well as a geographical entity, a territory which had a cultural as well as an administrative identity, that could be distinguished from its neighbours.[37] To put it frivolously, it might already have been possible to envisage playing inter-county cricket matches, as neighbouring villages challenged at football. To what extent was this true of the fifteenth century? When John Paston writes in 1465 that 'I wold make my doblet all worsted for worship of Norffolk' or his son in 1478 that James Hobart 'purposes to be a Norfolk man' by buying property at Hales, they are being jocular, no doubt, but jocularity of this sort clearly implies a widely held acceptance that 'Norfolk men' are distinguished from the rest of the country in some way.[38] A more clearly contrasting, even competitive, attitude to counties is found in William Paston's letter to his brother John in 1487, where he tells of the Earl of Oxford's boasting to the King of the fair gentlewomen of Norfolk and his determination to have his Essex men put on a good show when the King and his train come there 'that the Lankeschere men may see that ther be gentylmen of as grete sobestaunce that thei be able to bye all Lankeshere'. William goes on to tell his brother 'your contre is gretely bostyd of, and also the inabytors of the same'.[39] Such competition in beauty and display is a long way from county cricket matches. A little closer is Sir Henry Savile's invitation to William Plumpton for a week's field-sports in 1546, in which was promised a triangular cockfighting competition between birds of Lancashire, Derbyshire and Hallamshire.[40]

These examples are chosen because they are in a totally private context, with no relationship to the county-based institutions in which the gentry were inevitably involved. It is clear that the 'country' might have emotional connotations and be a focus of loyalty and affection, and the quotations from John Paston and Hobart cited above suggest that these sentiments were conventional enough to be smiled at. But what parts of the population felt such sentiments in any form? Did Margaret Paston and others writing of the 'country' or the 'shire' refer only to the gentry or, as seems certain in some cases,[41] imply that a much larger part of the population could be comprehended by these terms? Was Helen Cam right to consider that the community of the shire was the whole body of the county, not just the suitors of the county court? There is inevitably little evidence of what lesser men thought about the county, though the form of the 1381 and 1450 rebellions suggest that it was a natural context for their political actions.[42] But examination of the institution that symbolized the country may throw some light on who were expected to take part in some of its more important decisions.

The institutions governing and symbolizing the county in the early modern period, the quarter sessions of the commissions of the peace and the biannual sessions of the assizes, were not yet performing these functions during the fifteenth century.[43] The gathering of the assizes was certainly already an important event in the county calendar and not just for the settlement of litigation, but it does not yet seem to have acquired that major politico-social role that it had in Elizabethan times. For much of the fifteenth century the commission of the peace was quite small in most counties and attendance at quarter sessions was limited to a handful of JPs, most of them lawyers. Both in total numbers and in attendance there was quite a rapid change in the last decades of the century, but not yet was it the 'parliament of the shire'. Dr Maddicott, on the other hand, has demonstrated the continued importance of the county court in the fourteenth century and in the fifteenth century it still seems to have been the county court which symbolized the unity of the county and still the sheriff who was seen as its natural leader.[44] Dr Maddicott emphasizes the connection between the importance of the county court and the development of the commons in parliament.[45] Such a relationship remained important in the fifteenth century, even though the counties seem to be less active petitioners and there is less obviously a 'country' viewpoint being voiced in parliament.[46] In another way, however, parliaments provide new evidence of the nature of the 'county community', for from the 1407 election indentures allow some analysis of the attendance at the county court on the occasion of the supreme political act of the county as a unit: the election of its representatives to parliament.

It is, of course, only on such occasions that normally anything can be known about attendance at the shire court. Dr Maddicott was persuaded that at most county courts attendance was quite high, perhaps averaging about 150,[47] but the direct evidence of attendance at a normal fifteenth-century county court is very limited. We do have one snippet of evidence for an ordinary session in William Paston's petition against Walter Aslak, referring to the date 28 August 1424, 'beyng there thanne a grete congregacion of people bycause of the shire'.[48] But for the most part it is only for those sessions at which knights of the shire were elected and for which the indentures of return survive that knowledge of attendance at the county court is possible. Of course these were not typical sessions, but the returns do show the names of those whom the sheriff thought worth recording from those who appeared at the court for its most important, if only occasional, business. Analysis of attendance is thus relevant to any discussion of the 'county community' during this period.[49]

Nearly sixteen hundred indentures were presumably drawn up for shire elections for the forty-three parliaments between 1407, when the form was used for the first time, and 1478, the last parliament of the fifteenth century for which the returns survive. Of these some eleven hundred still exist in a state legible enough to extract approximate numbers of witnesses, if not always their names.[50] A reading of these and a more detailed analysis of those from East Anglia produced no evidence of fictitious names of attestors and a strong conviction that normally those listed were present at the election.[51] They were not, of course, all those who were there. Apart from the common use of such phrases as *et multos alios* after the list, there is a fair amount of evidence from other documents concerning certain elections (e.g. Buckinghamshire 1427, Huntingdonshire 1450, Suffolk 1455) to show that the attestors might form but a small proportion of those present.[52] Allegations in 1439 that some 2,000 men flocked into the Cambridge shirehouse claiming a voice and that there may have been more than 1,000 men at the Norfolk shire-court in 1461 may contain an element of exaggeration,[53] but it does seem probable that the 1429 statute restricting the numbers claiming the right to a voice in the election may have given some precision when a poll was taken but did not prevent large numbers of unqualified men appearing, many of them no doubt in the trains of gentlemen and intended to exhibit the latters' status and to put pressure on the sheriff. Normally elections would be arranged prior to the court and were made by acclamation: then the cheers of the commons would mean no more than the acclamation by the Londoners of a new King, confirming a sense of county solidarity, and providing the newly-elected knights with the knowledge that the commons of the shire were behind them. When, however, there was disagreement among 'the gentles of the shire', uproar and violence could ensue. The complaint against Sir James Ormond in 1439 claimed that after the sheriff had left the shire-court in protest against violence and the presence of outsiders, most of the commons also left, but there still remained about 500, not forty of whom were qualified to have a voice, the rest being 'gadered of oder shires, chamberdekyns and mennes servants of

Cambregge, threshers and all oder laborers, servauntes and noghtymen of the shire': a full, if not comprehensive, list of those whom almost all would have considered to be non-members of the county community.[54]

But from 1430 certainly, and no doubt before that, those whom the sheriff or his deputy chose to attest the indentures were rarely of this class. But were they necessarily drawn from the gentlemen? A survey of the eleven hundred county indentures mentioned above shows that four fifths of all those that survive contain the names of thirty or fewer attestors. There is a tendency for numbers to increase after 1422 and particularly after 1430, but there are considerable variations between counties. Some such as Warwickshire, Worcestershire and Sussex, as well as smaller counties like Rutland and Westmorland, invariably content themselves with small numbers of attestors. On the other hand some, not necessarily more populous, are more inclined to have larger numbers. Between 1422 and 1442 Essex indentures never and Hertfordshire ones very rarely have fewer than thirty, though numbers diminish later. Lincolnshire has consistently long lists of witnesses throughout the period, which makes Dr Rogers' use of them to analyse the composition of county courts more reasonable than it would be for many counties.[55] Shropshire, Wiltshire and Gloucestershire less consistently, but still frequently, have long lists of attestors. Norfolk and Suffolk indentures, which never had more than thirty attestors before 1432, begin to expand in size considerably thereafter and sometimes include large numbers. The same pattern is found with Nottinghamshire, Derbyshire and Kent, the last of which produced in 1472 the record number for the period of over one thousand attestors. The most notable change occurs however in the Yorkshire indentures, where the earlier practice of witness only by the attorneys of the magnate suitors gives way after 1439 to more normal, and often large, numbers of attestors.[56]

It is hoped to consider elsewhere the reasons for these variations in the lists of attestors. Their interest for the purpose of the present study lies in the indications they provide of views of the composition of the 'county community': for attesting the indentures of those elected to represent it must surely be recognition as part of that community. Fully to study the attestors and their status would require detailed knowledge of the individual counties, but something can be inferred from a survey of the way in which the attestors are described and the styles that some of them are given.

Early indentures vary greatly in the general descriptions given of the attestors. Sometimes they are 'suitors', sometimes 'honest and law-worthy men', sometimes 'electors' or 'residents', frequently without description. Until the 1420s very few indentures give a style to any individual below the rank of a knight.[57] Thereafter it becomes increasingly normal to style some men 'esquires' and a few counties begin to style some men 'gentlemen', though this does not become common until the 1460s.[58] Other styles are rarely employed. There is a yeoman in Staffordshire in 1433, a clerk in Cambridgeshire in 1453, and the occasional merchant,[59] but the only real exceptions are the indentures for Norfolk and Suffolk drawn up by what seems to have been a particularly status-conscious sheriff's clerk in 1447 and 1449. Besides knights, esquires and gentlemen, there are noted on these a number of franklins of both counties and nine yeomen in Norfolk.[60]

It is difficult to be confident about the status of attestors in the early part of the period. For what it is worth, the great majority of those on the short Norfolk and Suffolk lists seem to be esquires or lawyers, who would later be called gentlemen. But by the 1450s it is possible to be fairly sure that a considerable proportion of the attestors on most indentures, notably when the numbers are large, were below armigerous rank: e.g. of sixty-five attestors on the Suffolk indenture of February 1449, forty-one are not styled knights, esquires, gentlemen, or even franklins. It was thought appropriate to include such men in an indenture even when there were already more than a dozen gentlemen and above. More examples could be given, but it can be stated briefly that after the mid-thirties when esquires are normally recognized, there are few lists of attestors, large or small, where the unstyled are not more numerous than the knights and esquires. Even when the 'gentlemen' are recognized, there still remain substantial numbers of men who must have been of the rank of yeoman or below, in some cases very many.[61]

To sum up. It is unlikely that all those present at an election ever sealed as attestors. The average number of names is under twenty, but there are wide differences. At almost every election there were a few counties where particularly large numbers attested, perhaps when there was a contest or dispute, and there is a tendency for numbers of attestors to increase. Not in intention but in practice, the 1429 statute may (as Rogers suggests) have implied the right of all 40s freeholders to have a voice and therefore made it a more valued privilege.[62] The Cambridgeshire petition of 1439 shows that intensive, not to say violent, canvassing went on among the yeomanry before shire day.[63] Sheriffs tended to acknowledge this interest by usually including a number of 'non-gentles' among the attestors and, perhaps where there was doubt about the return, by adding the names of large numbers of freeholders who had been present to counter claims by the defeated party. The acceptance by the sheriff of such men's right to play a part in the most corporate act of the shire was an acceptance of their role in the community. Although we have no direct evidence of what these freeholders thought about their county, this electoral evidence does suggest that the 'county community' did in the fifteenth century comprehend all those freeholders, whose oath as jurors was, after all, effective in bringing freemen of their 'country' to trial, and in trying those who put themselves 'on their country'. They did not only attend county courts to listen to statutes, proclamations and the orders of their betters, but to participate there in one of its major functions.

Notes

1. e.g. A.M. Everitt, *The Community of Kent and the Great Rebellion, 1640–60* (Leicester 1966); J.T. Cliffe, *Yorkshire Gentry from the Reformation to the Civil War* (1969); A. Hassell Smith *County and Court* (Oxford 1974); J.S. Morrill *Cheshire 1630–60: County Government and Society during the English Revolution* (Oxford 1974); A.J. Fletcher, *A County Government in Peace and War: Sussex 1600–60* (1975); P.J. Clark, *English Provincial Society from the Reformation to the Revolution* (1977); D. MacCulloch, *Suffolk and the Tudors* (Oxford 1986). For general comment, see A.M. Everitt, *Change in the Provinces* (Leicester 1969); J.S. Morrill, *The Revolt of the Provinces* (1976).
2. For this point, see V. Morgan, 'The Cartographic Image of "The Country" in Early Modern England', *TRHS* 5th ser. xxix (1979), pp. 129–54.
3. Clark, *English Provincial Society*, p. 219.
4. A.M. Everitt, 'Country, County, and Town: Patterns of Regional Evolution in England', *TRHS* 5th ser. xxix (1979), pp. 79–108, at 89.
5. MacCulloch, *Suffolk*, pp. 105–7.
6. F. Pollock and F.W. Maitland, *The History of English Law* (2nd edn 1898), i. pp. 534–4.
7. H.M. Cam, *Liberties and Communities in Medieval England* (Cambridge 1933), pp. 245–7.
8. C. Holmes, 'The County Community in Stuart Historiography', *Journal of British Studies* xix (1979), pp. 54–73.
9. A. Macfarlane, *The Origins of English Individualism* (1978), esp. pp. 68–9, 162–3.
10. J.R. Maddicott, 'The County Community and the Making of Public Opinion in Fourteenth-Century England', *TRHS* 5th ser. xxviii (1978), pp. 27–44.
11. N. Saul, *Knights and Esquires: The Gloucestershire Gentry in the Fourteenth Century* (Oxford 1981), pp. 257–62.
12. I have not used Dr Carpenter's thesis, but her views are made clear in 'The Beauchamp Affinity', *EHR* xcv (1980), pp. 514–32.
13. A.J. Pollard, 'The Richmondshire Community of the Gentry during the Wars of the Roses', *Patronage, Pedigree, and Power in Later Medieval England*, C.D. Ross (ed.), (Gloucester 1979), pp. 37–59.
14. S.M. Wright, *The Derbyshire Gentry in the Fifteenth Century* (Derbyshire Record Society viii, 1983); G.G. Astill, 'The Medieval Gentry: A Study in Leicestershire Society, 1350–99' (Birmingham University PhD thesis 1977). Other unprinted county studies by Dr Rowney on Staffordshire (Keele PhD 1981) and Dr Cherry on Devonshire (Wales PhD 1981) have not been consulted.
15. Elsewhere she argues that in the fifteenth century any sense of 'county community' had yet to develop: Wright, *Derbyshire Gentry*, p. 58.
16. M.J. Bennett, *Community, Class and Careerism: Cheshire and Lancashire Society in the Age of Gawain and the Green Knight* (Cambridge 1983); idem, 'A County Community: Social Cohesion among the Cheshire Gentry, 1400–25', *NH* viii (1973), pp. 24–44.
17. Bennett, *Community*, pp. 1–52, 236sqq.
18. MacCulloch, *Suffolk*, pp. 105–7.
19. Hassell Smith, *County and Court*, esp. pp. 47–8, 333–42; MacCulloch, *Suffolk*, pp. 105–17.

20. I briefly touched upon these issues in R. Virgoe, 'The Crown, Magnates and Local Government in Fifteenth-Century East Anglia', *The Crown and Local Communities in England and France in the Fifteenth Century*, J.R.L. Highfield and R.I. Jeffs (eds), (Gloucester 1981), pp. 72–87, at pp. 81–2. The following expands these comments considerably, but makes no claim to final examination of the subject.
21. *Promptorium Parvulorum*, A.L. Mahew (ed.), (Early English Text Society extra ser. cii, 1908), p. 398. 'Cuntre' is also translated *patria* on ibid. p. 105.
22. e.g. *RP* v. pp. 181, 631. I have made no attempt at a full survey, nor analyzed usages in French. The Middle English Dictionary has examples from the early fifteenth century, most of them in a parliamentary context, *Middle English Dictionary*, H. Kurath *et al* (ed.), (Ann Arbor, USA, 1956), iii. pp. 652–3.
23. *Paston Letters* ii. pp. 134 (Earl of Oxford to Duke of Norfolk).
24. This survey of the Paston, Stonor and Plumpton correspondence has not been made line-by-line and no doubt examples have been missed, but proportions and order of magnitude are correct, *Paston Letters*; *Paston L&P*; *The Plumpton Correspondence*, T. Stapleton (ed.), (CS iv, 1839); *The Stonor Letters and Papers 1290–1483*, C.L. Kingsford (ed.), (2 vols CS 3rd ser. pp. xxix–xxx, 1919). I am aware of the unsystematic nature of the linguistic research, but hope that it will encourage a more thorough study of the subject.
25. See *Middle English Dictionary* iii. pp. 574–5 and the fourteenth- and fifteenth-century examples in *A New English Dictionary* (13 vols 1888–1928), ii. p. 1078.
26. *Paston L&P* i. p. 353.
27. Ibid. i. pp. 238, 161; *Chaucer's Works*, p. 94.
28. *Paston L&P* i. p. 114.
29. e.g. ibid. ii. pp. 576, 609, etc; *Stonor Letters* i. p. 151. In these and other cases the word probably signifies county, but could mean some less precise region.
30. Miscellaneous examples are Sir Andrew Ogard's letter of *c.* 1450 in Norfolk CRO, NRS14195; Lord Rivers' letter of 1483 printed in E.W. Ives, 'Andrew Dymmock and the Papers of Antony, Earl Rivers, 1482–3', *BIHR* xli (1968), pp. 216–19 at 226; and a petition of 1439, which is interesting in using both 'counte' and 'shire', while the answer orders a commission to 'worthy persons of the contray where the suppliant dwellith', E 28/62/73.
31. *Plumpton Correspondence*, p. 95; Ives, *BIHR* xli. p. 226; *Paston L&P* i. p. 131.
32. Pollock and Maitland, i. pp. 532–56; Maddicott, *TRHS* xxviii. pp. 40–1.
33. *Middle English Dictionary* iii. pp. 574–5, 652–3, & *New English Dictionary* for 'county'. The legal phrase *ponit se super patriam suam*, where 'patriam' certainly translated 'country', would suggest the colloquial usage was much earlier.
34. *Paston Letters* ii. pp. 154, 173–7.
35. Ibid. ii. p. 295.
36. Ibid. ii. p. 690; i. p. 218.
37. See footnotes 1 and 2 above.
38. *Paston L&P* i. pp. 77, 380.
39. Ibid. i. p. 409. The same examples are used in a similar context by Dr MacCulloch, *Suffolk*, pp. 105–6. This indicates the small amount of direct evidence to indicate 'county-mindedness' in the fifteenth century. It does not lessen its significance.
40. *Plumpton Correspondence*, p. 251.
41. There can be no doubt that when Lomnour warns in July 1461 that 'the country will rise', he is not referring to the gentry alone (or at all) and a number of examples clearly imply wider meaning for 'the country': *Paston L&P* i. p. 636; cf. i. p. 79 & ii. p. 765; *Paston Letters* ii. p. 765.
42. See for example, R.H. Hilton, *Bond Men Made Free* (1977 edn), pp. 216–20; R.A. Griffiths, *The Reign of King Henry VI 1422–61* (1981), pp. 629–35.
43. For this, see Virgoe, 'Crown, Magnates and Local Government'.

44. Maddicott, *TRHS*; A. Rogers. 'The Lincolnshire County Court in the Fifteenth Century', *Lincolnshire History and Archaeology*, i (1966), pp. 64–78. For the sheriff, see R.I. Jeffs, 'The Later Medieval Sheriff and the Royal Household' (Oxford D.Phil. 1960).
45. Maddicott, *TRHS* xxviii, esp. pp. 39–43; Maddicott, *The English Parliament in the Later Middle Ages*, R.G. Davies and J.H. Denton (eds), (Manchester 1981), pp. 61–87.
46. There are certainly some petitions from individual counties, devised, no doubt, in the same way as Dr Maddicott describes (e.g. *RP* v. pp. 53, 106–7, 326–7) but far fewer that concern the relationship between the crown, magnates and local government. For possible explanation, see Virgoe, 'Crown, Magnates and Local Government', pp. 73–7.
47. Maddicott, *TRHS* xxviii. p. 30.
48. *Paston L&P* i. p. 5.
49. I hope to discuss the form and contents of fifteenth-century election indentures elsewhere. Only that evidence which is particularly relevant to the 'county community' will be summarized here.
50. Thirty-seven counties should have made returns to each of these parliaments, but there are many gaps and no returns at all from the parliaments of Feb. 1413, Oct. 1416, 1461, 1463 and 1470. The returns are in C 219/10–17 and the following comments are based upon these, unless otherwise noted.
51. There is rarely confirmatory evidence of attendance. One exception is the Hunts. election of 1450, for which a separate petition survives confirming the attendance of those named in the indenture: J.G. Edwards, 'The Huntingdonshire Parliamentary Election of 1450', *Essays in Medieval History presented to Bertie Wilkinson*, T.A. Sandquist and M.R. Powicke (eds), (Toronto 1969), pp. 383–95. For further discussion of fifteenth-century elections and particularly the extraordinary Nottinghamshire indenture of 1460, see S.J. Payling, 'The Widening Franchise – Parliamentary Elections in Lancastrian Nottinghamshire', *England in the Fifteenth Century*, D. Williams (ed.), (Woodbridge 1987).
52. J.S. Roskell, *The Commons in the Parliament of 1422* (Manchester 1954); Edwards, 'Huntingdon Election'; R. Virgoe, 'Three Suffolk Elections of the Mid-Fifteenth Century', *BIHR* xxxix (1966), pp. 185–96.
53. C.H. Williams, 'A Norfolk Parliamentary Election, 1461', *EHR* xl (1925), pp. 79–86; R. Virgoe, 'The Cambridgeshire Election of 1439', *BIHR* xlvi (1973), pp. 95–101.
54. Virgoe, 'Cambridgeshire Election', p. 101.
55. Rogers, 'Lincolnshire County Court'.
56. This earlier Yorkshire practice was not quite invariable: e.g. in May 1413 sixteen witnesses not described as attornies of suitors attest the indentures (C 219/11), but the normal form of attestation begins only in 1442.
57. Only thirty-three out of the 339 surviving and legible indentures from before 1422 style men as esquire and thirteen of these are from the two parliaments of 1421.
58. The first return I have noted as styling some men as 'gentlemen 'or 'generosus' is that from Derbyshire in 1419, C 219/12/3. Even in 1467 only seven indentures include attestors styled 'gentlemen'.
59. Here I ignore the frequent inclusion in county indentures of 'electors' for one or more boroughs, for which see M. McKisack, *The Parliamentary Representation of English Boroughs during the Middle Ages* (Oxford 1932), pp. 54–60.
60. C 219/15. It is far from easy to see the criteria for these ascriptions from examining the names.
61. e.g. in Yorks., 1467, 150 out of 260; Suffolk, 1472, 209 out of 220.
62. Rogers, 'Lincolnshire County Court', pp. 67–8.
63. Virgoe, 'Cambridgeshire Election', p. 100. And compare Sir John Howard's allegation in 1460 that Berney and others had spent two weeks in Aylsham, Walsingham, and many other places encouraging some 500 men to attend the election, Williams, *EHR* xl. p. 82.

2

Late Medieval Wills and Pious Convention: Testamentary Evidence Reconsidered

Clive Burgess
University of London

Professor R. B. Dobson has recently commented on the number of scholars 'currently embarked upon the fascinating if often frustrating attempt to recapture late medieval religious priorities and sensibilities by means of probate registers'.[1] Any enquiry into the reasons why late-medieval conventional piety commands increasing attention would be obliged to consider the relative abundance of contemporary wills as an important factor. Wills, after all, contain a wealth of information about pious practice, and for many localities survive in sufficient number to invite an appraisal of inhabitants' religious *mores*.[2] It certainly proves possible to analyze pious practices among England's court and county elite, supplementing our impressions of the ruling classes thereby.[3] If the poor, having less use for wills, remain by comparison unapproachable,[4] members of the middling ranks of society – including merchants, shopkeepers, craftsmen, yeomen and priests – are accessible as their wills survive in plenty.[5] While little or nothing may be said with any confidence about the great majority of individuals who lived and died before *c.* 1350, thereafter the survival in large numbers of so personal a document as the will is at first sight an augury that it may prove possible to prise the ranks of late-medieval society apart, providing historians with detailed understanding of one aspect at least of the lives and beliefs of ordinary men and, more importantly, given the general dearth of information, ordinary women. Apart from the intrinsic interest of the topic, it is this promise which renders the study of late-medieval conventional piety via wills so intriguing. In addition, the number of wills available and their easily categorizable contents make it an enterprise which lends itself with particular facility to computer and data-base techniques. Statistical analysis may soon engulf the topic and the promise of such progress only adds to its attraction.

Why, then, does Professor Dobson also employ the term 'frustrating' when describing a pursuit with apparently so fruitful a prospect? Is there a catch? Not one but several are immediately apparent. There is, for example, the intractable problem of scribes who, when writing or transcribing wills, may or may not have standardized forms and added prefaces and phrases reflective of their practice or convenience rather than testators' use.[6] Moreover, although many late-medieval wills survive, many more have been lost. Surviving wills are probably more likely to represent the wealthier classes but ascertaining the social status of testators whose wishes survive is difficult and frequently impossible. The historian relying upon wills never enjoys certainty, that much is plain even from brief experience. Longer acquaintance discloses problems which, far from being catches, more resemble reefs waiting to sink any venturing unwarily to chart the sea of late-medieval faith. Probably the most debilitating problem has proved to be well disguised. Wills appear to yield abundant information, so much so that it is all too easy to assume that each provides a relatively realistic impression of a testator's pious intent. Historians extrapolating from this premise, who have sought to establish the characteristics of contemporary religious behaviour by, for instance, analyzing all the wills surviving for certain towns, have been so engaged sorting and interpreting wills' minutiae that they have neglected to question basic assumptions concerning the reliability of their evidence. But to do so is to discover the full force of Ernest Bevin's admonition 'Open that Pandora's Box [and] you never know what Trojan 'orses will jump out.'[7] It has consequences both far-reaching and destructive. While broad generalization based on will-analysis is clearly hazardous, it comes as something of a shock to realize that hoping for a reliable impression even of one testator's plans from scrutiny of his or her will is folly. Simply, the corroborative evidence which might permit deductions as to quite what proportion of any estate is being dealt with is seldom available. What indications there are suggest that testators were explicit about only a relatively small proportion of their estate.[8] This inevitably prompts queries. If specific testamentary provision represented part only of most testators' requirements, how small a part? Who was responsible for implementing the pious provision not specified in a will? Did a testator do what was necessary during life, or could significant matters simply be left to executors' discretion? How much, indeed, was left to executors? How reliable were they? Queries, unfortunately, which are as easy to ask as they are hard to answer. Wills were not designed to serve historians: fundamental aspects of both property bequest and pious provision were frequently omitted from them and it is seldom possible to determine which of the testator's interests was not specifically covered. But, ultimately, the detail and variety of wills' content proscribes any thought of discarding them.[9] So, if a gadarene rush, via computers or otherwise, to press wills into historical service must result in serious misjudgement of the intensity and character of late-medieval piety, it is essential that some of the shortcomings of wills be the more thoroughly considered. Adjustments may then be made to render their use, and resulting impressions, more accurate.

I intend in the following to rely on evidence surviving for the town of Bristol in the late-medieval period,[10] and should state immediately that protracted study of religious *mores* in Bristol has failed to reveal any particularly noteworthy innovation in the basic processes of piety in the century or two before the Reformation.[11] This has important implications. The very stability of pious practice fostered powerful customs: for many piety could depend on conventions so well established that neither prescription nor explanation were necessary. With the passage of time, these conventions had been dovetailed with perceived duties towards parish, family and associates, and, to labour the point, operated in the absence of written instruction. Hence, they are now well-nigh imperceptible. It is only with care and a good variety of evidence that something of them may be disinterred.

It is as well to consider, first, the specific purpose which wills were meant to serve and the manner in which this affects impressions derived from them. As far as pious provision was concerned, wills were made to implement part only of what most testators judged necessary and/or possible *after* death. So, inevitably, wills act as blinkers, emphasizing some aspects of testators' priorities and excluding others, shedding little or no reliable light, for instance, on the concerns with which individuals had been occupied during life. They focus particularly on the pious practices apposite immediately after death, that is, on the period of the funeral and its aftermath.[12] The services commissioned and offered in this period must not be taken as representing all that testators sought for their soul's benefit, although the agglomeration was typically sufficiently complex to render the assumption plausible. Important as these small-scale services were, both in signalling repentance and, bluntly, in accumulating grace to expedite progress through purgatory, the attitudes and activities an individual adopted and pursued before death were of much greater significance for the soul. Repentance and confession were essential for salvation; penitential acts and good works, moreover, might substantially lessen the purgatorial reckoning.[13] For the pious, the services provided at and immediately after death were little more than icing on the cake: the main response was made in life, of which wills yield hardly an inkling.

It follows that wills are perniciously deficient as indicators of the longer-term services that the wealthy commissioned.[14] Bristol affords numerous examples, which may doubtless be multiplied elsewhere, of testators who established their most costly and intricate *post obit* services before they died. Able to rest assured that all had been carefully arranged, they had no need to mention their services in their wills, except perhaps in passing. Such 'omission' is apparent only when supplementary evidence survives. Thus, the details of William Canynges' two perpetual chantries and of his munificence to St Mary Redcliffe are not apparent from his will because he had effected these wishes before death.[15] Mayors of Bristol, however, had responsibilities toward perpetual chantries which in some instances meant that the municipality registered founders' intentions; similarly Canynges' parish clearly thought it proper to celebrate the memory of so generous a benefactor.[16] Records were made which have, by good fortune, been preserved and, in the case of his perpetual chantries, even added to by central government records compiled at the time of Edwardian dissolution.[17] But almost every other founder and benefactor was less eminent and more obscure, although obscurity is no necessary indication of parsimony. It should be borne in mind that Canynges' most lavish enterprises, his two almshouses, remain shadowy when compared to his chantries.[18] Neither municipality nor parish had particular responsibility for them and any 'day-to-day' documentation they generated was not preserved. Ambitious *post obit* undertakings about which we now are ignorant – let alone smaller scale provisions – might both function and flourish.[19] With scraps of supplementary information for a few testators and nothing for the great majority, it is impossible to gauge precisely how deficient most wills are; but telling us little or nothing about the day-to-day provision in which men and women would undoubtedly have indulged, they are documents which also yield a decidedly deficient impression of *post obit* provision.

The second point also concerns a distortion which results from inadvisedly pressing wills into historical service. Each essentially is a statement of one testator's plans and intentions. Each tends to emphasize the individual, excluding the role that others may have played in his or her practices and priorities, and neglecting corporate activities in which a testator would probably have been involved. Wills' overriding concern with funerary practice, in fact, typifies their false perspective. For the funeral was arranged first and foremost to benefit the deceased testator's soul. By contrast, many of life's pious pursuits were altruistic in form, if not wholly in intention. It was, for instance, well established that the most efficacious means of assisting one's soul was charitable action, benefiting both the living and dead.[20] Men and women gave alms to the needy; they gave precious and sacred items and money to their parish church to improve the liturgy, to add to and beautify the building, and to glorify its patron saint; and to the parish priest and chaplains they gave money. In return they craved intercession from the poor, from parishioners present and future, and from the clergy. But premium was placed on the intercession of the dead, the most efficacious assistance of all. In addition to invoking the assistance of the 'very special dead', the saints, either by personal devotion or corporate cult, it is to be emphasized that prayers and suffrages were also offered for the rest of the faithful dead who, like the living and dying, were in need of assistance. This was done to ensure that when the time came each benefactor might similarly qualify for assistance from the living, but also, more importantly, to ensure that the dead would be obliged to intercede for their benefactors. The penitential scheme of the late-medieval church encouraged altruism by promising reciprocal benefits. Individuals were exhorted to provide and pray for others, implying that in any locality the body of the faithful was truly a cooperative entity. Wills, however, are one-sided: they permit a glimpse of testators' giving, but reveal little or nothing of what testators thought they would receive in return. They cannot illustrate reciprocation and so fail to represent one of the period's most crucial pious characteristics.

Further, fundamental as corporate activity was for much of late-medieval belief and action, wills fail to convey a spirit of community. Religious gilds and confraternities played a prominent part for many in day-to-day life and devotion but, beyond recording small-scale bequests to them, wills fail, for instance, to disclose what services were provided for members' souls, or the support that widows and orphans might expect.[21] Such benefits may nevertheless radically have altered a member's own religious provision and may similarly have reduced what he felt constrained to provide for his dependants in his will. Moreover, and more significantly, wills evoke almost nothing of the parish community. Yet it was by corporate activity that parishioners provided for clergy and maintained their parish church as a centre facilitating access to the sacraments and hence salvation. Late-medieval Bristol's parish archives shed light on those who participated to direct parish life, illustrating the tenacity and expertise of churchwardens, parish priests and prominent laity who protected and furthered the legal and propertied interests of parishes, and hence their prestige and efficacy as centres of worship and intercession. The existence and work of these agents had important implications.[22] Every parish was possessed of formidable forces for management and continuity. As a result, just as confraternity might modify the provision a testator was obliged to make, parish membership influenced plans and considerations. Reliable trustees existed who were practised in safeguarding the interests of parish and parishioners both. This explains why, as indicated above, arrangements could be made in life: parishioners might wish, understandably, to inaugurate their own services in agreement with parish officials, and could thereafter rest sure in the knowledge that wardens, priest and neighbours would respect and fulfil their wishes without testamentary prompting.[23]

While each testator was an individual, none lived in a vacuum. Life's common circumstances shaped everyman's planning. Membership of the parish community was one common factor which exercised powerful influences: stimulating certain devotions or intentions on the one hand, the parish community could on the other be relied upon to implement plans with little or no recourse to testamentary prescription. Other circumstances also shaped priorities and plans, having a similarly marked effect on the matters that any testator found necessary to prescribe in detail. The most influential, surpassing even parish membership in the gravity of its consequences, was kinship, either by marriage or blood. Each gave rise to powerful conventions which must be considered in turn.

It is worth noting, first, that late-medieval Bristol's evidence furnishes us with few wills for married women who predeceased husbands. Married men seem to have enjoyed in practice the rights vested in them in theory over any real and personal property their wives may have possessed before marriage; and although, with husbands' concurrence, wives might make wills, few bothered.[24] Legal convention, then, has displaced an unknown but far from negligible portion of late-medieval society from our purview. But if precious little can be said about the religious services, if any, that these women commissioned, it was not necessarily the case that each could only look to a service eventually established by the husband, primarily to benefit his own soul and permitting a late wife's soul to garner, as it were, only secondary benefit. By good fortune, one example survives which demonstrates that a husband might specifically commission a service for dead wives before his own death. Richard Vener died in 1413 and left instructions that his executors should sell twelve woollen cloths and devote the proceeds to profit his soul, the souls of his dead wives and those of all the faithful departed.[25] It was his wish that cash be distributed on his burial day, on the day of his month mind, and that it be spent to procure pious works – all of which was entirely standard. What is notable, however, is that his executors, using the proceeds of selling the cloths, were to pay one Sir Thomas Holme what had been agreed to complete his celebration for the souls of Vener's late wives 'for the present year'. It would appear that Vener died with obligations unfulfilled, which he sought to remedy. Moreover, his use of the word 'present' in these circumstances is interesting: it possibly suggests that he had been in the habit of extending his wives' chantry service year by year, paying the priest's salary as it fell due using current income from investment, commerce or livelihood, in any of which he may initially have been assisted by his wives' property. Whatever the case, he provided a chantry for his dead wives, but, had payment not been owing, we should never have been aware of the arrangement. How many other widowers acted similarly, though less explicitly, remains a subject for conjecture. It is nevertheless certain that he also requested that the service be extended for another year and that his own soul be added to the beneficiaries.

As to provisions made by widows for a dead spouse, there need, by contrast, be no doubt at all. Bristol's surviving late-medieval wills frequently reflect the phenomenon of husband predeceasing wife. The widow was almost invariably named either sole or joint executrix and was left the residue of the testator's estate with the instruction to dispose of it for the benefit of his soul as she saw fit. This arrangement, invariably blandly stated, is so common as to appear a protocol devoid of substance. Where no corroborative evidence survives it is impossible to guess what any testator intended, and speculation seems pointless. The temptation to discount the instruction is overwhelming – particularly where, as is occasionally the case, the widow's will has also survived and is of no particular interest. In such wills the common mixture of funerary provision and piecemeal bequest suggests that the responsibility for disposing of the husband's residue made very little difference. To regard the instruction as a nicety and nothing more seems perfectly justified.

But it would be wrong. In a number of cases, supplementary information, afforded in particular by the All Saints' archive, indicates well-established conventions at work. I have elsewhere and in detail discussed the provisions made by the likes of Henry and Alice Chestre, Thomas and Maud Baker *alias* Spicer, and Thomas and Agnes Fylour, all parishioners of All Saints'.[26] Their provisions and arrangements prove unquestionably that estate residues as entrusted to widows could indeed be sizeable, and moreover that *pre obit* inauguration was as much an option for widows as anybody else. Consider the Chestres: to judge from Henry's will, he would not appear to have been a rich man. The inescapable implication of information in the All Saints' Church Book, however, is that he was very wealthy but had devised the bulk of his estate to his widow without detailed specification either as to its extent or his wishes for its use. Similarly, Alice's will is relatively meagre. Nevertheless, the Church Book discloses that in the interval between Henry's death in 1470 and hers in 1485, she was lavish in both bequest and arrangement, possibly implementing some of his plans but doubtless pursuing her own pious interests too. This was to benefit both but has left no testamentary trace. Similarly Thomas Baker and Thomas Fylour profited from pious provision that neither had specifically requested but which was eventually entrusted to All Saints' and is, as a result, recorded in the Church Book. Documentation survives indicating that the parish faithfully discharged its responsibilities, and could do so without prompting from testamentary instructions. Agreements had been reached before death, and conventions, between husband and wife, executrix and parish, held sway. It is daunting to realize that failure on the part of any testator to specify an elaborate or long-term pious service is no guide as to his or her wishes; and that even if a will contains one such specification, there is no guarantee that this was all from which a testator might hope to benefit. It is daunting, too, to realize that a meagre will may be indicative more of the fact that the testator died with his wishes and estate well in order and with widow and parish prepared for what was to be done, rather than suggesting lack of funds or apathy toward religion. Estate residues devoted to pious purposes must be taken seriously: unequivocal evidence reveals widows discharging pious and social responsibilities with largesse and aplomb, so much so that Alice Chestre, for the benefit of future citizens and to her own and her husband's souls, saw fit to build a crane on Bristol quay![27] Bland and oft-repeated as the clause may be, 'estate residue to my widow and executrix, to be devoted in pious uses to the benefit of my soul as best she sees fit' must in reality have betokened the most significant part of many a provision.

If the bonds of marriage galvanized widows into activity as spiritual lieutenants for dead spouses, then conventions of equal or greater potency operated between testators and the heirs of their body. These conventions had similarly crucial effects on the provision of pious services and on the composition of wills. Two sets of circumstances will presently be investigated: one concerns mature heirs, the other concerns minors. But first, a cautionary note. When relying on wills for guidance as to the descent of property to offspring it must be borne in mind that practice in this matter might vary. The basic obligation incumbent on property holders was to ensure that patrimony descend to offspring, as an extension of which many parents doubtless felt bound to bequeath heirs a reasonable proportion of the land and chattels they had accumulated during life.[28] But in Bristol the situation was muddied by the possibility of alternative practice which blurred the distinction between inalienable real property and alienable movables. In common with counterparts in London and elsewhere, Bristol's citizens held by burgage tenure, as a consequence of which they might devise real property to whomsoever they chose, in just the same way as they might bequeath their movables.[29] Heirs of the body may have had very strong claims to their progenitors' real property but Bristol's testators were not strictly required to abide by them. Thus for the historian attempting to interpret wills and gauge testators' wishes, the situation in late-medieval Bristol vis-a-vis property and heirs is hopelessly intractable. Too many unspecified variables cast conflicting shadows: offspring may commonly have inherited patrimony but at the same time testators might use borough customs to ensure a different settlement, and, as with other conventions, quite possibly without specific testamentary reference. A testator's commitments, plans and priorities, obvious enough at the time, are now all too often indecipherable.

As far as mature heirs were concerned, then, it is perfectly plausible that the portion that was their due had been so well defined and was sufficiently widely known to mean that detailed testamentary delineation and 'transfer' was superfluous. Or, by the time that the testator died, he may already have devised to heir or heirs their inheritance or dowry, in which case testamentary prescription was again superfluous.[30] The very existence of issue, while obviously crucial in determining the shape and scope of plans, need not be apparent since testators needed only to clarify their short-term, small-scale pious provision and bequest of chattels.

But more was involved. Heirs may have had a certain claim to their inheritance, but it is to be emphasized that testators expected a return for fidelity toward offspring, the more so since burgage tenure did permit alternatives. Consider: had testators not had surviving issue, or had they chosen to neglect them, they might have devoted all their estate to pious uses. Parents obviously felt justified in expecting some return, particularly for the property that they themselves may have accumulated. Just as widows were expected to provide for services from property ostensibly devised for their sustenance, so children, themselves frequently nominated executors, were assigned the responsibility, for instance, of 'finding' a priest for a given number of years or an anniversary service for their parents.[31] And it is in this respect that wills are particularly misleading. For the instruction to find a priest for seven years at a salary of £6 per annum seems to imply that £42 had been set aside by the testator to foot the bill. Testators' true intentions, however, as to their legatees' reciprocal responsibilities become apparent only with closer scrutiny. Richard Vener's plans again repay examination.[32] Proceeds from selling twelve cloths were to provide for essentially small-scale pious provisions, as noted earlier. His explicit plans for the rest of his estate were as follows. To his daughter Margaret he bequeathed a number of his more valuable movables – a mazer, spoons, a cauldron, blankets and so on – and to her children, sums of money. To his daughter, Agnes, he left the residue of his estate but did not specify whether she was to devote this to pious uses for the benefit of his soul. Vener appointed her husband, Robert Ledbury, co-executor with one Laurence Brokke (not otherwise mentioned in the will except as a recipient of a bequest of one mark), and, more significantly, devised Agnes and Robert his dwelling house in the parish of St Mary le Port, Bristol. In default of their heirs, this property was to revert to Margaret and her husband, John Teffent, in default of whose heirs it was to revert to Vener's nephew, Nicholas Derlyng, and his heirs. But regardless of which branch of the family would ultimately have kept this property, Vener was determined to have a return: an annual payment of 12d was to be made to sustain a lamp burning before the Lord's body (presumably the reserved Sacrament) in the chancel of St Mary le Port. It is possible that Vener would have profited from a more ambitious service provided by the disposal of his estate residue. Come what may, Vener's soul and the souls of his other nominees were to benefit, in a modest but symbolically significant way, from a service provided by the recipients of his dwelling house.

Others made similar specifications. John Foster in 1492 devised his daughter and son-in-law the messuage in which they already lived in Corn Street, provided they keep it in good repair and pay annually 10s to the Prioress and Convent of St Mary Magdalene, Bristol, 2s to the Abbot and Convent of Tewkesbury, 2s to the churchwardens of St Werburgh's, Bristol, and, additionally, 10s to Foster's own almshouse in Steep Street, Bristol.[33] Effectively their rent was to benefit Foster's soul and help sustain his most ambitious pious work. Similarly, Agnes Wellishote, when she died in 1457, devised her daughter Agnes Gaywode properties in Bristol and left her the residue of her estate; Agnes Gaywode was, in return, to commemorate her mother's anniversary in the parish church of St John the Baptist for twenty years.[34] The principle is clear. So when, some twenty years later, Agnes' husband, John Gaywode, was silent as to the specific provision he sought in death, there can be little doubt that Agnes and his children would have commissioned worthwhile services: the former having received the residue of his estate and instructions, as sole executrix, to dispose of it as she saw fit, and each of the latter a substantial legacy of real property.[35] And it is to be emphasized that just as Gaywode omitted specific instructions as to the form that his pious services were to take, so others, possibly those whose heirs were already in possession of their inheritances, might specify the services they required without reiterating which legacy was to be harnessed, or even which beneficiary was to find the service.

It is all too easy to assume that testators paid for their own *post obit* services. This is mistaken. Rather than reserving cash for dispersal in regular instalments, testators relied on practices evolved to ensure that heirs and devisees provided services for benefactors. And it is to be borne in mind that the service a will specified – be it a lamp, an anniversary, or even a chantry of two or three years' duration – was not necessarily the most ambitious undertaking from which a testator would have profited. It may conceivably have been subsidiary, simply the return a devisee was obliged to discharge to 'earn' his or her right to relatively unimportant property. The main service may have been inaugurated *pre obit*, or left to the discretion of executrix or executors. Seldom in the position to reckon the precise value of their estate residue or the duration of the service it might support, and under no obligation to give comprehensive detail as to their property plans, testators were frequently content to leave their main service to vague instruction or tacit arrangement. Wills are all too often deceptive as to the relative significance of any particular devise, any particular service, or any particular beneficiary's duties. Important and well established as the convention of reciprocal provision may have been, it is now frequently obscure and formidably difficult, if not impossible, to disentangle, to the lasting detriment of historical reconstruction.

If we turn, secondly, to consider heirs who were minors, another convention presents itself which, while ostensibly operating to protect heirs' interests, nevertheless had significant ramifications. The convention was long-established, but was applied in a single eventuality by the fifteenth century. Should a testator die leaving both widow and infants, immovable property would be reserved, entrusted usually to the widow until the heirs came of age, and the testator's movable estate split into three: one third to the widow, another to the children, the remainder devoted to procuring pious works to benefit the testator's soul.[36] The procedure was not particularly common in late-medieval Bristol. In the fifteenth century, roughly 5 per cent of the sample, some twenty testators, gave specific instructions that it be adopted, almost all the examples occurring in the first thirty years of the century. Many points arise: this discussion will concentrate on three. First, to the question of why the procedure was adopted by certain testators, the answer obviously lies in the fact that it was evidently perceived as a fair way of solving the problem of how a parent might provide for issue without neglecting his soul. But it also seems reasonable to suggest that as all who relied on the convention were survived both by a wife and young children, a good proportion of them died young and perhaps suddenly, possibly of plague or (in a predominantly mercantile community) at sea. It is, therefore, probable that many of the testaments in question were not deathbed documents. After all, the convention had much to recommend it as a provisional arrangement to be made by a man not actually expecting imminent death but nevertheless mindful of the unforeseen. Second, it may be noted that few of the wills in question mention real property. This is not to imply that those testators who omitted any reference to it had none. Clearly, it was accepted that the widow and mother would assume responsibility for any realty during the interval between the testator's death and his heirs' majority, a principle so well established that it needed no prescription. The third point is the corollary of the second and elaborates an aspect of conventional practice alluded to earlier. Few of the wills in question mentioned realty; a high proportion were simply personalty wills. Some prescribed what was to be done with each third in some detail; others simply concentrated on the pious uses. John Gy, for instance, who made his will in 1424, specified that his goods be divided into three, said that 'everything following was to be paid for from his share', and proceeded to devote the bulk of his will to detailed instructions for his funeral and the various small-scale observances that were to accompany it.[37] Unbidden, his widow and executrix, Alice, may in the fullness of time have provided long-term services for his soul; but the point to be emphasized is that, save the first clauses which mention that his movables were to be split into three, the rest of his provision resembles many other wills which dwelt almost entirely on funerals.[38] The convention of 'thirds' was particularly well established: John Gy thought a cursory reference to his children adequate; how many other testators were there who, content to rely on the convention, simply devoted their will to prescribing the disposal of their 'third'? As suggested earlier, it was not always necessary to mention heirs in wills; nor was it necessary to give comprehensive instructions for the estate. Many extant wills may well be dealing only with a small proportion of testators' movable goods. Agnes Spicer, who died in 1456, certainly left two distinct wills: a realty will registered in the Great Red Book of Bristol, and another, unspecified but clearly a personalty will, registered by the Prerogative Court of Canterbury.[39] By good fortune her realty will survives. How many others were lost or never registered, leaving us only with testators' personalty wills bearing no indication as to the limitation of their competence? In the absence of supplementary information, it is impossible to determine how many testaments are concerned merely with the disposal of a third of testators' movables: that is, with a tiny proportion of the total estate. Insofar as this convention was specifically employed almost entirely before 1430, and as the circumstances recommending it are hardly likely to have ceased thereafter, many later wills are surely misleading.

It is, however, salutary to explore the implications of this convention further. By good fortune, corroborative material survives for one of the few specific examples from the late fifteenth century. William Rowley, a member of a mercantile family prominent in late-medieval Bristol, died in 1478.[40] The circumstances of his death are obscure, although his wish to be buried within the church of Carmelite friars 'apud Burdeaux', bequest of 'fifty francs in money of Acquitaine' to these frairs, and reference to merchandise and maritime ventures suggest a merchant who died in Gascony. References to Gascony and to an unconcluded commercial interest apart, his will merits no special note. His wife, Elizabeth, apparently survived him, as did four daughters; but Rowley devised no realty, nor issued any clear statement as to plans for dispersing his movable estate. His intentions are signalled by bequests to Elizabeth, significantly, of the third part of his silver, his merchandise and of any debts due to him. Also, he appointed his father, one Thomas Rowley, his executor and entrusted him with his soul's and his daughters' share. Thus, Thomas Rowley was instructed to dispose of £10 in alms, and to find a suitable chaplain to celebrate a trental for his son's soul, as he had done formerly for William's brother, Richard; he was to be guardian for his four grand-daughters and their legacy; and, finally, was entrusted with the residue of William's estate to dispose of it for the benefit of his late son's soul, as he saw fit. The will is modest and, even if one were aware of the family's prominence, its contents give no pause for further examination. The extent to which convention obfuscates reality in this instance is made manifest only by documentation generated by subsequent, unforeseen occurences. Thomas died only a month or so after William. The *Little Red Book of Bristol* records the re-assignation of guardianship, in September 1479, to Margaret Rowley, Thomas's widow and William's mother, to be exercised under supervision of the Mayor of Bristol and named trustees, one of whom was William's uncle and Thomas's brother, also called William Rowley.[41] Had Thomas's death not succeeded his son's so closely, apparently before the latter's will had been proved, so formal a procedure of re-assignation may not have been necessary; but it was this event which first reveals that the share reserved for the four girls was very substantial indeed, amounting to £524 13s 4d to be divided equally among them. Additional information recorded in the Patent Rolls may be adduced in confirmation.[42] By 1492, the first and third daughters, Margaret and Alice, had married; the second, Elizabeth, had died; and the youngest, Joan, by dint of Elizabeth's decease, now heir to one third of the legacy, had been betrothed. She died at the age of twelve-and-a-half, before matrimony but not before she had made a will appointing her intended, one John Prout, and his father (or possibly brother) as her executors, and naming John her beneficiary. A quarrel ensued. The Mayor and Commonalty of Bristol claimed that so young a child might not make a testament, acting effectively in the interests of the two surviving daughters; John disputed this and claimed Joan's share, said now to be worth 250 marks and £8 4s 5d. Prout won. But the point to be emphasized is that William Rowley was a very wealthy man with a movable estate apparently worth in excess of £1,500: much more than ever would have been assumed from his will. One can only speculate as to the pious services his widow, heirs and mother would have been either obliged or inclined to provide for him. How many other simple and relatively modest wills concealed large fortunes may never be known, but it is clear that 'safe' assumptions and 'modest' estimates may be wildly inaccurate.

Many conventions operated to determine and safeguard the disposition of property, the provision of pious observances, and the procedures of exchanging property for services. It would be possible, for instance, to analyze the contrivances to which individuals resorted to establish perpetual chantries and guarantee future supervision and maintenance.[43] These were conventions which, while of importance to founders, parish authorities and even town government, made a variable, and all too often negligible, impact on wills. But their examination would add little to the point I seek to make. Wills blinker us to testators' wider concerns. The influences exercised by the circumstances of everyday life, by parish community, and by family, were potent pressures to which each individual was subject and which each might exploit – pressures which in turn, constrained and liberated. The courses of action they prompted needed no testamentary prescription. As a result, wills may best be regarded as documents to which, in the main, details were consigned: the small-scale observances of the funeral, the precise service required in return for minor property devise, the after-thoughts not previously seeming important or feasible. If mentioned, testators' most important plans and main objectives, in contrast to the detail devoted to the short-term and small-scale, appear both tidy and vague. Brief allusion was all that was necessary to confirm previous arrangements or to set agreed and conventional practices into operation. Wills were, of course, used to enunciate important principles: they affirmed the nomination of executors and might reveal the principles determining the disposal of the estate. But nominees often had to proceed largely on their own initiative and they too may well have sought the help of others and relied on established customs. Conventions played a fundamental, although now inevitably obscure, role in shaping and effecting what Professor Dobson called 'religious priorities and sensibilities'.[44] Wills alone are an inadequate guide to the pious practice and procedure of individuals and communities alike.

As a final illustration of many of the principles and practices referred to above, an example may be described which vividly illustrates social and pious convention as each combined to operate in a family and parish in pre-Reformation Bristol. It should serve once and for all to emphasize that impressions derived from wills alone are a blank façade disguising an intricate reality.

The example concerns one John Newman, a butcher of Bristol and parishioner of St Mary le Port, who died in 1513. A document dated January 1517/18, which is transcribed in a late nineteenth-century local history journal but whose original has apparently perished, reveals that he was murdered by his servant, Denys Grene, on 31 August.[45] He was murdered, however, after making various provisions with the full agreement of his wife and parish. The document reveals that wife and parish sought to ensure that Newman's wishes, no less than the benefit of the other parties, would be realized. It starts by listing many men of 'good evidence and sadness' who swore that they had, on 22 June 1513, gathered in the parish church in the presence of John Boys, the parson, to partake in and witness the arrangements that Newman sought to make 'unto the wealth of his soul'. They thereafter refer to themselves as 'Recorders' and describe what occurred. Newman, although poor, had recently married Johanna Luke, widow of Thomas Luke, another butcher. Johanna 'brought with her' £100 or more in money and plate. Newman and

Johanna, however, were disposed and also probably obliged to devote a portion of the money to procuring services profiting their own souls and the soul of Thomas Luke. With Johanna's assent, Newman purchased a messuage in the Shammells in Bristol, paying its owner £20, which he had from Johanna, and promising to pay a further £20 for it.[46] In the meeting on 22 June he enfeoffed the Recorders with this property, retaining its use for as long as he and Johanna lived, but providing thereafter that the property and its revenues were to be held and administered by feoffees and their heirs and assigns in perpetuity. They were instructed to use its revenues to hold an anniversary in St Mary's for his soul, Johanna's soul and the soul of Thomas Luke at an annual expense of 3s 4d. They were also to find a lamp to burn before the blessed Sacrament at the high altar of St Mary le Port for ever at a cost of 8s annually. Any surplus accruing was to be used by the feoffees to find an honest priest to sing for the souls of John and Johanna and Thomas within the chapel of St Wilgefortis recently built in St Mary's church, 'among other good doers there forever'. Presumably this chantry would either have been intermittent or the revenues in question combined with others from similar arrangements to support a permanent priest in the chapel. Nevertheless, on 22 June the Recorders are said to have entered into the messuage in Newman's presence and the presence of other witnesses, bringing forth a posnet of brass to establish their seisin. Thence all repaired to a tavern called the Boar's Head. In the tavern, Newman rehearsed his 'will and intent' concerning the above arrangements, affirmed the same and moreover, with his cap in his hand, desired that the Recorders and their heirs and assigns, 'would stand and be seised to the use above written' and promise to perform and fulfil his will. Those present declared that they would 'and there quieted unto him', whereupon Newman paid for the wine that the assembled company consumed.

The document reports that on 31 August 1513 Newman was 'feloniously murdered' by his servant. Johanna, now John's widow and executrix, 'trusting verily the foresaid will of the same John, by him in manner and form above written, declared it to be good and effectual in conscience'. She is said to have paid the £20 still owing on the messuage in the Shammells, after which the Recorders declared that they were indeed seised of and in the property, to the use of Johanna for her life and thereafter to the further use and performance of the will and intent of John Newman – effectively to the benefit of Johanna's and her husbands' souls. Significantly, the Recorders then announce that they had often heard John Newman say that his son William was entirely disinherited because he was unthrifty and would not be ruled by his father, preferring instead the company of 'strong thieves'. This must account for his reported earlier arrest on suspicion of felony and consequent imprisonment for six months or more in Newgate prison, Bristol, until such time, the Recorders report, as his father had paid for his release, after which, it is said, William and his father never met. This remarkable document ends with the Recorders affirming the truth of its contents, all of them announcing their readiness to swear on the Holy Evangelists that what they had asserted contained 'very truth' as was the 'voice and fame in Bristol and its suburbs'.

Whether the parish was successful in its attempt to ensure that the Newmans and Luke benefited from the services prescribed is at present impossible to determine; in that there were eminent local men among the Recorders, it would be surprising had they failed. Either way, clearer vindication of many of the axioms employed in the foregoing discussion is hard to imagine. The example demonstrates beyond any doubt that individual and parish might combine *in life* to settle the services that were to be provided in death. The agreements – oral, in this instance – were binding, and the subsequent action taken by the parishioners of St Mary le Port demonstrates just how seriously a parish community took its responsibilities towards its own members. It also demonstrates that widows could indeed be trusted to act in the spiritual interests of a dead spouse, and that any such relict might rely on the help and guidance of the parish to effect the requisite services. Individual, parish and family interests were thoroughly inter-mingled, although in the case in question the existence of a malcontent, with at least some claim to his father's estate, probably prompted the parish to attempt verification of Newman's wishes and its own rightful responsibilities. Had Newman not been murdered, and, probably more pertinently, had he not had a disinherited heir, then his wishes and arrangements would have gone unrecorded. For it is to be noted that Newman did leave a will, registered in the Prerogative Court of Canterbury.[47] It was made on the day of his death, presumably in the interval between mortal injury and demise. He declared that he was whole in mind and memory. He bequeathed his soul to God, the Blessed Virgin and the whole company of Heaven. He ordered that his body be buried in St Mary le Port. He devised all his goods, movable and immovable, to his wife Johanna, whom he appointed sole executrix and charged with doing what was best for the health of his soul. It was witnessed by three men in addition to one John Coke, his 'gostely father', who had written down his wishes. His will is short, very tidy and decidedly vague. It is utterly unremarkable. Ordinarily it would not merit a second glance.[48]

A strong sense of irony proves invaluable for those who seek to plumb the well-springs and comprehend the manifestations of late-medieval popular piety. The very abundance of what appears to be the most promising documentary source – that is, of contemporary wills – accounts for perhaps the most besetting problem accompanying their use. Historians have devoted inordinate attention to wills' contents, to the neglect of establishing a methodology which takes adequate account of the implications of alternative documentation. Blinkered, they have used wills very carelessly. For reasons which I hope are now plain, it should be remembered that in the absence of other materials, wills can yield only a limited impression of either devotional attitude or religious practice, at least for the middling ranks of society. It may by contrast be true that wills surviving for members of the elite may afford fuller impressions. Noble and knightly provision would more probably have been on a scale demanding detailed prescription, and, in some cases, sufficient additional material survives to permit an impression of the practices and attitudes of some such individuals in life.[49] But what is true for a tiny minority may not be applied generally. It is a mistake to expect townspeople's wills to yield sufficient information to grant similar analysis of testators as individuals; only the survival of copious extra information permits any such assessment, and this is rare. Among the citizens of fifteenth-century Bristol, only William Canynges can be examined in any detail. For the great majority of townspeople, it would be nearer the truth to recognize that the impression afforded by their wills is but 'key-hole' vision, and to recognize too that by themselves such glimpses make very little sense. Wills, after all, were documents made to govern part only of what was to be done after death by men and women who were also parishioners, quite probably gild members, and almost certainly citizens and spouses. These loyalties may at times have been in competition, but they undoubtedly determined and facilitated practices and attitudes which now elude us. Ultimately, wills were useful for taking care of details, but – ironically, once again – as far as long-term or important business is concerned, were frequently used simply to outline essential principles. Rather than offering mirrors of the soul, wills are all too often undeniably vague. This may account for the tranquillity, amounting almost to sterility, that one recent commentator selects as the salient characteristic of late-medieval urban piety. But it is to be emphasized that if faith and practice in this milieu appears 'insular, inert, and shallow, untouched by the new devotions, perfunctory almost in the old ones', then this is simply the testamentary impression. While following well established procedures, and although dovetailed with a host of other considerations, the reality of town, parish and even family piety must surely be accounted richer and more vital.[50]

Notes

Strictly, wills dealt with the devise of real property and testaments with bequests of movables. Nevertheless in practice people might deal with real and movable property in one document, a last will and testament. For convenience I shall apply the noun 'will' and adjective 'testamentary' to documents directing the *post obit* disposal of estates.

1. R.B. Dobson in *EHR* cii (1987), pp. 477–8: review of N.P. Tanner, *The Church in Late Medieval Norwich 1370–1532* (Toronto 1984).

2. The number and location of late-medieval wills is detailed in A.J. Camp, *Wills and their Whereabouts* (4th edn 1974); cf. J.J. Scarisbrick, *The Reformation and the English People* (Oxford 1984), ch. 1.

3. e.g. J. Rosenthal, *The Purchase of Paradise: Gift-Giving and the Aristocracy 1307–1485* (1972); M.G.A. Vale, *Piety, Charity and Literacy among the Yorkshire Gentry 1370–1480* (BP 50, 1976); N. Saul, 'The Religious Sympathies of the Gentry in Gloucestershire 1200–1500', *TBGAS* xcviii (1980), pp. 99–112; P.W. Fleming, 'Charity, Faith, and the Gentry of Kent 1442–1529', *Property and Politics: Essays in Later Medieval English History*, A.J. Pollard (ed.), (Gloucester 1984), pp. 36–58.

4. Common law encouraged all freemen to make wills and married women were also entitled to do so. Men of servile status might make wills but, if they did, few survive: M.M. Sheehan, *The Will in Medieval England* (Toronto 1963), pp. 233–41, and Tanner, *Norwich*, pp. 114–16.

5. See Tanner, *Norwich*; J.A.F. Thomson, 'Piety and Charity in Late Medieval London', *JEH* xvi (1965), pp. 178–95; J. Kermode, 'The Merchants of Three Northern English Towns', in Clough, *Profession*, pp. 7–49; P. Heath, 'Urban Piety in the Later Middle Ages: The Evidence of Hull Wills', *CPP*, pp. 209–34.

6. Scarisbrick, *Reformation*, pp. 10–11; Tanner, *Norwich*, p. 117; cf. R.A. Houlbrooke, *Church Courts and the People during the English Reformation 1520–70* (Oxford 1979), p. 101.

7. *The Oxford Dictionary of Quotations* (3rd edn Oxford 1979), p. 44.

8. For some examples, see my '"By Quick and by Dead": Wills and Pious Provision in Late Medieval Bristol', *EHR* cii (1987), pp. 837–58.

9. This quandary is trenchantly summarized by contrasting K.B. McFarlane's reported concurrence 'with traditional antiquaries in finding in funeral monuments, heraldic achievements and wills, if read aright, the most important evidence of men as individuals' (McFarlane, *Nobility*, p. xxxvii) with his much gloomier reaction to the problems of interpreting the so-called Lollard wills, as expressed in *Lancastrian Kings and Lollard Knights* (Oxford 1972), p. 207.

10. For present purposes, this may be taken as comprising about 350 wills located mainly in the PRO (PCC wills) and Bristol RO Great Orphan Book; municipal and commercial archives in *Bristol GRB* and *Bristol LRB* and supplemented by E.M. Carus-Wilson, *The Overseas Trade of Bristol* (Bristol Rec. Soc. vii, 1937); and parish archives inc. accounts, inventories, ordinances and deeds deposited in Bristol RO, some of which is printed, e.g. in *The Church Book of St Ewen's, Bristol, 1454–1584*, B.R. Masters and E. Ralph (eds), (Bristol and Gloucestershire Arch. Soc. Records Section vi, 1967).

11. An impression which is not necessarily restricted to Bristol, see Tanner, *Norwich*, pp. 138–40, and Heath *CPP*, p. 228.

12. F. Pollock and F.W. Maitland, *History of English Law* (2nd edn Cambridge 1968), ii. p. 340.

13. C. Burgess, '"A fond thing vainly invented": Purgatory and Pious Motive in Later Medieval England', *Parish, Church and People*, S. Wright (ed.), (1988), pp. 56–84, which describes the development of the sacrament of penance and outlines its effect and influence in the later medieval period.

14. Burgess, *EHR* cii (1987), elaborates this point.

15. His will is registered in Bristol RO Gt. Orphan Bk. ff.199v–201.

16. For the relevant municipal and parish archives, see E.E. Williams, *The Chantries of William Canynges in St Mary Redcliffe, Bristol* (Bristol 1950), pp. 255–87.

17. Printed in 'Chantry Certificates, Gloucestershire', J. MacLean, *TBGAS* viii (1883–4), pp. 232–51 and summarized in Williams, *Canynges Chantries*, pp. 32–41.

18. The references to his almshouses are conveniently collected in M.D. Lobel and E.M.

Carus-Wilson, 'Bristol', *The Atlas of Historic Towns*, ii, M.D. Lobel and W.H. Johns (eds), (1975), p. 14 n.33.

19. For instance, neither of the perpetual chantries established by the Halleways and the Spicers in the 1450s in the parish churches of All Saints' and St James', Bristol occur in their founders' wills. Apart from the mid-sixteenth-century chantry certificates, we depend for our knowledge of each on the chance survival of chantry accounts and (for Halleways' chantry) on foundation deeds enrolled in *Bristol LRB* ii. pp. 199–206.

20. See also Burgess, *Parish, Church & People.*

21. On fraternities, see Scarisbrick, *Reformation*, ch. 2; C.M. Barron, 'The Parish Fraternities of Medieval London', *The Church in Pre-Reformation Society*, C.M. Barron and C. Harper-Bill (eds), (Woodbridge 1985), pp. 13–37, esp. pp. 26–7.

22. See also Burgess, *Parish, Church & People.* Cf. R. Hutton, 'The Local Impact of the Tudor Reformations', *The English Reformation Revised*, C. Haigh (ed.), (Cambridge 1987), pp. 114–38.

23. Parishes had strong interests in complying with parishioners' wishes, as the latter almost invariably contrived financial or liturgical profit for the parish from the faithful discharge of long-term *post obit* services, see Burgess, *Parish, Church and People* .

24. Pollock and Maitland, ii. pp. 403–36; Sheehan, *Medieval Will*, pp. 234–9; *Bristol GRB*, introduction, pp. 55–9. Of fifteenth-century Bristol wills, only four represent wives predeceasing husbands: Margaret Yonge d.1406 PROB 11/2A (PCC 13 Marche) ff.100v-102; Christina Chesewell d.1407 Bristol RO Gt. Orphan Bk. ff.105v-106; Margaret Stephens d.1417 ibid. f.128; Maud Esterfield d.1491 PROB 11/9 (PCC 20 Dogett) f.157.

25. Bristol RO Gt.Orphan Bk. f.120v.

26. For references and details, see Burgess, *EHR* cii (1987).

27. Provision or repair of public amenities e.g. roads and bridges was a good work and beneficial to the soul, see Tanner, *Norwich*, pp. 137–8; Thomson, *JEH* xvi (1965), pp. 187–8; Kermode in Clough, *Profession*, pp. 31–2.

28. Pollock and Maitland, ii. pp. 260–313, 325–30; Camp, *Wills*, p. x; Sheehan, *Medieval Will*, pp. 269–74, 280–1.

29. Pollock and Maitland, i. p. 645; ii. p. 330; Sheehan, *Medieval Will*, pp. 274–81; *Bristol GRB*, introduction, 5sqq; *Borough Customs*, M. Bateson (ed.), (Selden Soc. xxi, 1906), pp. 90–102, 201–4.

30. William Canynges' sons received their portions well before his death, but as both predeceased him he had to leave instructions for the ultimate devise of his property after the deaths of his daughters-in-law to a nephew and niece. For a simpler example, see Henry Chestre PROB 11/6 (PCC 1 Wattys) f.4v; and Burgess, *EHR* cii (1987), p. 852.

31. See also Burgess, *EHR* cii (1987).

32. Bristol RO Gt. Orphan Bk. f.120v.

33. PROB 11/9 (PCC 9 Dogett) ff.65–66.

34. PROB 11/4 (PCC 12 Stokton) ff.92–v.

35. Bristol RO Gt. Orphan Bk. ff.191v–3v.

36. Pollock and Maitland, ii. pp. 348–56; Sheehan, *Medieval Will*, pp. 263–4; *Bristol GRB*, introduction, pp. 69–73; Bateson, *Borough Customs*, ii. pp. 136–7; *The Register of Henry Chichele*, E.F. Jacob (ed.), (4 vols Canterbury and York Soc. 1937–47), ii. pp. xxxv–vii.

37. Bristol RO Gt. Orphan Bk. ff.144v–45.

38. See for example, the wills of John Stone d.1414, Thomas Bewflour d.1426, John Nancothan d.1469, William Coder d.1473, and William Hynde d.1473, Bristol RO Gt. Orphan Bk. ff.125v, 154v–55, 189v, 197v–99.

39. *Bristol GRB* ii. pp. 207–8; PROB 11/4 (PCC 7 Stokton) f.52v.

40. Bristol RO Gt. Orphan Bk. ff.209–v.

41. PROB 11/6 (PCC 36 Wattys) f.278v; *Bristol LRB* ii. pp. 197–9.

42. *CPR 1485–94*, pp. 413–14.

43. C. Burgess, 'Chantries in Fifteenth-Century Bristol' (Oxford D.Phil. thesis 1981), pp. 237–91. I hope to publish an article on this subject in the near future.

44. Dobson, *EHR* cii (1987), pp. 477–8.

45. J.R. Bramble, 'Ancient Bristol Documents II: A Curious Deed belonging to the Parish of St Mary le Port', *Proceedings of the Clifton Antiquarian Club* i (1884–8), pp. 136–41. The date of 1508 in the transcript is given in error for 1513: Newman, killed in the year of the deed, definitely died in 1513.

46. The name 'Shambles' denotes an area associated with the slaughter of animals, the sale of flesh, and hence butchers.

47. PROB 11/17 (PCC 30 Fetiplace) f.239.

48. Note also the provision made for John and Juliana Hyham by the latter's second husband and executor Thomas Slye, but for whom no wills survive; see *Bristol GRB* i. p. 251.

49. See for example, M.A. Hicks, 'The Piety of Margaret, Lady Hungerford (d.1478)', *JEH* xxxviii (1987), pp. 19–38 & esp. n.2 for bibliography; and also M.G. Underwood, 'Politics and Piety in the Household of Lady Margaret Beaufort', in ibid. pp. 39–52.

50. Heath, *CPP*, p. 229.

3

Women's Work, Women's Role, in the Late-Medieval North

P.J.P. Goldberg
University of York

It is no longer permissible for the medievalist to work on a variety of manorial, urban, taxation and even legal sources without acknowledging that women were actively involved in economic life.[1] Indeed it is hardly possible to understand the society and economy of the later Middle Ages if one ignores the position of women in that society. I have argued elsewhere that the differing social–structural responses to epidemic plague in Northern England and Tuscany owe much to differences in social customs in relation to marriage and household formation, which are themselves intimately linked to the economic status of women.[2] I have also argued that for the towns of late-medieval Yorkshire, and for England as a whole from at least the early modern period, a north-west European pattern of late companionate marriage, of life-cycle servanthood, and of a significant proportion of the population at any period never marrying, allowed women to fill a wide range of occupations when economic expansion overtook the supply of labour.[3] This last was certainly true of the economy of the Yorkshire region and more widely in the decades following the Black Death.[4] Nearly all my work to date has been concerned with the experience of urban women, and the women of York in particular. What then of the experience of rural women?

It is possible to explore the economy of a significant part of Yorkshire for the later fourteenth century, and something of the economic role of women within that economy, from poll tax sources.[5] These throw light on the relationship between town and country, between agriculture and industry, and between status and household. Of particular interest is the evidence relating to servants and to children remaining with their parents. This may prove especially valuable when tied to evidence relating to migration and to marriage that I hope to obtain from alternative sources.[6] This then is very much work in progress and some of the observations made must necessarily be of a highly speculative nature.

Much of this present paper is derived from an analysis of the surviving poll tax returns for the West Riding and Howdenshire in the East Riding of Yorkshire for 1379.[7] The West Riding returns vary in quality between the twelve constituent wapentakes, although none are as detailed as the Howdenshire returns. The second poll tax was levied in theory on all lay persons over the age of sixteen. Married couples were assessed together and a differential assessment with a minimum rate of fourpence (4d) was employed. Artisans and other more substantial persons, including franklins and farmers of manors, were taxed at sixpence (6d), a shilling or more.[8] Within these Yorkshire returns such higher rate taxpayers are invariably described by occupation, although there may be numbers of craftworkers not deemed to be of sufficient substance to be taxed as artisans. It may be that there is some justification in using occupational by-names as evidence for occupations in such cases since surnames still appear unstable at this date within this region. Millers, for example, are very rarely designated, though the surname 'milner' is often encountered. In the Ainsty a few individuals so named are assessed at sixpence, indicative that these were indeed millers and that the assessors here chose to class them as artisans. For the purposes of this present analysis single women having an occupational by-name will be presumed to be of that calling unless there is evidence that this is a family name possessed by other members of a particular community. This method will inevitably introduce a margin of error, but it may be noted that the pattern of occupations so derived is remarkably consistent and corresponds well with the evidence for female craft work derived from occupational designations of higher rate female taxpayers only. Some occupational by-names are, moreover, specifically feminine, as, for example, semester, sewester, laundere, norys or *nutrix*, all professions unlikely to merit taxation at the higher rate.[9] The same method of identifying professions has been applied to persons of both sexes in the case of larger urban communities.

Other than for Howdenshire the returns rarely note the occupation of a married woman where this differs from, or is in addition to, that of the husband. For Claro Wapentake, however, the husband's occupation is stated after his own name and not that of the couple as is more usual elsewhere. Where the occupation is stated after the wife's name, therefore, this may be assumed to refer specifically to the wife. In nearly all these cases the wife is stated to be a 'brewster'. Joan, the wife of William Palfrayman of Kirk Deighton, however, is assessed as a weaver (*textrix*) separately from her husband. Dependents, i.e. children, servants and other relatives, are often recorded immediately following the head of household, but for the wapentakes of Barkston Ash, Morley, Skyrack, Staincliffe and Ewecross single persons are regularly listed together at the end of the return for each community without any indication of the household unit to which they might belong. This is also true of the returns for individual communities within the other wapentakes, but sometimes details of household affiliation are provided and household units can thus be reconstructed. For the wapentakes of Strafforth, Tickhill, Staincross, Osgodcross, Agbrigg, and Claro, a variety of measures relating to household and occupational structure may thus be derived. It is further possible to compare measures derived from specifically rural communities primarily engaged in agriculture against those derived from more urban, craft-based communities.

A number of communities were loosely classified as urban on the basis of size and economic structure, but closer analysis suggests certain more specific definitions. Towns tended to be characterized by a relatively low adult sex ratio, i.e. women outnumber men, and by a relatively high proportion of servants. Thus the poll tax sex ratios for Howden and Pontefract were 84.7 and 92.8. The proportion of servants to all taxpayers in Pontefract was 17.4 per cent. This contrasts with a sex ratio of 99.2 and a proportion of the population in service of only 4.5 per cent for Strafforth Wapentake (excluding Doncaster, Bradfield, Rotherham and Ecclesfield). For rural Howdenshire, where, as noted before, the returns are rather more comprehensive, the total sex ratio was somewhat higher at 94.4. The structure of urban craft or trade-related households also demonstrates certain specific characteristics. A very high proportion of all servants can be associated with such households, but relatively few contain children of age to be taxed. The ratio of children to servants tends thus to be very low for many urban communities, viz. 0.14 at Pontefract, 0.16 at Ripon, and 0.18 at Doncaster. This may be compared against equivalent ratios of 0.53 for Claro, 0.86 for Strafforth, and 1.40 for Tickhill Wapentake. The proportions of servants specifically associated with craft households tend to be rather smaller in rural communities, but these proportions are not insignificant considering the relatively small numbers of households known to be engaged in craft activity. On the basis of this analysis some larger communities initially classified as urban appear anomalous. Ecclesfield and Bradfield, for example, with tax populations of 313 and 398 respectively are thoroughly rural in structure despite possessing rather larger numbers of artisans than their neighbours. The same is also true of Sheffield with a tax population of 527, but relatively few servants and a high child to servant ratio (1.13).

The same pattern of analysis may be applied to specific occupations. The trades of tailor, souter or shoemaker, weaver, smith or marshal, and wright or carpenter have been considered here since they are well represented in both village and town. The rural sample is drawn from the six wapentakes noted before, and the urban sample from Pontefract, Wakefield, Ripon, Doncaster, Tickhill and Rotherham, towns with a combined tax population of 3,275. Sex ratios associated with servants do not differ radically between town and country save in weavers' households. Here female servants are rather more common in rural districts (urban servant sex ratio = 400, rural servant sex ratio = 150) and this would accord with other evidence, discussed shortly, that weaving was more feminized outside the town. Servant groups associated with wrights and carpenters tend to be comparatively feminized in both town and country (urban servant sex ratio = 75, rural servant sex ratio = 80). Conversely, servant groups associated with smiths and marshals tend to be male dominated (urban servant sex ratio = 260, rural servant sex ratio = 200). The striking difference between town and country is again seen in the high proportion of children retained in rural artisan households. The child to servant ratio in the group of towns ranges between 0.07 for wrights and carpenters, and 0.27 for weavers. For the rural sample, however, the equivalent ratios range from 0.55 for souters to 1.72 for wrights and carpenters. The sex ratios associated with these children tend to be more balanced and thus show little correlation with servant sex ratios. Within the households of smiths and marshals over the six wapentakes, for example, there are twenty-three daughters and twenty-eight sons recorded as against twenty-two female servants to forty-four male. In the cases of souters and weavers dependent female children actually outnumber male children, though sample sizes are comparatively small. Since the poll tax was levied only on persons aged sixteen and over, there can be little doubt that such retained children and servants of either sex were economically active. At Howden retained children are specifically, albeit confusingly, described as servants to indicate their economic status. This is sometimes made explicit within the tax records. Isolda, the daughter of Richard Broune and his wife, is described as '*textrix*' and separately assessed at the higher rate. Likewise Emma, one of four recorded servants of John Dicas, a tanner of Fryston, is assessed as a webster also at the higher rate.

The West Riding poll tax evidence thus suggests that service as an institution was comparatively widespread, but that it was less comprehensively developed within rural areas than was true of the towns.[10] In rural communities the retained labour of children represents a significant productive element within the household alongside, or in place of, servants. Young countrywomen, moreover, were at least as likely to be found living in their parental homes as dependent labour than as servants in the households of others, whereas young men were more likely to be found as servants. Service sex ratios associated with rural craft households tend, therefore, to be relatively high; male servants outnumbered female by three to two, as in Strafforth (craft servant sex ratio = 140.7) and Claro Wapentake (craft servant sex ratio = 150), although ratios for all servants are often lower. In the towns the equivalent ratios are rather lower, as at Pontefract (craft servant sex ratio = 117.9) or Ripon (craft servant sex ratio = 88.5).

These patterns are mirrored in the 1377 poll tax returns for the county of Rutland and for the Coquetdale Ward of Northumberland.[11] These earlier returns are assessed on a population aged fourteen or more. Using by-name evidence alone to identify craft households, the frequency with which children are retained in such households is again apparent. Indeed for Rutland excluding Oakham (tenants of the king) the craft child to servant ratio is 1.44, but for Oakham itself it is only 0.11. The craft-servant sex ratio in rural Rutland is especially high at 242.9, though the sex ratio for the entire tax population is lower at 161.9. Significantly the sex ratio of dependent children is much lower, i.e. more feminized, in craft households (sex ratio = 69.6) than in all households (sex ratio = 101.0). This would suggest that in rural Rutland crafts drew disproportionately upon male servants and female children. It is tempting to conclude that the retention of female children between the ages of fourteen and sixteen, an age group excluded from the 1379 poll tax, was an especially common phenomenon in craft households.

Certain observations follow from the findings just discussed. On the one hand young countrywomen may have acquired trade-related skills either through service or within their natal home, and these may be related to trades practised later in life. On the other hand a much higher proportion of children of both sexes appear to have been retained at home in rural communities than was true of towns where servant labour was more normal. Young people may thus often have been less economically and emotionally independent of their parents during their adolescence than was true of their urban counterparts. This may have had implications for marriage formation in as much as parents may have played a larger role in arranging marriages and providing for the couple at marriage. The evidence from matrimonial litigation in the Church court may support this view.[12] Depositions from a matrimonial cause of 1466 tell how a group of people, including the prospective groom and his mother, the vicar of Rotherham and one Nicholas Keeton, '*generosus*', assembled at the house of the prospective bride and her parents to discuss the proposed marriage. Only after the father's offer of dowry of 25 marks was agreed were the couple asked if they were willing to be married.[13] Another such conference is described in a cause dated 1453. Once again the young woman was living in her father's house at Eastburn near Driffield. When asked why she was unwilling to marry a man approved by her father she replied that it was because his parents called her 'lass'.[14] Conversely, when in 1490 Elena Couper of Welton near Hull contracted marriage without her parents' consent she was obliged to beg temporary lodgings with a friend so as to escape her father's wrath. She was called a harlot by both her father and her mother, but in order to gain her father's agreement she threw herself at his feet crying, 'I desire no more of your goods but your blessyng'. This strong-minded woman then tried to persuade her partner that they might lawfully live together, but he, the typical male, replied, 'we must tarry tyll the houce be reddy'.[15]

The greater freedom away from parents of town life, coupled with the prospect of meeting other young people, surely served to attract the young of both sexes into the town. This may have been especially true of the labour-starved years of the later fourteenth century when wage-labour was at a premium. Thus Richard, the son of Thomas de Queldryk, was presented in 1364 for leaving his work as a ploughman and his home in Sutton upon Derwent to settle in York.[16] The imbalance of poll tax sex ratios between town and country would suggest, however, that young women tended to be more mobile than young men. This might be suggested from the West Riding data, though the evidence should be treated with circumspection as some returns are clearly unsatisfactory and it must be doubted whether single persons are always fully enumerated. The total tax sex ratio for rural Strafforth Wapentake is 99.2, but for the towns of Rotherham and Doncaster within the wapentake it is 94.5 and 86.0 respectively. For rural Howdenshire, where the returns inspire more confidence, the equivalent ratio is 94.4, but for Howden itself only 84.7. The more satisfactory nominative returns of the 1377 poll tax likewise demonstrate that urban sex ratios tended to be low. The town was not, however, attractive exclusively to the young. Elena Blakburn and Alice Spurn, recent migrants to York from across the Pennines, were both said to be forty in a matrimonial cause of 1418.[17] When after eight years the monks of Meaux caught up with John Helmyslay, a villein who had fled their grange at Wharram and had married under an assumed identity, his wife, a free woman of good family, immediately fled to York. She was said still to be living there when she tried to have the marriage dissolved some years later in 1410.[18] The greater provision of hospitals, maisonsdieu and casual charity may also have attracted the elderly and widowed to settle in the town.[19]

The skewed nature of urban sex ratios must have meant that not all women could have found marriage partners within the town even had they so desired. What is less certain is how often rural migrants subsequently returned to the country to settle or to marry. A matrimonial cause of 1430 provides details of the movements of two servants from Poppleton near York in the four years prior to their marriage in Poppleton eighteen years earlier. John Dalton was in service with a tailor at York for three years before returning to live with his father at Poppleton prior to his marriage. Joan Dalton served in York, firstly Thomas Legate, until Martinmas and then until Pentecost a baker, John Croxton, whose wife was her blood relative. She then returned for the remainder of the year to Poppleton, but was again in service at York for the following hiring year before her marriage.[20] John Semer was in service at Bishophill in York for six years until the Martinmas of 1394, and was living at Ouseburn aged twenty when he made his deposition in a cause in 1396.[21] Agnes Nevill of Menethorpe had likewise been in service with a York widow the year prior to her deposition in 1372.[22] The departure of some adolescents from village communities and their subsequent return, perhaps to work heritable land, but often, it may be surmised, to marry, would have proportionately reduced the size of the unmarried population as reflected in the poll tax returns. Unfortunately the 1379 West Riding returns tend not to be of sufficient quality to demonstrate this, but it is apparent from the more comprehensive returns of the 1377 poll tax. The proportion of the tax population aged fourteen or more who were currently married was 58.4 per cent at Carlisle, 57.9 per cent at Hull and 57.4 per cent for York.[23] For Rutland the equivalent proportion was 65.8 per cent.[24]

The total sex ratios described for Strafforth Wapentake and, with more confidence, for Howdenshire, do not demonstrate the sort of bias against single female taxpayers for which the poll taxes have traditionally been criticized. Indeed, despite considerable local variation, the overall pattern shows a modest preponderance of females over males. In rural Rutland, however, the 1377 mean sex ratio is rather higher at 103.5. It is tempting to conclude that this reflects a difference in sex-specific labour requirements between a predominantly pastoral region and an arable region. Pastoral agriculture, that typified Howdenshire and much of the West Riding, tends to be less seasonalized and to draw upon female labour for various specific occupations, notably washing and shearing sheep, milking both cows and sheep, and the manufacture of butter and cheese.[25] Women may also engage in a variety of other part-time activities associated with sheep farming and the production of woollen cloth, viz. spinning and carding wool, and weaving. Parts of the West Riding further provided a variety of industrial and craft occupations that may have served to prevent a drift of labour of either sex to towns outside the region. Thus the leather trades, and souters or shoemakers in particular, are conspicuous in a number of villages associated with livestock farming. In the returns for Methley in Aggbrigg Wapentake, for example, are listed six souters, four tanners and a beast merchant. Souters, tanners, saddlers and skinners are likewise conspicuous in the towns of Ripon, Pontefract and Doncaster. Metalcrafts are prominent in the south-east part of the riding including Sheffield. The village of Greasbrough near Rotherham alone contained eight smiths, far more than could be sustained by purely local demand. Woodcrafts are likewise well represented, especially in the wapentakes of Strafforth and Claro, and textile manufacture is especially

prominent in Staincliffe, Claro and Osgodcross wapentakes, in Howdenshire, and at Wakefield and Rotherham. The village of Gargrave near
Skipton, for example, contained two weavers, a chaloner, two fullers and
a dyer. At Skipton itself were four weavers, two fullers and a draper.

Differences in the prevailing agricultural economy may also account for
differences in the circumstances of single females. The poll tax rarely
distinguishes widows, though it may reasonably be assumed that all those
female-headed households containing children and most such households
containing servants represent widows. In Rutland female-headed households were as likely to contain male dependents as female, but in the West
Riding male dependents are comparatively uncommon. Thus in Rutland,
of forty-four female-headed households, seventeen contained male children as against nineteen that contained female chidren, and thirteen
contained male servants as against eight that contained female servants.
In Strafford Wapentake, out of sixty-three such households, only fourteen
contained sons as against forty-two that contained daughters. Much the
same pattern is found again for Tickhill and Staincross wapentakes.
Taking the two together, female-headed households containing daughters
appear to be twice as common as those containing sons. Households
containing servants are more rare, but again the balance is tilted in favour
of females. It may thus be that for widows holding dower land, male labour
was at a premium in arable Rutland, but that in a pastoral economy female
labour was actually preferred. The opportunities for single women to
support themselves were actually wider within a pastoral economy. There
is relatively little by-name evidence for independent female traders in
Rutland, but, as shall shortly be considered, there is much evidence for
women working as weavers and smiths, in addition to other more
traditional occupations, within the West Riding and Howdenshire. Some
women traders engaged labour in their own right. Four of the eleven
websters identified for Tickhill wapentake, for example, are listed
alongside dependents within the poll tax. Women with little or no land
might work as labourers. In this respect women may have found more
opportunity within a pastoral economy caring for livestock and dairy herds
than within an arable, though it is difficult to assess the significance of
such by-names as 'cowhird' and 'calfhird' as borne by women at Kirk
Deighton near Wetherby and Rufforth near York.

One of the most common by-employments for women was brewing.[26]
The rural West Riding returns list some thirty-one brewsters, and the more
detailed Howdenshire returns a further forty-four. It is evident that the
poll tax data are seriously deficient as most brewsters were married women
and the occupations of wives are not consistently recorded. Only for the
wapentakes of Claro and the Ainsty do the West Riding returns list
brewsters in any number, though these same returns also apparently

include a number of male brewers. It may merely be that the assessors for these two wapentakes chose to regard brewing as an activity that merited a higher level of taxation, but the proximity of these wapentakes to York, the only substantial city within the wider region, may be significant. The presence of some male brewers suggests that the industry here was on a large scale and it seems probable that some ale was sent to York where there was demand not just from a resident population, but from numerous visitors to the markets and shops or on various kinds of business. The majority of brewsters appear, however, to have been married women, though some were clearly widows. This is apparent from the small number of brewsters assisted by their daughters, as for example Margaret Broune of Wetherby, and is explicitly stated in a few instances within the How-denshire returns, for example Isabella Wryght, brewster of South Duffield. It is unlikely that many unmarried women are represented as independent brewsters as brewing required a degree of capital investment rarely open to the young and single, but an interesting partnership between Agnes Milner, webster, and her daughter Agnes, a brewster, is recorded at Barmby on the Marsh in Howdenshire. A number of married brewsters are associated with households containing dependents including servants, though only occasionally is the husband also associated with a trade. This observation would tend to support Marjorie McIntosh's findings from the court rolls of the manor of Havering for the period 1380–1460 that the majority of brewsters were married to agriculturalists, and to 'men of middling economic level'.[27] A small number of women are also found as hostilers, but these were probably mostly widows.

Poorer women, including the young and unmarried, may often have relied on the spinning and carding of wool to earn or supplement a meagre living, while others traded as seamstresses. These occupations were not generally regarded by the poll tax assessors as of sufficient substance to merit artisan status. The Howdenshire returns do include two kempsters, though only one is assessed at the sixpenny rate, whereas at Cliffe one Margaret Semester is assessed as an artisan and at Lindeley in Claro Wapentake, Matilda Schawe is supported by her daughter Margaret, 'semster'. Altogether the West Riding returns allow twenty-one seam-stresses or sempsters to be identified, almost exclusively from surname evidence. Kempsters and spinsters are even more poorly represented since these employments were too universal to constitute useful by-names. How many spinsters worked with the more productive wheel rather than the traditional, though highly versatile, distaff is uncertain. An Isabella Whelespynner is found at Bishopthorpe and this by-name might suggest that the wheel was still uncommon in 1379. By the fifteenth century spinning wheels are not infrequently noted within wills and they may have become increasingly common.[28] It is, however, possible that the increase in productivity consequent upon technological advance would have served to depress the wages paid to spinsters. The poverty of the spinster appears a commonplace. Alice de Bridelyngton of Beverley, a deponent in a matrimonial cause of 1367, was described as '*non coniugata operatrix lane anglice* spynner'. She lived with another spinster, who had allegedly left her husband, and was herself accused of prostitution.[29] Isabella Foxhole of Houghton, noted in a cause dated 1418, was said to make a meagre living by carding and spinning wool. She was the daughter of a villein and had previously been in service to one John Carrow of Pontefract who was married to her aunt. Her status again made her vulnerable to allegations of immorality, and it was alleged that her motives for trying to enforce a contract of marriage against a Pontefract man she had known and slept with as a servant were purely financial. The court, however, ruled in her favour.[30] A number of spinsters from within the county are known to have been presented between 1360 and 1364 for receiving 'excessive' wages. Two, Matillis Swan and Alice de Skyren (Skerne, near Driffield) were also presented under the same statute as weavers, and Margaret Pocher was similarly presented as *filatrix et messor*.[31] The strong bargaining position of wage-labour at the time of the second plague is, however, unlikely to have continued through the fifteenth century, and it may be remembered that by the mid-sixteenth century West Riding cloth was said to be more competitive than that of York because spinsters and carders could not afford the high cost of living in the city.[32]

The regional economy depended on large numbers of carders and spinners of wool to support the manufacture of woollen cloth. The craft of the weaver is much better represented within the surviving returns as its status as an artisan craft is unambiguous. One hundred and ninety-nine weavers, both male and female, may be identified from designations alone for the rural parts of the riding, and a further seventy-three for the towns of the region from designations and by-names. In general female websters are found most in those parts of the Riding where male weavers are also most common. Altogether some seventy-seven websters can be identified from designations and by-names, the greatest concentration being in Claro Wapentake north-west of York. In rural Howdenshire at the same date twenty-four female websters are recorded, six in the village of Barmby on the Marsh alone. A number of these women are associated with adult children and this pattern would again indicate that many websters were widows. Margaret de Skyres of Hoyland (Tickhill Wapentake) even retained two sons and two daughters in her household. Sometimes, however, it is the daughter that is described as 'webster' or '*textrix*' as in the case of Isabella, the daughter of Elena Wall of Hunsingore or Isolda, the daughter of Richard Broune and his wife of Burton Leonard. A number of others maintained servants. The household of Elizabeth de Snayth, *webster*, assessed at a shilling, contained her daughter, another female relative and a male servant. Much more rarely, married women are distinguished, as for example the wife of John del Croft of Wetherby, *textrix*. In general, however, the poll tax fails to record the occupations of married women and it seems probable that a number of married women may have worked as weavers without being so described. A further nineteen websters may be found in such urban communities as Pontefract, Ripon and Tickhill, and only two in the surviving York returns for 1381.[33] This pattern might suggest that the female webster was more commonly located in the country than the town. This may be related to the rural economy of the West Riding and Howdenshire. The evidence of an inquisition into breaches of the York weavers' charter of Henry II dated 1399 suggests that much rural cloth weaving was seasonal, most cloths being produced in winter or in April and May.[34] These represent slack seasons within an essentially pastoral economy and it may be concluded that much weaving constituted a by-employment within an agricultural community rather than a full-time means of support. The same may be true of such small 'urban' communities as Wakefield and Tickhill. The inquisition data suggests a rather higher concentration of female websters in and around Wakefield than the poll tax would allow. The part-time nature of the rural industry might suggest that the poll tax returns may not record websters consistently, but the evidence would equally support a real growth in the industry over two decades. This would be consistent with the evidence for the continued growth of the textile districts of the West Riding over the course of the fifteenth century, but it is more difficult to assess the implications of this for female employment since the industry may also have become more urbanized.[35]

A number of women may have found employment in trades associated with finishing cloths, notably fulling and, more rarely, dyeing. Fifteen female walkers and fullers may be identified from the rural returns, but only two dyers. At Ripon, however, two female litsters or dyers may be noticed assessed at the artisan rate, the one assisted by her daughter, the other by a female servant. Women may also be found trading in finished cloths. Nearly one quarter (113 of 454) of the individuals dealing in cloth noted in the York aulnage account of 1394–5 were female.[36] This compares favourably with the equivalent proportion of less than 7 per cent at Winchester over the same year and may reflect something of the enhanced status of women within the Northern economy.[37] Some more substantial female cloth traders may have been the widows of merchants. One Isabella who accounted for twelve cloths in 1395–6 can be identified as the widow of Adam Holman of Wakefield, assessed at the rate of two shillings in the poll tax of 1379. Emma Erle of Wakefield who accounted for forty-eight cloths in 1395–6 had been claimed in marriage by John de

Topcliffe, a Ripon spicer and cloth merchant, in a matrimonial cause of 1381, but the court upheld an earlier contract to one John Archier of Healaugh.[38] Many women were, however, of more humble status as the surname 'huckster' associated with a number of York traders suggests. In Coventry special provision was made for the 'woman that bereth a dossen in her armes' whereby she was exempt from the normal rule that restricted cloth traders to the drapery on Fridays.[39]

Female hucksters and chapmen did not confine their activities to dealing in cloth. They can be identified from a variety of sources as general traders and may be associated with a number of communities noted within the 1379 poll tax returns for the West Riding.[40] From these it is possible to distinguish ten female chapmen, three merchants and a peddler. Half the female chapmen are located in Strafforth Wapentake in the south-east of the riding and it is probable that this reflects the greater willingness of the collectors there to assess such women at the artisan rate of sixpence. The actual number of female general traders throughout the riding is therefore likely to have been much higher. Most of the women recorded were probably widowed, as for example Alice Broune of Wath who was assessed alongside her daughter.

The names of Rose Burford and Margery Russell loom large in the literature devoted to medieval women traders, but the evidence for women merchants of substance is comparatively rare. Nichola de Irby, a York merchant's widow, left a ship, the *Anneys de Yhork*, at her death in 1395, and the fishmonger, John Rodes, bequeathed his cogship to his wife Margaret in 1457.[41] On a more modest scale Alice Upstall, also the widow of a York merchant, left her one male servant her pack saddles.[42] A more comprehensive source is provided by the enrolled customs' accounts. Wendy Child's edition of the Hull accounts for the period 1453–1490 suggest that very few women were involved in overseas trade.[43] Seven of the eleven female merchants noted appear only once within the customs' accounts. All were probably widows. A few appear to have engaged in trade shortly after their husbands' deaths and it may be that their activity represents little more than the conclusion of business left unfinished at the time of their being widowed.[44] Thus Margaret, the widow of Roger Bussell, Alice, the widow of John Day, and Joan, the widow of Richard Doughty, are all observed uniquely in the year following the deaths of their Hull merchant husbands in 1483, 1472 and 1489 respectively.[45] Katherine Lamb of York is noted once in 1489, some five years after her husband's decease, but from the following year her son Thomas is regularly noticed within the customs' accounts.[46] Only two women can be distinguished as substantial overseas merchants in their own right. Dionisia Holme of Beverley exported wool and woolfells in some quantity between her husband's death in 1465 and her own death in 1471.[47] Still more active was Marion Kent, the widow of John Kent, himself a wealthy merchant of York. She is observed in the surviving accounts for 1470–3 trading in lead, cloth, flax, madder, wax and even trenchers and games tables, but is absent from the accounts for 1483 and 1489–90 despite living on until 1500. Marion demonstrates that male prejudices were not insurmountable, but her mercantile career seems to have lasted only so long as her children were under age.[48] This rather limited evidence that the widows of merchants engaged in trade should not detract from the probability that wives were active partners in their husbands' businesses. When in 1421 John Astlott, a young Hull merchant, went overseas for several weeks, he gave his fiancée, Agnes Louth, his keys and left her to manage his business. This Agnes did, but John's expedition was not a success and on his return he found that Agnes had been persuaded by her parents to break off the marriage. To add insult to injury, Agnes allegedly withheld from John her account of the goods sold in his absence.[49]

Turning to other craft activities represented in the 1379 poll tax, women are frequently noticed trading as smiths and marshals. Some twenty-seven are noticed from the rural West Riding and a further nine in the towns of the region. Often they can only be identified from by-names, but they are specifically designated as artisans paying the tax at a higher rate with sufficient regularity as to allow some confidence in this method. A few smiths are known to be widows since they were assisted by their children, as for example Alice Wod, smith, who had both a son and a daughter over the age of sixteen living with her at Hiendley in Staincross Wapentake. The marital status of other independent female smiths and marshals is less certain, especially in view of the numbers of daughters trained in smithcraft identified from the same returns, though in Claro Wapentake the wife of William Brame, tanner, is described as a smith, and the couple are assessed together at a shilling. In this same village the wife of Nicholas Hamund, sutor, is specifically designated a mason, and elsewhere in Claro an Isabella Mason is assessed in association with her son and a female servant. The by-name 'wright' is similarly encountered in association with single women, but here there are no examples of such women being assessed at the higher rate. This is despite the evidence that wrights or carpenters frequently made use of the labour of their daughters. The evidence for female tanners is likewise inconclusive.

Three service occupations may also be noted, those of the miller, the laundress, and the nurse. This last is particularly well represented since in this instance there seems little reason to doubt by-name evidence. In total fifteen nurses are listed within the West Riding returns. Most, it may be surmised, were wet-nurses and child minders employed by generally well-to-do families. Elizabeth, the wife of Thomas de Swanland, a Beverley draper, for example, remembered her former nurse Alice in her will dated 1404.[50] The rural aristocracy likewise appear to have demanded wet-nurses for their children as is suggested from a matrimonial cause of 1366. When Elena, the wife of Gervase de Rouclif, gave birth to a son one Martinmas, Elena, subsequently the wife of Thomas Taliour of Skelton, was asked to act as wet-nurse since she had just left service, having herself given birth the previous month. On this occasion Elena refused because she said she loved her baby and did not wish to prejudice its survival by suckling another. One and a half years later, however, she was still feeding her child when Elena de Rouclif gave birth to a daughter. This time Elena agreed to become her wet-nurse, and the same day she was born took the infant to be baptized two and a half miles away in the parish church of St Olave's in York. The same source contains the deposition of one Cecily de Shupton of York who was employed in the home of Elena de Rouclif for a month between her giving birth and being churched, i.e. to use nineteenth-century terminology, as a monthly nurse.[51] Only three laundresses and a 'kerchieflavender' are noted from by-name evidence. This was an exclusively female occupation, though probably only part-time in most cases, and women were often presented for washing clothing on church festivals.[52] The female miller, again noted from by-mame evidence, is more commonly noticed and may represent an operative of a hand-mill. The importance of hand-mills worked by women is suggested by the conflict concerning their use between the townsfolk and the abbey at St Albans in the fourteenth century. In the mid-fifteenth century a Wakefield woman, Alice Barlawe, bequeathed a set of millstones ('*par molar*'), but it may be remembered that some years before Margery Kempe had herself briefly managed a horse-mill.[53]

This discussion by no means pretends to offer a definitive account of women's work in the West Riding in 1379. The poll tax merits much more detailed analysis, though it could be argued that even this preliminary survey has made light of the very real problems of the source material. But the analysis does suggest a framework for further research. Service as a social institution for both sexes does seem to have been widely established, especially in craft-based households, but not to the degree found in neighbouring York. On the other hand, adolescent children are frequently found living at home in village society and only rarely in the town. As at York, women are found engaged in a variety of non-agricultural occupations, though the West Riding poll tax is an indifferent source for such low status occupations as spinster, shepster, huckster and lavender or launderess that are so well represented in the 1381 returns for Oxford and Southwark, and no source at all for those women whose livelihood was exclusively on the land.[54] Our analysis does suggest, however, that the prevailing agricultural economy and the proximity of major urban communities may have had a profound effect on economic opportunity and the sexual composition of the labour force. Unfortunately it is not immediately possible to relate these observations to a suitable demographic model; the evidence is simply not good enough. Analysis of rural cause paper depositions may provide some clues. A preliminary suggestion is that people in rural Yorkshire married slightly earlier than their urban counterparts.[55] This would accord with the less developed pattern of service and with the evidence of children remaining with their parents after sixteen. It would also accord with the relative paucity of evidence for unmarried women supporting themselves, but this may prove illusory. On balance, however, the evidence of the 1379 West Riding poll tax returns would seem to offer little discouragement to those who would argue for the prevalence of a Western marriage regime at this date, but perhaps only limited difficulties for those who would prefer a 'medieval' or non-European system.[56]

Notes

1.   There is a growing body of literature on women and work in later medieval England. See for example R.H. Hilton, *The English Peasantry in the Later Middle Ages* (Oxford 1975), pp. 95–110; R.H. Hilton, *Class Conflict and the Crisis of Feudalism* (1985), pp. 194–215; S.C.A. Penn, 'Female Wage-earners in Late Fourteenth-century England', *Agricultural History Review*, xxxv (1987), pp. 1–14; essays by B.A. Hanawalt, J.M. Bennett, and M. Kowaleski in *Women and Work in Pre-industrial Europe*, B.A. Hanawalt (ed.), (Bloomington 1986), pp. 3–36, 145–64; D. Keene, *Survey of Medieval Winchester* (Oxford 1985), pp. 387–92; essays by K.E. Lacey and D. Hutton in *Women and Work in Pre-Industrial England*, L. Charles and L. Duffin (eds), (1985), pp. 24–99. Still of real value is E. Power, *Medieval Women* (Cambridge 1975), pp. 53–75.

2.   P.J.P. Goldberg, 'Women and Work in Two Late Medieval English Towns: A Study in Social Topography', *Regional and Spatial Demographic Patterns in the Past*, R.M. Smith (ed.), (Oxford forthcoming); P.J.P. Goldberg, 'Female Labour, Status and Marriage in Late Medieval York and Other English Towns' (Cambridge PhD thesis, 1987), pp. 296–329.

3.   P.J.P. Goldberg, 'Marriage, Migration, Servanthood and Life-Cycle in Yorkshire Towns of the Later Middle Ages', *Continuity and Change*, i (1986), pp. 141–69.

4.   P.J.P. Goldberg, 'Female Labour, Service and Marriage in the Late Medieval Urban North', *NH* xxii (1986), pp. 18–38.

5.   For a detailed discussion of the poll taxes as a source see Goldberg, thesis, pp. 27–48.

6.   Notably from the cause papers housed in the Borthwick Institute of Historical Research, York (hereafter BI). See my forthcoming paper '"For Better, For Worse": Marriage and Economic Opportunity for Women in Town and Country'.

7.   'Rolls of the Collectors in the West-Riding of the Lay-Subsidy (Poll Tax) 2 Richard II', *YAJ* (1879–84), v. pp. 1–51, 241–66, 417–32; vi. pp. 1–44, 129–71, 287–342; vii. pp. 6–31, 145–86; 'Assessment Roll of the Poll-Tax for Howdenshire . . . (1379)', *YAJ*, ix (1886), pp. 129–61. All subsequent references are derived from these sources unless otherwise stated.

8.   *RP* iii, pp. 57–8.

9.   These particular by-names are unlikely to have been inherited.

10.   Very little has been written about rural, life-cycle servants, but not for want of

evidence. See Hilton, *English Peasantry*, pp. 30–5; R.M. Smith, 'Hypothèses sur la Nuptialité en Angleterre aux XIIIe-XIVe Siècles', *Annales E.S.C.* xxxviii. pp. 129–31.

11. E 179/269/51; E 179/158/29. I am most grateful to Dr R.M. Smith for providing me with typescript editions of this poll tax material.

12. Parental involvement is implicit in much rural matrimonial litigation surviving contained in the York cause papers, BI CP.E, F. This contrasts with the pattern of apparent individualism suggested by the urban evidence, cf. Goldberg, 'Marriage, migration, servanthood', pp. 155–60.

13. BI CP.F.242.

14. BI CP.F.189.

15. BI CP.F.280.

16. *Yorkshire Sessions of the Peace 1361–4*, B.H. Putnam (ed.), (Yorkshire Archaeological Society Record Series c. 1939), p. 71 (assize roll 1136/173).

17. BI CP.F.79.

18. BI CP.F.59.

19. M. Rubin, *Charity and Community in Medieval Cambridge* (Cambridge 1987) argues that the later Middle Ages were characterized by a hardening of attitudes to the poor, but this does not accord well with evidence from the Yorkshire region, cf. the proliferation of maisonsdieu in York and in Hull over the later fourteenth and fifteenth centuries. I have greatly benefited from discussing these problems with Dr P.H. Cullum. See our forthcoming paper '"Ad Laudem Dei et Utilitatem Pauperum": Piety and Charity in Late Medieval York'.

20. BI CP.F.201.

21. BI CP.E.221.

22. BI CP.E.121.

23. Goldberg, thesis, table 2.1, p. 33.

24. Calculated from E 179/269/51.

25. Some agricultural (inc. pastoral) economies offered greater opportunities for female employment than others: see J.M. Bennett, *Women in the Medieval English Countryside: Gender and Household in Brigstock Before the Plague* (New York 1987), pp. 89–90. For female agricultural work generally see B.A. Hanawalt, 'Peasant Women's Contribution to the Home Economy in Late Medieval England', *Women and Work*, pp. 9–13; Hilton, *English Peasantry*, pp. 101–3; K. Casey, 'The Cheshire Cat: Reconstructing the Experience of Medieval Women', *Liberating Women's History*, B.A. Carroll (ed.), (Urbana 1976), p. 228; Penn, 'Female Wage-earners', pp. 1–14; Power, *Medieval Women*, pp. 71–2; A. Clark, *Working Life of Women in the Seventeenth Century* (1919), pp. 46–50, 60–62.

26. J.M. Bennett, 'The Village Ale-Wife: Women and Brewing in Fourteenth-Century England', *Women and Work*, pp. 20–36.

27. M.J. McIntosh, *Autonomy and Community: The Royal Manor of Havering 1200–1500* (Cambridge 1986), pp. 173–4.

28. e.g. York Minster Library, St Leonard's Hospital register, M2/6e f.36 (Margaret Usburn, York); BI Prob. Reg. 2 f.140 (William Lydeyate, York); 5 f.40 (Agnes Ragett, Coxwold).

29. BI CP.E.102.

30. BI CP.F.81.

31. Putnam, *Yorkshire Sessions*, pp. 58, 69, 71.

32. H. Heaton, *The Yorkshire Woollen and Worsted Industries* (Oxford 1920), p. 55.

33. *The Lay Poll Tax Returns for the City of York in 1381*, J.N. Bartlett (ed.), (Hull 1953).

34. *Calendar of Miscellaneous Inquisitions* vi, pp. 242–9. Simon Penn found 'a widespread female presence as rural cloth workers' in later fourteenth-century Herefordshire, Somerset, and the Allestree wapentake of Derbyshire, all pastoral districts: Penn, 'Female Wage-earners', pp. 4–7.

35. J.N. Bartlett, 'The Expansion and Decline of York in the Later Middle Ages', *EcHR*, 2nd ser. xii (1959), p. 32.
36. *The Early Yorkshire Woollen Trade*, J. Lister (ed.), (Yorkshire Archaeological Society Record Series lxiv, 1928), pp. 48–94.
37. Keene, *Medieval Winchester*, p. 389; Goldberg, 'Women and Work'.
38. BI CP.E.124.
39. *The Coventry Leet Book*, M.D. Harris (ed.), (Early English Text Society, OS cxxxiv, cxxxv, cxxxviii, cxxxxvi, 1907–13), p. 100.
40. Hilton, *Class Conflict*, pp. 197, 201, 203, 208–9.
41. BI Prob. Reg. 1 f.89; 2 f.357Av.
42. BI Prob. Reg. 2 f.640.
43. *The Customs Accounts of Hull 1453–1490*, W.R. Childs (ed.), (Yorkshire Archaeological Society Record Series cxliv, 1986).
44. M. Kowaleski, 'Women and Work in Medieval English Seaports' (typescript paper, Berkshire Conference, 1984), pp. 6–8.
45. Childs, pp. 180, 198, 214; BI Prob. Reg. 4 f.79; 5 ff.87, 350.
46. Childs, pp. 213, 224; BI Prob. 5 ff. 228, 448.
47. Childs, pp. 94, 116–9, 128, 132–3; BI Prob. Reg. 3 f.302; 4 f.31.
48. Childs, pp. 128, 142, 148, 154, 158–61, 167, 170–2, 179; Prob. Reg 3 f.320; 4 f.53v; *The York Mercers and Merchant Adventurers 1356–1917*, M. Sellers (ed.), (Surtees Society, cxxix, 1918), pp. 64, 67.
49. BI CP.F.46.
50. BI Prob. Reg. 3 f.105v.
51. BI CP.E.89.
52. *Depositions and other Ecclesiastical Proceedings from the Courts of Durham*, J. Raine (ed.), (Surtees Society xxi, 1845), pp. 30, 33.
53. *The English Rising of 1381*, T.H. Aston and R.H. Hilton (eds), (Cambridge 1984), p. 68; BI Prob. Reg. 2 f.239; *The Book of Margery Kempe*, H.M. Allen and S.B. Meech (eds), (Early English Text Society, OS ccxii, 1940), p. 11.
54. *Oxford City Documents 1268–1665*, J.E. Thorold Rogers (ed.), (Oxford Historical Society xviii, 1891), pp. 8–53; E 179/240/307.
55. The rural deposition material is unfortunately less comprehensive than that analyzed for York and other Yorkshire towns (Goldberg, 'Marriage, migration, servanthood'), but age data and patterns of litigation appear both to suggest that marriage was earlier in the countryside. See note 6 above.
56. For the 'medieval' evidence see Z. Razi, *Life, Marriage and Death in a Medieval Parish* (Cambridge 1980). For a 'northwestern' view see Smith, 'Hypothèses sur la Nuptialité', pp. 107–36, and Goldberg, thesis, pp. 221–71. See also the debate currently pursued by Professor Razi on the one hand and Drs Poos and Smith on the other in the pages of *Law and History Review*.

4

Prince Henry and Wales, 1400–1408

Rhidian Griffiths
National Library of Wales, Aberystwyth

Henry V is rare if not unique in the annals of English kingship in the quality of his posthumous reputation. Shakespearean depictions of fifteenth-century history find little favour with modern historians, who may be sceptical of the fulsome praise accorded the King in the exchange between the dukes of Bedford and Gloucester which opens *The First Part of King Henry the Sixth*:

> King Henry the Fifth! too famous to live long!
> England ne'er lost a king of so much worth.
>
> England ne'er had a king until his time.
> Virtue he had, deserving to command:
> . . .
>
> What shall I say? his deeds exceed all speech:
> He ne'er lift up his hand but conquered.

Yet this portrait, derived as it is from Hall and Holinshed, does little more than confirm what his contemporaries at home and abroad thought of the second Lancastrian King. The 'noble prince and victoriouse kynge' admired by the English author of the *Brut* was acknowledged even by the Burgundian Chastellain, no friend of England, as a 'prince of justice' who showed no favour and condoned no wrong done to anyone.[1] Nothing succeeds like success, and Henry was conspicuously successful in those things expected of a late-medieval King: he was pious and orthodox; he was just, and administered good governance; he was a vigorous and competent soldier who was almost always on the winning side. It is tempting to speculate whether his successes could and would have been maintained had he lived, and whether his greatest success of all was to die in his prime, a few weeks short of his thirty-fifth birthday, before his extraordinary energy (and luck) gave out. On the whole, however, it can be agreed that 'the simple record of . . . [his] achievement is sufficient to establish him as a great king',[2] a statement which echoes the unwontedly extravagant assertion of the cautious Bruce McFarlane that Henry was 'all round . . . the greatest man that ever ruled England'.[3]

Dissentient voices are few, and not many would endorse A.J.P. Taylor's dismissal of Henry as 'a mere condottiere'.[4] Yet even to reduce him to that level is to confirm the overriding and abiding impression of him as first and foremost a soldier; and though recent work has rightly concentrated on aspects of his government and his administration of justice, he remains largely the victor of Agincourt and the conqueror of Normandy. It has long been acknowledged that the apprenticeship for this military career was served in Wales when Prince Henry was attempting to suppress the rising inspired and personified by Owain Glyndŵr, but these years when he 'grew up and learnt his trade' are often too readily dismissed as an insignificant prelude to later events. On the contrary this was an important formative period during which the prince learnt lessons which would prove of value to him as King.

There was no reason to suppose on 15 October 1399 when Henry was created Prince of Wales that he would, in the words of the chronicler Jean Creton, have to fight to possess his inheritance; but fight he did, although not for the reason that Creton supposed, that Wales would remain loyal to Richard II.[6] Nor was there any reason to suppose that the unfurling of the banner of another Prince of Wales, Owain Glyndŵr, on 16 September 1400 would have such far-reaching consequences for the Principality. Though there were rumblings of discontent as far afield as Anglesey, the ravaging of Rhuthun and other English boroughs in north-east Wales was not perhaps to be taken as a sign of impending doom, even if the authorities feared collusion between the malcontents in this area and those of Cheshire, where there had been a short-lived uprising in January 1400. Rebellion on a small scale was endemic in the northern March of Wales, and Henry IV assumed no doubt that his punitive expedition across north Wales in the autumn and his establishment of strong garrisons at strategic points would be the end of the matter. Henry Percy, Justiciar of Chester and of north Wales, who was left in charge, administered a policy of conciliation, issuing pardons and protections to all who would seek the King's peace: at his side was the thirteen-year-old prince, recently returned from his father's expedition to Scotland, and now forming his first impressions of a land that was to play an important part in his life during the eight years following.[7]

Prince Henry withdrew to his manor of Kennington for the winter, but the problem of Wales had come to stay. From the ill-fated hour of *tenebrae* on Good Friday 1401 when the garrison of Conwy was at mass and the brothers Gwilym and Rhys ap Tudur of Penmynydd took the castle, the Lancastrian crown was to know no peace for many a long year either in the Principality or the March. Prince Henry came to Conwy to observe the besieging of the castle first by Henry Percy and then by Sir Hugh le Despenser, the prince's governor. It was Henry IV's declared view that a negotiated settlement for the surrender of the castle was unthinkable and that the Welsh should be properly punished, but the eventual outcome whereby nine Welshmen were executed and thirty-five pardoned and allowed to repossess their lands reflected badly on royal authority and began the steady eclipse of the crown's power in Wales.[8] Events now gathered momentum. During the summer Glyndŵr gained an important victory in the valley of the Hyddgen in mid-Wales, and the prince petitioned the King's Council to ordain justices for the south, since disaffection appeared to be spreading.[9] In addition he himself was at the end of August instructed to go to Wales with the array of Gloucestershire, Worcestershire, Herefordshire and Shropshire to crush the rising, his first known commission as the leader of an expedition to Wales, in name if not in deed. But this must have been a frustrating time. The 372 townsmen of Shrewsbury secured exemption from military service which, under the terms of the commission of array, was unpaid and therefore unpopular: the prince may have had great difficulty in raising any kind of army, and perhaps achieved little bar the revictualling of the castle of Aberystwyth.[10] While the insurgents in Wales made further headway, attacking Caernarfon and besieging Harlech, the crown grew more impotent as the uprising began to take on the form of a guerrilla war characterized by sporadic and unpredictable outbursts of unrest.

It was perhaps the Percys who stood the best chance of bringing the Welsh to peace. Thomas Percy, Earl of Worcester, commissioned King's lieutenant in south Wales in the autumn of 1401, followed like his nephew Hotspur a policy of conciliation, apparently with some success, and came up with a grand strategy for quelling the rising by a combined English attack simultaneously from north and south on the Welsh heartland: but whether because of lack of means or lack of will, or simply because it was a Percy policy, this initiative was not, it seems, followed up, and the insurrection gained ground.[11] In February 1402 Glyndŵr captured his old adversary Lord Grey of Rhuthun (the man whose dispute with Glyndŵr over land had precipitated the initial rising in 1400) and in June at Bryn Glas near Pilleth in Radnorshire he took Edmund Mortimer, the uncle of the Earl of March. Yet the royal response was dilatory. It was not until the end of July that Henry IV succeeded in organizing his forces to punish those who in the prince's words planned 'to destroy him and us and the whole English nation'.[12] The army raised had three divisions, and the prince took command of that which set out from Chester. He seems to have enjoyed better success than his counterparts, not in punishing the Welsh but in strengthening garrisons and in victualling the hard-pressed castles of Harlech and Caernarfon. The second division, commanded by the earls of Stafford and Warwick, disappears altogether from view, while the King himself at the head of the third met disaster in appalling weather which he attributed to Welsh sorcery.[13] In military terms this inglorious campaign achieved nothing except to prove that Wales would not be pacified by large-scale offensives and seeking after field engagements. English armies, it was said, made so much noise as they clanked their way up the river valleys into the principality that the Welsh, forewarned, could withdraw to the mountains, swoop down and plunder their baggage.[14] The best that could now be hoped for was the maintenance of the English garrisons as vestigial symbols of royal authority. Is it perhaps an indication of uncommon military maturity on the part of the fifteen-year-old prince that he had already recognized this, and had concentrated on that very task of getting supplies through?

It may have been this proven aptitude for soldiery which prompted Henry IV in March 1403 to invest his son with the powers of King's lieutenant in Wales, a commission to be held for a year from 1 April, with specific instructions to maintain a line of strong garrisons from north to south Wales as bases for attacks on Welsh territory: tacit recognition of the failure of English offensives so far. To fulfil the commission the prince was to have a standing army of 4 barons and bannerets, 20 knights, 500 men-at-arms and 2,500 archers, significantly a contract army in view of the evident failure of the county levies, to be paid for by the Exchequer.[15] The appointment argues a marked degree of trust in the prince, not yet sixteen years old, since his office as lieutenant carried with it the power to grant pardons and receive into the King's grace. It was also a rebuff to the Percys, whose work in Wales had been snubbed, and whose by now fragile allegiance to Henry IV was not to last. Yet this was the shape of things to come, since the English strategy henceforth would be to maintain defences in the March of Wales and engage in forays on the insurgents as occasion arose. It was on the basis of this commission that the prince, at the head of an army which had as its nucleus his own household, led a raid into Glyndŵr's home country of Cynllaith Owain and fired his abandoned castle at Sycharth, following on to Glyndyfrdwy and razing to the ground Glyndŵr's lodge there. Scorched earth tactics were freely adopted on both sides, and English troops found it impossible to live off the land: even oats to feed the horses had to be carried from England.[16]

This lieutenancy begun not unpromisingly in April was, however, short-lived. When at the end of May the prince wrote to his father's Council to plead for help for the beleaguered garrisons at Harlech and Aberystwyth, and to ask for money to pay the wages of his troops, he made plain the flaw in the whole arrangement, namely over-dependence on an Exchequer which was proving inconstant. Henry succeeded in dispatching to Harlech early in June a company of Cheshire men whom he followed, bringing wages and supplies for the garrison there and at Aberystwyth; but the Welsh were still elusive and disaffection was spreading.[17] Flintshire was becoming increasingly turbulent, and the consequences for the adjacent earldom of Chester could be serious. There was a deepening crisis in south Wales where Glyndŵr had gained Cydweli, one of Lancaster's own lordships, and had for a short time held Carmarthen, the administrative capital of the Principality of South Wales.

Across everything in mid-July came the revolt of the Percys, which diverted the prince's attention from Wales and was to mark the end of his active service there for 1403. In the battle of Shrewsbury, the only field engagement he is known to have fought during this period, he played a vital tactical role, proving his mettle as a commander by leading his forces round behind the rebels' right flank and putting pressure on them from both sides to hasten the royal victory.[18] Despite a wound to his face he refused to leave the field, to the admiration of contemporary chroniclers and subsequent biographers who embroidered the story into legend. Yet the psychological effect on the prince of this 'sory bataill'[19] must have been even more marked than any physical discomfort he suffered. Henry Percy had been his early mentor and the Earl of Worcester his governor and until a few days before a member of his household: he had watched their gradual estrangement from his father; he perhaps retained the same respect for them that he had for the deposed Richard II;[20] but he had also acquired an independence of thought and action which left his own loyalties to the new King, his father, unquestioned.

With his position as lieutenant made untenable by lack of means, Henry withdrew from Wales, leaving royal authority there at a low ebb. On 1 December the King's esquire Miles Water was granted lands worth £47 6s 8d in the lordship of Brecon provided he defend Brecon town for nothing, not the only grant of its kind which suggests a measure of desperation on the part of the crown.[21] In November Edward Duke of York had been appointed lieutenant in south Wales for a year; Gilbert Talbot managed to relieve Beaumaris, but attempts to protect Cardiff from the Welsh failed. In the early months of 1404 the Earl of Arundel was put in charge of north Wales, with Sir Thomas Burton installed at Aberystwyth trying to contain insurgents who were increasingly powerful and confident, and were now threatening the peace of the border counties.[22] It was not until June that Prince Henry reappeared on the scene, in response both to the pleas of parliament earlier in the year and to Welsh attacks on Herefordshire. As he reminded Archbishop Arundel, he was not bound by indenture to serve there, having no commission as lieutenant and receiving no income from the Exchequer; and he was to spend much of his time writing begging letters to the Council. From July to November he maintained at his own cost a household company of fifty men-at-arms and 100 archers at Hereford and Leominster, to safeguard the entrance to the Wye valley.[23] Apart from the occasional firelighting foray into Wales it was defensive rather than offensive warfare, but it served its purpose and earned the gratitude of the gentry of Herefordshire and of the Council.[24] It was the beginning too of a sustained and largely successful attempt to preserve intact the bulwark of the March. Throughout the winter of 1404–5 troops were stationed at strategic points (Monmouth, Radnor, Hay-on-Wye) in a concentration of resources which paid dividends when in March 1405 the Welsh suffered a reversal at Grosmont at the hands of Gilbert Talbot, followed by another defeat at Pwll Melyn near Usk in May.[25]

It was at this time that the prince's commission as lieutenant was formally renewed, to run for a year from 27 April, specifically for north Wales and with an army of 500 and 2,650 to be augmented to 600 and 3,000; yet again, however, its fulfilment was interrupted.[26] In May Henry was summoned from Chester to his father's side, to combat the rebellion of Archbishop Scrope in the north of England. Though the troops retained for north Wales served until June at least, it is difficult to ascertain the scope of their activities, which probably involved policing the March and reinforcing castles; still less can it be determined whether Henry returned from the north to join the Earl of Arundel, Grey of Codnor, Sir John Greyndore, Lord Bergavenny and others who were bearing the brunt of the defence of the March at a difficult time, when a French force sent to aid Glyndŵr made a brief appearance in south Wales.[27] The lieutenancy was again renewed in 1406 and forces were maintained in Henry's name for service in the March throughout the year, but it is not clear what they were doing there nor whether he himself was active in Wales. As early as New Year's Day 1406 Henry IV in proroguing the parliament which was to have met at Coventry had spoken of sending his son to Wales

> to make war on the rebels there, to punish
> them, and finally to conquer them, God willing.[28]

Yet even as late as June the commons were still pressing for the prince to go to Wales, which suggests that he had not already done so.[29] It seems reasonable to suppose that he spent some time in Wales during the year, but it is no more than supposition; what is certain is that on 8 December he attended his first meeting of his father's Council, thus opening up a field of interest which was to engage his attention more and more during the remaining years of Henry IV's reign.[30]

By now too the crisis in Wales was slowly receding. Throughout the year resistance in Anglesey had been crumbling and by November a full submission had been obtained; at the other end of the country the lordship of Gower was likewise received into the King's grace.[31] During the following summer, 1407, Henry moved into central Wales to lay siege to Aberystwyth which had been in Welsh hands since at least 1405. He used cannon to bring the garrison to the point of surrender, but made the mistake of leaving after the agreement had been struck and before the castle was delivered; Glyndŵr interposed and reclaimed the castle, and it was not until the summer of 1408 that it was finally recaptured in what proved to be Prince Henry's last campaign in Wales. Early in 1409 Gilbert and John Talbot regained Harlech from the Welsh, and the former was to play a prominent part in the mopping-up operations of succeeding years. Troops were retained in the prince's name for service in Wales until his accession to the throne in 1413, to bring the country to peace, but it is unlikely that he himself again saw active military service there. He had proved himself a defender of the realm, earning the frequently expressed gratitude of the commons in the loyal addresses that were a commonplace of the parliaments of Henry IV's reign; perhaps too he had helped to vindicate the Lancastrian title to the throne.

Central to any understanding of the significance of the prince's military activities in Wales is the question of finance and the resources he had at his disposal for the pursuit of war. Henry IV had come to the throne as a great landowner, and his attitude to royal lands and revenues was, initially at least, in keeping with his background. He assumed not unjustifiably that his son would be able to finance the pacification of Wales from his patrimonial revenues, which amounted in the case of the Principality to a little over £5,000 a year gross [32]: but by 1403 it had become apparent that revenue from Wales could not be relied upon, for the simple reason that owing to the insurrection it had ceased to exist. Admittedly the prince had at his disposal revenue from the duchy of Cornwall where the tin mines were enjoying a period of prosperity, so that income from the duchy was some £3,700 a year; this money, however, was according to well-established practice absorbed by the prince's household and not used in direct support of military endeavour.[33] The story in the earldom of Chester is very different. From 1403 Chester bore the exclusive costs of the garrisons of north Wales as well as a whole range of incidental costs of the prince's expeditions, and both there and in Cornwall every attempt was made to increase revenue by collecting arrears and exploiting all available sources of income.[34] Following a review of finances in February 1404 the prince's Council instigated a process of resumption of lands alienated by Richard II, in a bid to secure every last penny. Yet in spite of all these efforts Henry remained from his appointment as his father's lieutenant in Wales in March 1403 largely dependent for a war income on the Exchequer, a department with which he had a turbulent relationship.[35]

The Exchequer had supported military dispositions in Wales as early as the autumn of 1400 when it had paid for the large garrisons installed for three months in the northern castles, and money for the campaigns of 1401 and 1402 came from the same source. What was different about the lieutenancy of 1403 was the recognition of a regular obligation to support an army in Wales at a cost of £8,000 a quarter; but like almost everything that the hapless Henry IV touched, the plan went awry. The first instalment of the £32,000 due for the year was paid in advance in February 1403; the second came promptly in March and the third in June, followed by a sum of 100 marks in July, making the total for two quarters £8,666 13s 4d, a little over half the required sum. The collapse of the Exchequer in the summer of 1403 put an end to this arrangement, and it was not until parliament met at Coventry in October 1404 that direct Exchequer support for the prince could be renewed through the medium of two treasurers of war, Sir John Pelham and Lord Furnival, who transferred cash into the hands of Henry's receiver-general John Wynter. There survives for the period November 1404 to May 1405 an account of this John Wynter which shows that two-thirds of the total paid was given in cash, obviously much to be preferred to the assignment which had been used in 1403 and on other occasions.[36] A commander in the field who had to pay his soldiers' wages in Carmarthen did not wish to have to send tallies to King's Lynn to get his money. From 1406 there is a marked increase in the number of payments to the prince on the Exchequer Issue Rolls for the maintenance of armies in Wales, reflecting both a healthier Exchequer and perhaps the prince's own growing influence in central government. That payments were continued in his name, although he was not (it seems) on active service demonstrates the unique standing he had acquired as supreme commander of forces in Wales: as early as 1404 Henry IV had insisted that it should be so because money entrusted to others had not been properly spent.[37] That so many of the payments should be made in cash argues the prince's recognition that effective military operations required consistent and ready financial support.

It was a recognition born of frustration which Henry expressed more than once in his letters. Writing to the Council in 1403 to plead for more cash, he urged that he had already pawned jewels and plate to raise loans, a device he had recourse to again the following summer.[38] During the years 1403–4 in particular he borrowed directly from corporations, religious houses and individuals: the expedition which he led in the autumn of 1404 to relieve the castle of Coety in Glamorgan was the occasion of a whip-round in parliament.[39] He shared to the full the bitter anxiety of Edward duke of York who, when serving in the summer of 1404 as King's lieutenant in south Wales, had to urge the garrisons at Carmarthen, Cardigan and Newcastle Emlyn to stay at their posts a little longer, since every effort was being made to find money to pay their wages.[40] The war was not merely a war against geography and guerrilla tactics: it was a war against chronic shortages of cash and resultant problems of indiscipline and desertion.

One aspect of Henry's response to the problem was his creation within his household of a war fund known as the secret treasury (*prive tresor*), into which was paid miscellaneous revenue of all kinds. It does not appear to have existed before August 1403, and it may be that the experiences of that year precipitated its formation: in succeeding years it was a useful source of ready money to meet military and personal needs. John Waterton, scion of a staunch Lancastrian family, who had been raised in the service of the duchy and was the prince's receiver in Cornwall, acted as keeper of this secret treasury, and it was to him that jewels and plate were transferred along with money derived from lands, loans and assignments on taxation. When in 1404 the prince maintained his household at Hereford and Leominster Waterton was able to release nearly £700 towards its costs.[41] The relief expedition led by Gilbert Talbot to Beaumaris in December 1403 included members of the prince's household whose wages were paid by Waterton, and it was he too who paid the wages of the garrison of Cardigan and arrears owed to the constable of Harlech after the latter castle's fall to the Welsh in the spring of 1404.[42] In later years as the flow of money from the Exchequer became more regular and the emergencies perhaps less critical, the secret treasury was absorbed into the prince's chamber, and it was there that loans were received for the expedition to France in 1411 in support of the Duke of Burgundy.[43]

What therefore was the value to Henry of this military apprenticeship? The obvious answer is that he learnt to be a soldier. He certainly acquired experience of leadership and command which perhaps heightened his impatience to become King and may have contributed to his estrangement from his father in the latter's last years; yet in purely military terms the record is not particularly impressive. Admittedly the evidence is uneven, but it seems that Henry's direct experience of fighting in Wales was rather limited: one pitched battle (Shrewsbury), fought not against the Welsh but against the Percys; a few sieges; some raids and relief expeditions. It was all good practice, but was not over a period of eight years an outstanding record of campaigning. Of greater worth in the long term were his experiences in financial planning and the organization of war: not so much the art of war *per se* as the art of war management. The relief expeditions taught him the importance both of adequate supply and of keeping supply lines open. Shortages of cash and attendant problems of discipline brought home to him the importance of a reserve of readily accessible money. Maintaining a defensive posture in the March of Wales and biding time until the rising should collapse gave him an insight into the organization required to sustain a laborious war of conquest. So the prince who had kept the castles of north Wales stocked with bows, arrows and victuals and had enabled most of them to weather the storm was the King most thorough in his organization of supply and artillery for expeditions to Normandy. The prince who supervised the exaction of all available revenues in Chester and his other lands for the maintenance of the war effort was the King who engaged in 'an ubiquitous and vigorous attempt to improve the collection of crown revenue, increase its yield, and ensure that it was spent effectively' on military pursuits.[44] The prince who established a secret treasury to meet the immediate needs of war was the King who at Harfleur kept a store of £30,000 in gold coins and £2,000 in silver, and organized the Agincourt expedition from his Chamber.[45] He was more, even as a soldier pure and simple, than 'a mere condottiere'; but it is perhaps to these aspects of finance, supply and the organization of war rather than to active military service that we must look if we seek in the prince the prototype of the efficient, businesslike and thoroughly professional King that was Henry V.

Notes

All MS references are to documents in the PRO.

1. J.H. Wylie and W.T. Waugh, *The reign of Henry the Fifth* (Cambridge 1914–29), iii. pp. 423–4.
2. *Henry V: the practice of kingship*, G.L. Harriss (ed.), (Oxford 1985), p. 201.
3. K.B. McFarlane, *Lancastrian Kings and Lollard Knights* (Oxford 1972), p. 133.
4. A.J.P. Taylor, *A personal history* (London 1983, repr. 1984), p. 233.
5. McFarlane, *Lancastrian Kings*, p. 122.
6. John Webb, 'Translation of a French metrical history of the deposition of King Richard the Second', *Archaeologia*, 20, 1824, at p. 204.
7. J.E. Lloyd, *Owen Glendower* (Oxford 1931); P. McNiven, 'The Cheshire rising of 1400', *Bull. John Rylands Library*, 52, 1969–70, pp. 375–96.
8. Keith Williams-Jones, 'The taking of Conwy castle, 1401', *Trans. Caernarvonshire Hist. Soc.*, 39, 1978, pp.7–43.
9. CPR *1399–1401*, 538, 554; E28/10, 27 Aug.
10. HMC xv (10), p. 27; *Anglo-Norman letters and petitions*, M.D. Legge (ed.), (Oxford 1941), p. 314.
11. Ibid., p. 308.
12. Ibid., p. 318.
13. CCR *1399–1402*, 587; *The chronicle of England, by John Capgrave*, F.C. Hingeston (ed.), (RS 1858), p. 279.
14. *Duo rerum Anglicarum scriptores . . .*, Thomas Hearne (ed.), (Oxford 1732), i. p. 236; *The Brut*, F.W.D. Brie (ed.), (London 1908), ii. p. 363.
15. CPR *1401–05*, p. 216; E404/18/300.
16. PPC ii. pp. 61–2.
17. Ibid., pp. 62–3; E101/404/24(1), f.12–13.
18. A.H. Burne, 'The battle of Shrewsbury: a military reconstruction', *Trans. Shropshire Arch. Soc.*, 52, 1947–8, pp. 141–52.

19. *A Chronicle of London 1089–1483*, E. Tyrrell and N.H. Nicolas (eds), (London 1827), p. 88.
20. McFarlane, *Lancastrian Kings*, p. 121.
21. *CPR 1401–05*, pp. 320, 354, 390–1.
22. Ibid., p. 311; E101/405/1, No. 22; J.H. Wylie, *History of England under Henry the Fourth* (London 1884–98), i. p. 445; E404/19/324; E101/43/36.
23. *Anglo-Norman letters*, p. 359; E101/404/24(1), f.16v.
24. *PPC* i. pp. 235–6.
25. E101/44/1; *PPC* i. pp.248–50.
26. *CPR 1405–08*, pp. 6,8.
27. *Chronique du religieux de Saint-Denys*, L. Bellaguet (ed.), (Paris 1839–52), iii. pp. 324–8.
28. *Report on the dignity of a peer*, Vol. i–iii in *Journals of the House of Lords*, lxvi, 1824, p. 1022.
29. *RP* iii. p. 576.
30. *PPC* i. p. 295.
31. Glyn Roberts, 'The Anglesey submissions of 1406', *Bull. Board of Celtic Studies*, 15, 1952–4, pp. 39–61; *Glamorgan County History*, III, T.B. Pugh (ed.), (Cardiff 1971), p. 184.
32. SC11/862.
33. SC6/813/22, 25.
34. Anne E. Curry, 'Cheshire and the royal demesne, 1399–1422', *Trans. Hist. Soc. Lancashire and Cheshire*, 128, 1978, pp. 113–38.
35. What follows is discussed in greater detail in Rhidian Griffiths, 'Prince Henry, Wales, and the royal Exchequer, 1400–13', *Bull. Board of Celtic Studies*, 32, 1985, pp. 202–15.
36. E101/44/1.
37. *PPC* i. p. 266.
38. Ibid., pp. 231, 233, ii. pp. 62–3; *Anglo-Norman letters*, pp. 355–7, 359–60.
39. E404/20/186, 220, 268, 270, 290; /21/265.
40. *PPC* i. pp. 271–3.
41. E101/404/24(1), f. 14r.
42. E101/405/1, Nos. 22, 23, 24, 27.
43. SC6/775/12.
44. *Henry V: the practice of kingship*, p. 176.
45. Ibid., p. 177.

5

What was the Legal Profession?

N.L. Ramsay
British Library and University of Kent

In the early years of the legal profession, from the late thirteenth century to about the mid- or late fourteenth century, lawyers generally appear in records as clerks or as holders of certain offices, if their occupation is indicated at all. The legal practitioner's prestige was not such that men aspired to be called lawyer. A common view of lawyers' greed for money is expressed in Langland's statement that:

Thow myght bet mete the myst* on Maluerne hulles,
Than gete a mom of hure mouth* til moneye be hem shewid[1]

[bet: better; mete: measure]
[mom: murmur, sound]

From the mid- to later fifteenth century onwards, lawyers are disguised in the records as gentlemen, although many of them did not practise; men now wished to be regarded as lawyers even if they were not active professionally. Yet the essence of the problem is not the labels behind which men hid or which the historian may wish they had borne; it is instead that there was no one 'legal profession' or even a profession divided into what would today be called barristers and solicitors. Rather, there were several types of activity whose practitioners were seen as lawyers. The classic signs of a profession – such as a clearly defined and delimited membership with a corporate identity and a clear detachment from the laity – are therefore not to be found except in certain of the sub-groups of what historians may regard as the legal profession.

Furthermore, these groupings were not exclusive: a lawyer might belong to two or three of them, in that his legal activities or private life cut across our definitions of the groups. For instance, a member of an Inn of Court – and thus one whom contemporaries might refer to as a man of court – might practise as an attorney and reside in his inn merely on an irregular basis, when business brought him to London. Modern definitions of barrister and solicitor cannot be applied strictly to lawyers of the early or mid-fifteenth century, because the lawyers' activities simply were not so specialized.

There *were* legal terms for certain types of lawyer, but these were principally limited to the office to which a lawyer had been appointed, such as serjeant-at-law (and king's serjeant-at-law), a lifetime appointment, or attorney – as an authorized appointment that was most commonly limited to a particular case. Outside legal records, such terms as 'apprentice' or, in full, 'apprentice-at-law', or 'learned in the law' (*iurisperitus* or *legisperitus*) are frequent, but these are purely descriptive and are not often found on, say, the Close, Pardon or Patent Rolls, even after the Statute of Additions in 1413 had made some sort of occupational definition usual. Fortescue, in his *De Laudibus Legum Anglie*, shows his awareness of this in the way he refers to 'those men learned in the law whom the people call apprentices'.[2]

Caxton, in his translation of *The Game and Playe of the Chesse* published in 1474, took a different way of describing lawyers, by the courts in which they worked:

> I suppose that in all Christendom are not so many pleaders, attorneys and men of the law as be in England only, for if they were numbered all that belong to the courts of the Chancery, King's Bench, Common Pleas, Exchequer, Receipt and Hell, and the bagbearers of the same, it should amount to a great multitude.[3]

But such an approach was Westminster-oriented and omitted those lawyers who practised in the provinces. Besides, lawyers who practised in one court might well be active in another, at Westminster or in the provinces, with the sole clear-cut exception of the Court of Common Pleas, where a singularly well defined and small group, the serjeants-at-law, had by the fifteenth century succeeded in having firmly established their monopoly of pleading in the court.[4]

J.H. Baker has suggested that 'membership of an inn [*sc.* of Chancery or of Court] was probably conceived, by 1450, as being the clearest indicator of professional status and as a warrant for claiming the vague qualification "learned in the law" which afforded protection against the stringent laws of maintenance'.[5] It is certainly the case that the claim of membership of an inn was advanced by defendants in maintenance suits,[6] but this was just one of several possible lines of defence, and, at least in the first half of the fifteenth century, it is likely that many apprentices were not members of any Inn of Court or of Chancery, while only a minority of all attorneys are likely to have belonged to either sort of inn at any time in the century.

But what is perhaps most relevant to the purposes of this discussion is that the inns do provide the clearest indicator of a sense of corporate spirit among lawyers. In a way similar to an Oxford or Cambridge college, the Inns might attract a feeling or loyalty or goodwill from their members – a feeling that resulted from their residential and convivial side and which is manifested in the songs and 'disguisings' which were performed in them during the Christmas vacation.[7] The testament of John Grenefeld, for example, includes a bequest to the fellowship (*societas*) of lawyers of Cliffords Inn, in 1448,[8] while it was to the company of Davys (or Thavies) Inn that Richard de Denton in about the 1410s or 1420s addressed a petition asking to be supplied with food and drink while conducting litigation in London.[9] The corporate identity of the inns was not reduced by their lack of legal incorporation.

On the other hand, the social attraction of the Inns was (or should have been) one bar to their being seen as affording, merely by their membership, proof of a man's legal capabilities: many members of the inns of Chancery and, as the fifteenth century progressed, of the inns of Court had joined simply because they offered one means of gaining a legal education. Rather than to serve as clerk to an established lawyer it was a pleasanter and more independent life for a young man to learn law by attending readings on the statutes and participating in moots, and sometimes going to watch and listen in the Westminster courts. The latter course required financial support over a period of a few years, but was far more commonly followed than that of clerkship, which was presumably seen as socially less desirable. Besides, membership of an inn did not rule out some personal control, for instance by the principal of the Inn of Chancery, or even, perhaps, some direct instruction on a one-to-one basis. In 1499 Eleanor, widow of Sir Roger Townsend (Justice of the Common Pleas, 1485–93), left five marks a year to find (i.e. fund) her son-in-law Ralph Castell in Staple Inn 'yf he be Rewlid by my cousyn there',[10] while personal instruction or at least control is implicit in the decision of the mayor and aldermen of London in *c*. 1432 to send an orphan to Grays Inn to be instructed by Richard Hungate.[11]

The importance of the inns of Chancery and of Court as controllers of their members is demonstrated in the way in which the principals of the inns of Chancery in the 1440s and 1450s were held responsible for preventing their younger members from rioting; after a riot in 1459 the principals of Furnivals Inn, Cliffords Inn and Barnards Inn were all committed to prison.[12] Control of the Chancery Inns was very much a matter of the personal supervision of their principal and steward, however, and it may be that one element of the rise of the inns of Court was the stronger institutional control which they appear to have exercised over their members – if that is not to take too much at face value countless references to disciplinary action in the early records of Lincolns Inn.

At the same time, the increasing dominance of the inns of Court, and especially of their educational function,[13] may lead to underestimation of the importance of the attorneys, who decreasingly belonged to the inns of Court and even, probably, inns of Chancery. They were retained just as much as the pleaders (the apprentices and serjeants), albeit in a different pattern, but they were less likely to be the object of maintenance actions, in that they were generally men of lesser social and political status. In any case, their retention was likely to have been buttressed by formally warranted appointment as attorney, enrolled on the Close Roll or (most commonly) plea roll.

Membership of one of the inns and the claim to legal expertise were two of the ways in which men could assert that they were lawyers; such ways help to show how the legal profession saw itself, and membership was a touchstone by which people outside the profession could identify a man as a lawyer. In a broader way, they contributed to distinguishing lawyers as members of a trained profession rather than merely followers of an occupation. That is to say, lawyers, like the members of a gild, were seen as needing to adhere to certain rules of conduct and to be subject to penalties if they failed to maintain due standards. In the sixteenth century, the inns of Court assumed control over the right to plead in the higher courts (other than the Common Pleas), thanks to the elevation into a public degree of their 'call to the bar' of utter (or outer) barristers. Before then, the inns of Court can only be said to have exercised internal or private control over a sector of the profession. With the exception of the serjeants-at-law, no group of lawyers was sufficiently clearly defined or limited in number to be able to form a fraternity or other form of society; it was the law courts, as guardians of the public interest and to punish fraudulence, that upheld what they regarded as the minimum standards of competence. Thanks in part to statutory provisions, the courts would punish ambidexterity (the taking of a fee from both sides) and the consequent likelihood of one side's secrets being disclosed to the other party.[14] The judicial hand was strengthened by making all the attorneys who had been allowed to act in a particular court into officers of that court, who were thus made subject to its rules. In 1402, for instance, statute 4 Henry IV, c. 18, had the effect of making attorneys of the Common Pleas into officers of that court, and it provided that they were to be examined for fitness.[15]

The fourteenth-century development of the practice of making enfeoffments to uses was to bring a great deal of work for lawyers, and it was a *sine qua non* of their employment as feoffees that they were trustworthy. Is it reasonable to suggest that the increasing frequency with which they were relied on as feoffees, from the late fourteenth century onwards, is one indication of the generally successful maintenance of a fairly high standard of honesty by the legal profession? Lawyers were peculiarly dependent on their reputation, of probity as well as of competence, if they wished to be employed in such a long-term way.

To categorize lawyers by the court in which they practised was Caxton's approach,[16] but he was content to refer only to the Westminster courts. These were certainly the most important courts, in terms of both the bulk and the nature of their work, and so they were the courts where the most prominent lawyers practised. Nonetheless, there were some lawyers who operated in only one town or part of the country. Although it has already been pointed out that the categorization of lawyers by or within the type of legal activity in which they were principally engaged – that is, as pleader or as attorney – can produce false distinctions, it is nonetheless unavoidable to examine these groupings in some detail.

The clearest grouping, and therefore the one requiring least analysis, is that of the serjeants-at-law. Every single serjeant in the fifteenth century is known, and their (small) total number can be stated for any date in the century: they could be counted on the fingers of two hands, if not one.[17] Since they enjoyed a monopoly of pleading in the most active and lucrative court in the land, the Court of Common Pleas, they were not so likely to be found pleading in other courts; they supplemented their income, however, by giving their advice and by being retained as counsel on an annual basis at a premium rate of at least two marks and commonly 40s or more. They could look forward to appointment as a permanent royal judge, and they associated with judges more than with their fellow practitioners, the apprentices, while their sense of corporate spirit was fostered by their occupation of Serjeants' Inns in Chancery Lane and Fleet Street. Once called to the degree of serjeant (in an elaborate and costly ceremony, including the giving of gold rings and a feast that may well be compared to a university doctoral inception feast), they ceased to live in an Inn of Court and, when in London, lived thereafter either in one of the Serjeants' Inns or in chambers or a house of their own. Wherever they went, they were distinguished by their dress – the close-fitting coif (like a white skull-cap, tied below the chin) and perhaps a tabard or else a mantle, as well as the long robe of rayed (striped) cloth that all lawyers favoured.

Pleaders below the rank of serjeant might aspire to that degree – although a few reckoned that the greater honour was actually less lucrative, and resisted the summons to give gold and take up the serjeant's distinctive coif. A great many remained 'apprentice-at-law' (*apprenticius legis* or *apprenticius ad legem*) for their entire career. The word apprentice was a catch-all term, comparable to that of 'man of court' and only exceeded in vagueness by that of 'gentleman'. An apprentice was neither young nor at the learning stage, but it was only gradually, in the course of the fifteenth century, that the word was largely superseded by the broader term 'learned in the law' (*iurisperitus*, or, more and more commonly, *legisperitus*). What might be seen as a transitional form, *apprenticius in lege peritus*, is used in the brass memorial inscription of John Edward, a Gloucestershire practitioner who died in 1462.[18]

Many of the lawyers found referred to as apprentices were relatively obscure men, and although the term is used in the law reports (or Year Books), it is not particularly frequently encountered in other contexts. It had no legal significance, and it remains unclear whether a man referred to as apprentice was necessarily an active practitioner. The earliest statement of the number of apprentices practising in the Westminster courts is a list drawn up in about 1518 for Cardinal Wolsey:[19] there were thirty-seven apprentices 'supposed now to be present at this term' and twelve 'supposed now to be absent from this term', thus forming a total of about fifty. They had mostly been members of an inn for at least fifteen years. It is impossible to give any reliable estimate as to how many apprentices may have practised outside London – whether as many as in London, or more, or fewer – although the smaller volume of litigation that was surely conducted in the county courts and other local courts suggests that there were fewer. On the other hand, they enjoyed a major role in the county as givers of counsel and by discharging lesser judicial functions (as Justices of the Peace and as stewards of religious houses and the larger lay landowners). They were brought together by such activities and by being feoffees-to-uses and arbitrators, as well as by their periods of residence in inns of Court (and perhaps occasionally of Chancery) in London. Their testaments show that their chief friends and associates in private life were often other apprentices.

Attorneys had become a professional type of lawyer by the closing years of the thirteenth century, in the sense that some are found very frequently on the membranes of the Common Pleas rolls which record attorneys' warrants, and that in 1292 their total number and their fitness to practise had been put under judicial control.[20] By a Commons petition of 1402[21] they were to be limited in number to between four and six per county, and it is clear that these totals were generally exceeded. In 1455 the Commons complained that whereas there should be only six 'common attorneys' in the counties of Norfolk and Suffolk and two in the city of Norwich (making a total of fourteen), there were actually twenty-four and more.[22]

Sampling of the rolls of the Common Pleas, King's Bench and Exchequer for the four terms of 1480 has led J.H. Baker to suggest that there were then about 210 attorneys active in all these courts. About a seventh of the total also occupied a major clerical office in one of the three courts, so that the total number of attorneys active in the central courts, excluding those who held clerical office, was around 180.[23] It must however be borne in mind that some – perhaps several dozen – attorneys are likely to have been active and yet not to have had warrants entered in that year, while others are likely to have followed a purely local practice and never or only rarely to have gone to Westminster. For instance, Canterbury Cathedral Priory in 1453–4 retained William Tame to act for it in the local town court, and yet it retained other men to act in the central courts: it is therefore likely that Tame will not generally be found in the records of attorneys in the central courts.[24]

Baker's sample makes allowance for the fact that there were also always many men who appear as warranted attorneys and yet cannot be called active or professional attorneys, since they were only acting on an occasional or one-off basis, perhaps being, for instance, a neighbour or friend or a law student or an apprentice who was making use of his location and general expertise.

The evidence of institutional and private account rolls makes clear how much the attorneys varied in their activeness and social importance (and thus in their ultimate wealth). In any one county two or three were likely to cream off the best business, being the feed (or retained) attorneys of the greater landowners and serving them in other legal roles, such as that of steward or as under-steward (as the post of steward became more of a sinecure, given to an apprentice).

It is not yet possible to show how likely it was for an attorney to have gone to an Inn of Chancery. It was probably more frequent for him to gain his expertise through service as clerk to an established lawyer. For instance, an inquiry held in 1443 into the behaviour of Henry Hatewronge found that he was educated at the local school (not named; he was born at Well in Cambridgeshire and lived at Newmarket with his parents), became clerk for three years to Thomas Fulthorpe, Justice of the Common Pleas, and then, by Fulthorpe's licence, became clerk (*serviens et clericus*) to Robert Cavendish, King's serjeant-at-law, until Cavendish's death seven years later (1439). Only after this did he become an attorney in the King's courts.[25] Hatewronge never became prominent; the career of Edward Cullyford shows what a more successful attorney might achieve. He too, is likely to have begun as a lawyer's clerk, for he worked for Robert Hylle of Spaxton (Somerset) from c. 1416 to 1423, writing a cartulary and other documents for him.[26] He was the county's Clerk of the Peace, 1431–7,[27] and MP for Bridgwater at about the same time (1431), while before his death (which occurred by 1447) he also served as coroner and undersheriff.[28] He died leaving property in Bridgwater and with one serjeant-at-law as a feoffee and another as an executor, while he had his own clerk, John Tracy, as another executor.[29]

The careers of these two attorneys illustrate the extent to which local officials are likely to have been men of considerable legal expertise, even if their office was a lowly one; Henry Hatewronge in 1444 was acting as no more than an escheator's officer.[30] One problem that is raised is the question of whether the holders of any such local offices as coroner, undersheriff, escheator or the like can be deemed likely to have been lawyers *ipso facto* , or whether it was merely incidental to their careers that many lawyers took such offices. My own research suggests that the office of undersheriff, and that alone, was commonly held by a lawyer (usually an attorney, although sometimes an apprentice or at least future apprentice). It is unfortunate that no lists of medieval undersheriffs have yet been published.[31]

A similar problem is raised in the case of officials of the central royal courts, where it is clear that far more men than in a shire's administration were court officials first and foremost, and active as, say, attorneys only in a subsidiary capacity. These men mostly remain shadowy figures, but the few whose careers have so far been investigated were undoubtedly lawyers who were professional to their fingertips. William Wakefield, for instance, was a Common Pleas prothonotary, with responsibility for the keeping of fines and files of writs, from Richard II's reign onwards. He was appointed to the Commission of the Peace in Essex (1406), had various commissions of oyer and terminer, and was probably clerk of the justices of assize and of gaol delivery on the south-eastern and south-western circuits in the last years of Richard II.[32] He is perhaps to be identified with the husband of Joan, daughter and heiress of Sir Robert Tresilian, Justice of the King's Bench.

Particularly intractable is the problem of the Chancery and its officers' relations with the common lawyers. Its principal clerks, other than the Clerk of the Crown, were mostly celibate (in accordance with an ordinance of *c.* 1388–9), but in the reign of Henry VI there was a steady infiltration of its posts, from the lower level upwards, by married laymen.[33] No doubt related to this, as well as to the increasing volume of litigation coming to Chancery as a result of the Chancellor's protection of the beneficiaries of enfeoffments-to-uses, is the fact that from the first quarter of the fifteenth century onwards apprentices and attorneys are increasingly found acting instead of the Chancery clerks as sureties or pledges for the prosecution of bills there. Previously, in the late fourteenth century, it had quite often been the Chancery clerks who were sureties.

Another indicator of the sort of changes taking place in the fifteenth-century legal profession is the way in which Chancery clerks appear less and less distinguishable from the general run of lawyers. At the top of the profession, the serjeants-at-law had a scarcely changed career pattern and range of work, while the career pattern of apprentices was also more or less unaltered, although it probably became more London-oriented as the county courts continued to decline in importance. But if a line must be drawn, however uncertainly, to delimit the legal profession and distinguish it from the mere bureaucrats and petty local officials – men who perhaps had legal knowledge but who cannot be presumed to have been professional lawyers – then the line must be deemed to have shifted in the course of the fifteenth century, to accommodate many of the central court officials. At the same time a new class of lawyer, the solicitor, was springing up: at this date they were lawyers who acted as attorneys on a very local basis, seemingly relying on other attorneys for the prosecution of litigation in the Westminster courts. Meanwhile the attorney was meta-morphosing into the attorney-general; as these two categories were becoming predominant in the country, the apprentices became based more in London, receiving clients at the inns of Court. The division between attorney or solicitor, on the one hand, and apprentice or pleader, on the other, was becoming sharper. In London, too, some scriveners were coming to act more like lawyers, executing wills as well as drafting them, and drafting bills for Chancery litigants: they may be seen as middlemen who helped to bridge the increasingly wide chasm that separated the professional lawyer from the layman.[34]

Notes

1. Piers Plowman, C text, Prologue, lines 163–4, The Vision of William concerning Piers the Plowman . . . , W.W. Skeat (ed.), (2 vols Oxford 1886), i. p. 15.
2. 'et aliis iuris peritis quos apprenticios vulgus denominat': J. Fortescue, De Laudibus Legum Anglie, S.B. Chrimes (ed.), (Cambridge 1942), p. 22.
3. Cited by J.H. Baker, 'The English Legal Profession 1450–1550', Lawyers in Early Modern Europe and America, W.R. Prest (ed.), (1981), 16–41, at p. 16.
4. J.H. Baker, The Order of Serjeants at Law (Selden Soc. supplementary ser. 5, 1984).
5. Baker, 'English Legal Profession', p. 17.
6. Ibid. p. 36 nn.6 & 8.
7. See J.H. Baker, 'The Old Songs of the Inns of Court', LQR xc (1974), pp. 187–90.
8. PROB 11/3 (PCC 35 Luffenam) ff.282v-3 dated 8 June & proved 24 June 1448.
9. SC 1/50/143 addressed 'a la treshonorable, tresage compagne de David Inne in Holborn'.
10. Canterbury Cathedral Archives, register F, f.116v (testament dated 9 November 1499). Cf. Paston L&P i. p. 21 No. 28.
11. Calendar of Letter Books of the City of London . . . Letter Book K, R.R. Sharpe (ed.), (1911), p. 143.
12. C.M. Barron, The Parish of St Andrew Holborn (privately printed, 1979), p. 22; Six Town Chronicles of England, R. Flenley (ed.), (Oxford 1911), p. 146.
13. See E.W. Ives, 'The Common Lawyers', in Clough, Profession, pp. 181–207, at pp. 199–209.
14. Statute of Westminster I c.29; SR i. p. 146.
15. Ibid. ii. pp. 138–9; discussed by M. Hastings, The Court of Common Pleas in Fifteenth Century England (Ithaca, New York 1947), pp. 109–10.
16. See above n.3.
17. See Baker, Serjeants.
18. C.T. Davis, Gloucestershire Brasses (1899), p. 61. Edward is also described as famosus in the inscription.
19. Baker, 'English Legal Profession', p. 28, & n.54.
20. J.C. Meier, 'The Beginnings of Professionalism among English Attorneys 1266–1300' (Iowa Univ. PhD thesis 1977).

21. See above n. 15.
22. See the discussion by Baker, 'English Legal Profession', p. 25 and n.40, and *RP* v.326–7 No. 57; for the number, 24, *pace* J.H. Baker, see C 49/30/6.
23. Baker, 'English Legal Profession', p. 24; J.H. Baker, 'Lawyers Practising in Chancery, 1474–1486', *Journal of Legal History* iv (1983), pp. 54–76.
24. Canterbury Cathedral Archives, prior's roll 9. For another such instance, see N.L. Ramsay, 'Retained Legal Counsel, 1275–c. 1475', *TRHS* 5th ser. xxxv (1985), pp. 95–112. at p. 102 n.37.
25. C 145/311.
26. See *The Hylle Cartulary*, R.W. Dunning (ed.), (Somerset Record Society lxviii, 1968), p. xiii. Hylle was the son of a justice of King's Bench and himself practised in the West Country.
27. L.E. Stephens, *The Clerks of the Counties, 1360–1960* (Society of Clerks of the Peace and Clerks of County Councils, 1961), p. 155.
28. CP 40/771 m.114.
29. Lambeth Palace Library, Reg. Stafford f.151 (testament dated 11 July 1444 & proved 27 January 1447).
30. A.F. Bottomley, 'Personnel for the Administration of Cambridgeshire in the Reign of Henry VI' (London Univ. MA thesis, 1952), p. 86.
31. Very incomplete lists for Middlesex and London are given by N.L. Ramsay, 'The English Legal Profession c. 1340–c. 1450' (Cambridge Univ. PhD thesis, 1985), pp. xliii–v, appendices 6 & 7.
32. M. Gollancz, 'Gaol Delivery in the Fifteenth Century' (London Univ. MA thesis, 1936), pp. 116–21; see also Hastings, *Common Pleas*, pp. 118, 124.
33. See R.L. Storey, 'Gentleman-bureaucrats' in Clough, *Profession*, pp. 90–119, at pp. 98–100.
34. See further Ramsay, *TRHS* 5th ser. xxxv, p. 111.

6

The Profits of Expertise: The Rise of the Civil Lawyers and Chancery Equity

Mark Beilby
Formerly of Oriel College, Oxford

1. Introduction

Frederick Maitland once wrote that, 'except as a diplomatist, chancery clerk, or a teacher, the civilian would find little do in England'.[1] In fact, the secretariat of the Chancery was one of the few spheres of late medieval life in which, at least until the mid-fifteenth century, the civil lawyer made little impression. My purpose in this paper is to explain how and why the equity side of the Chancery grew in the fourteenth and fifteenth centuries, and more particularly why the civilians were for a long time excluded from this office of state, yet ultimately came to dominate it. Section 2 of the paper outlines the origins of the Chancery to the late fourteenth century. Section 3 traces the growth of Chancery through the development of petitioners' rights to conscience and highlights the essential role played in this development by the civilians. Section 4 examines the relationship of Chancery to arbitration and this is followed by a brief conclusion.

2. The Origins of Chancery

Most authorities agree that the equitable justice of the chancellor started to develop in the later fourteenth century.[2] A parliamentary petition of 1415 complains about the growth of what is clearly equity justice, and ascribes it to the malevolent influence of Richard II's keeper of the rolls John Waltham.[3] This petition explicitly mentions the three characteristic features of English equity: the initiation of legal proceedings by the subpoena, the requirements of the defendant to answer an oath, and use of romano-canonical procedure.[4] In this petition, which proved unsuccessful, the commons' complain that the English common law has been under threat since Waltham held the great seal. The commons' complaint should not be taken at face value, for the hegemony of the common law was not being challenged, but it does reflect a general assumption among contemporaries that a change had occurred in the administration of justice and that a new channel of judicial remedy had been opened up.

The development of the equitable jurisdiction of the chancellor was the result of demands from below.[5] It grew out of petitions made to the king's council by supplicants for whom the common law provided no adequate remedy. The council, which in the fourteenth century was dominated by chamber knights,[6] had neither the time nor the capacity to deal effectively with these petitions. As a consequence, it became common practice for petitions for redress to be passed from the council to the chancery.[7] It was inevitable that this should happen since the Chancery was particularly suited for the dispensation of judicial remedies, the chancellor was himself a leading member of the council, the Chancery was already the department which issued judicial writs, and the fact that it had long exercised a common law jurisdiction endowed it with a staff conversant with legal forms. By the reign of Richard II and the keepership of John Waltham, therefore, the equity side of Chancery was a recognized supplement to the common law courts.

Just what was meant by the word equity and where it was applicable needs to be carefully considered. Put simply, it was the subjective ruling of the chancellor based, not on precedent, but on the circumstances of each case. It was applicable in those suits in which the common law could offer no satisfactory solution. Equity evolved slowly and it is not until the first half of the sixteenth century and the publication of Christopher St German's *Doctor and Student* that any clear definition was produced. St German declared that equity pertained where the literal application of the law would frustrate the object the legislator had in mind or else where it would run contrary to the dictates of natural law. In such circumstances, equity excepted from the common law on grounds of reason and above all conscience.[8] Conscience, indeed, was the guiding principle of the equity that St German described. Conscience that is, as discovered and utilized by the lawyers of the ecclesiastical courts.

It is incontrovertible that the gradual development of the Chancery as a court of conscience owed a great deal to the procedures of the ecclesiastical courts. The lawyers in the dioceses had frequent recourse to conscience as a means of reconciling litigants. To give one representative example, which comes from the Ely consistory in 1376, Dr John Newton, the diocesan official principal, sought to effect such a reconciliation between Agnes atte Hull and John Weston in a marital suit. He ended his summation with the words ' . . . and in these words we dismiss the case and leave the matter to their consciences'.[9] This resort to conscience by the lawyers and judges of the ecclesiastical courts was no mere legal formula. Rather, it was an enduring cornerstone of medieval justice that right and law could not be disregarded without danger to one's mortal soul.

One canonical device, above all others, reveals the debt the equitable jurisdiction of the chancellor owed to the ecclesiastical courts, namely, the *Denuntiato Evangelica*. This enabled a litigant, in certain secular causes, to bring an offender before the ecclesiastical courts after two admonitions, so long as one admonition was held before reputable witnesses. Herman Coing has demonstrated that the *Denuntiato Evangelica*, like Chancery equity, was both a supplementary judicial system and one based on conscience.[10] But, the resemblance is closer even than Coing has suggested. From the late fourteenth century onwards, canonists were justifying recourse to the *Denuntiato Evangelica* on strikingly similar grounds to those later employed by St German to justify the equitable jurisdiction of the chancellor. Canonical writers such as Antonius de Butrio claimed that the *Denuntiato* was enforceable in the event of default of justice by the prince or the secular authority. The prince had an inalienable duty to dispense the law of nature to whichever of his subjects who petitioned him for redress of their grievances. Should he fail in this duty, then the petitioner had a right which was good in conscience and which the ecclesiastical courts should enforce by means of the *Denuntiato*.[11] In other words the ecclesiastical courts, on grounds of conscience, brought secular causes within their purview to ensure the application of the law of nature. The *Denuntiato*, therefore, as defined by late fourteenth-century canonists, was to all intents and purposes the same as Chancery equity in its most highly developed form.

3. The Development of a Petitioner's Right in Conscience

The growth of equity, as St German understood it, is shrouded in mystery. Much of the rest of this paper will be devoted to tracing the development of the Chancery petitioners' right in conscience and to demonstrating the fundamental role played by the civilian in this development.

Unfortunately the surviving records of Chancery proceedings are so scarce as to make it impossible for the historian to be sure when procedural innovation took place. The bulk of the manuscripts deposited in the Public Record Office are petitions from suitors and replications from defendants. These hint tantalizingly at Chancery procedure but are seldom explicit. Nevertheless, there is circumstantial evidence to suggest that the commons' petition of 1415 was correct to identify the chancellorship of John Waltham as a turning point in the development of the Chancery. The period between 1377 and 1382 was an exceptional one in the history of the medieval Chancery. This was because the Chancery was then (for the last time before the reign of Edward IV) dominated by university-trained lawyers with practical experience of the ecclesiastical courts. The office of chancellor was successively held by Simon Sudbury, William Courtenay and Robert Braybroke. All were civil law graduates who had practised as advocates in the consistory courts. Moreover, in 1382, the great seal was held jointly by John Waltham and Walter Skirlow. Skirlow is noteworthy as the only lawyer with practical experience of the church courts to serve in the secretariat of the Chancery after 1377 and before the mid-fifteenth century.[12] Indeed, only a handful of law graduates held office of any sort in the Chancery between 1382 and 1448. Of these, one, Richard Clitherow, received his bachelor's degree in civil law some thirteen years after first practising as a chancery clerk.[13] Finally Richard Ronhale and Ralph Greenhurst were employed in the Chancery as diplomatic experts alone and probably took no part in the day to day running of either the equity or Latin side.[14] So, there appear to have been few lawyers involved in the Chancery secretariat while the equity justice of the chancellor was flowering. It should be borne in mind, moreover, that at any given time there were around one hundred permanent Chancery officials.[15] It is surely no mere coincidence that the commons' petition should associate the introduction of the subpoena into Chancery and the consequent growth of equity which (as we have seen) had unmistakable romano-canonical origins, with a key period, albeit short, when lawyers versed in the decretals and the *corpus juris civilis* and boasting practical experience of the ecclesiastical courts held sway.

In the late fourteenth century and early fifteenth century the Chancery was a kind of closed shop dominated, like all medieval departments of government, by nepotism. Thus, Walter Skirlow owed his preferment entirely to the patronage of Archbishop Thoresby, who was successively master of the rolls and chancellor.[16] Skirlow came from the same geographical area as Thoresby, became first his secretary, then his official principal, then a clerk of Chancery.[17] The Chancery was a clique dominated by successive generations of a handful of well-connected families.[18] Furthermore, some of the clerks who dominated the Chancery secretariat before the reign of Edward IV, were apprenticed during the reign of Richard II. To give one example, Nicholas Wymbysh was appointed to the Chancery as a teenaged apprentice in 1391 and was still active fifty years later.[19]. Moreover, many of the most senior clerks who served Henry V and his successor came from the same area of South Yorkshire and North Lincolnshire as did Skirlow and Thoresby. So, Thomas de Kirkby, Richard de Selby and William de Normanton were all clerks of the first form and, as their names imply, Howdenshire men.[20] Consequently the rights, privileges and offices of the Chancery became, to all intents and purposes, hereditary. To give but one example, between 1345 and 1400, the office of clerk of the hanaper was held solely by the kinsmen of Archbishop Thoresby.[21] The effect of this institutionalized nepotism was to produce, in the chancery, an insular, introspective antiquarianism. Under the watchful eye of the master of the rolls, the Chancery clerks were taught esoteric, time-honoured skills. Documents had to be copied in a particular manner and the Chancery apprentices were even forbidden to mix socially with the apprentices-at-law living nearby. The insularity of the Chancery curtailed not only the social life of the secretariat, but also their ability to assimilate technological innovation. For instance, the only Chancery clerk who enjoyed Thoresby's patronage, but who did not originate from Yorkshire, Lincolnshire or Nottinghamshire, was John de Branketre, who was born near Norwich and served as a Chancery notary during the 1360s.[22] Branketre had come to Thoresby's attention while serving as a notary in the Worcester diocese, before that, he had been a household servant of the Black Prince. As Pierre Chaplais shows,[23] Branketre introduced a number of innovative techniques for the framing of diplomatic documents. It is most instructive that none of these innovations survived their author. It is a fair assumption that the insular fourteenth-century Chancery was unable or unwilling to adopt sophisticated notarial techniques introduced by an outsider.

The self-perpetuating, introverted character of the fourteenth-century Chancery secretariat is fundamental to our understanding of the development of the equitable justice of the chancellor. For an essentially romano-canonical judicial procedure was put into practice by an institution whose personnel had precious little practical knowledge of such procedures and who had their own, rigidly observed methods. As a consequence, conscience-based equity seems to have been assimilated into the existing Chancery forms. To illustrate, it has been demonstrated that those judgements which survive from the equity side in the late fourteenth century and fifteenth century are, in their *form*, identical to the judgements earlier evolved in the Latin, common law side of Chancery.[24]

The services of those seemingly ideally suited by training and legal experience to the conduct of equity justice, the university-trained lawyers of the ecclesiastical courts, were clearly not required by the early fifteenth-century Chancery. Indeed, the only Chancery clerk, of the first half of the fifteenth century, to study one of the learned laws, Richard Sturgeon, spent three years as a *civilista* at New College yet never troubled to take his bachelor's degree.[25] This was for two reasons. Firstly, the number of petitions was not so great as to overburden the existing resources of the Chancery. It is not until 1426 that one can find evidence of the chancellor being forced to delegate the examination of witnesses to the master of the rolls. In that year, John Frank, a non-graduate clerk who had risen through the ranks of the Chancery, examined witnesses at Leicester.[26] During the reign of Henry VI, however, as is well attested,[27] there was a quadrupling in the number of petitions which came before the chancellor. Fundamental to this expansion in the equity side of Chancery was a decision of Henry V to suspend the assizes for the duration of his French campaign. Henry seems to have referred a number of petitions to his chancellor, Thomas Langley, by way of letter issued under the signet. Thus in 1419, he wrote to Langley: 'we send you closed . . . a supplication of grevious complaynt put unto us by Roger Wodehill . . . that ye do calle before you bothe partis specified in the same supplication . . . yat ye do unto them bothe right and equite'.[28] Judging from the numbers of petitions from each year preserved among the early Chancery proceedings (PRO class C 1), it was not until the minority of Henry VI that the increase in equity proceedings became both marked and consistent.

The second, more fundamental, reason that a knowledge of the civil law was not thought of particular use by the early fifteenth-century Chancery was that the equitable justice it dispensed was not yet fully developed and differed in one vital respect from that defined by St German. Before the mid-years of the fifteenth century, the plaintiff did not commonly seek the assistance of the chancellor because he had a right that was good in conscience and which did not come within the purview of the common law. Rather, the petitioner asserted that his pursuit of a legal remedy at common law had been obstructed by a powerful opponent or, during the reign of Henry V, by the suspension of the assizes. Never, in this early period of Chancery equity, did the petitioner claim to be judged by any standards save those of the common law. So a typical petition from the early fifteenth century, shows how John Claypole, rector of Wooton in Northamptonshire, petitioned against Sir Henry Bylcock who had kept him from his church. Bylcock had been enabled, claimed Claypole, to disregard a sentence of the court of Arches because of the support of the powerful Lord Grey of Ruthin. Lord Grey had evidently threatened Claypole with physical violence if he sought a common law remedy.[29] Petitioners from the mid-fifteenth century onwards, on the other hand, admitted that they had no redress at the common law and sought a remedy from the chancellor on the grounds that the common law was either defective or contrary to natural law and that they wished to be judged by a different standard, that of good conscience.

There is no conclusive evidence that the Chancery was a court of equity, as St German would have understood the word, before the reign of Edward IV. It has, however, been suggested that the document entitled 'Orders of the High Court of Chancery' (*Renovacio*) demonstrates that the equity side of Chancery in the reign of Henry V was much the same as it was in the reign of Henry VIII. This document, if taken at face value, shows that as early as the second decade of the fifteenth century the master of the rolls, as well as the chancellor, was daily hearing equitable causes. Moreover, it suggests that it was common practice to keep register books of these causes, and that masters extraordinary were already employed to assist the regular Chancery masters in their administration of equity justice. The Hargreaves manuscripts, however, are far from reliable. It is much more likely that the *Renovacio* originates from the reign of Henry VIII when the equity side of Chancery was long established as a court of conscience.[30]

It was in the mid-years of the fifteenth century that the Chancery became a court of conscience. A court, that is, which did not obey the standards of the common law and which established its own, founded on conscience and the natural law. As Chancellor Stillington said in 1469, 'in Chancery a man shall not be prejudiced by mispleader, or for default of form, but by conscience'.[31] From the reign of Edward IV onwards petitions no longer simply alluded to the petitioner's inability to gain a common law remedy because of the power of his adversary. Rather they conceded that the petitioner had no claim at common law, but had a right in conscience which the chancellor should recognize. The change had been brought about by a startling growth in petitions arising from enfeoffments to use and from sentences in commercial courts given in causes of mercantile debt. The significance of these petitions was that in the former category, the petitioner's demand was not recognized at common law, while in the latter the petitioner rejected the sanctions of the common law or of customary usage and sought to be judged according to a quite separate judicial standard. In both categories the petitioner claimed a right in conscience. This was the equity which St German described.

That enfeoffment to use and mercantile debt transformed the Chancery can by seen clearly from a numerical breakdown of the petitions in each bundle deposited in the Public Record Office and catalogued as C 1. Bundle C 1/5, dating from the early years of the fifteenth century, contains 207 petitions. Of these none concern enfeoffments to use and only one arises from mercantile debt.[32] Yet, out of 302 cases in C 1/38, dating from the latter half of Henry VI's reign, 155 appertain to uses. Moreover, bundle C 1/64 contains 1,165 petitions, over 99 per cent of which concern mercantile debt. In all fairness, it must be conceded that the counting of Chancery petitions can produce contradictory and even misleading results. To give one recent example, Mr Pronay has estimated the average number of cases dealt with during each year of Wolsey's chancellorship at 770, while Dr Metzger maintains that the true figure was a mere 543.[33] Nonetheless the evidence is conclusive. The judicial business of the Chancery had changed.

Enfeoffment to use arose when landowners conveyed their property to nominees, who would ultimately re-enfeoff them as instructed. Obviously, this type of agreement was open to abuse and as a consequence, from the reign of Richard II onwards, conditions were commonly attached to protect the rights of the feoffer to re-enter.[34] These often proved unsatisfactory, since the right to re-enter descended to the heir of the feoffer, heedless of the claims of the beneficiaries of the initial conveyance. The common law offered no protection since it did not recognize enfeoffment to use.[35] Litigants in cases arising out of uses were obliged therefore to petition the chancellor for an equitable remedy. The remedies the chancellor provided were a product, not of feudal law, but of law of contract. Thus, he applied to enfeoffment to use the civilian principle that the promisee in a contract, unless the promise be performed, and the plaintiff in action on delict, should have the power of recovering damages by action.[36] So, the use was simply another contract which was actionable, much as a debt would be, if either party failed to perform their contractual obligations. Moreover, the Chancery also applied the civilian principle that once an heir was invested with the rights of an ancestor, he also assumed his liabilities. This enabled the chancellor to intervene against an heir in a case of disputed uses in a manner which was quite unacceptable to common lawyers with their traditional reverence for title by descent.[37]

There was a considerable variety in the disputed enfeoffments to use which were brought before the chancellor in the mid- and late fifteenth century. They ranged from the complaint of John Lopham, a Cambridge glazier, concerning a messuage in the city centre,[38] to that of Earl Rivers and the Duchess of Bedford against the executors of the extensive estate of the late Sir John Fastolf.[39] Each case required the pragmatic application of civilian contract law. Sometimes, the chancellor and his staff were called upon to judge a case which fell in the no-man's-land between the common law and equity,[40] and which necessitated labyrinthine legal argument. All cases ultimately rested on conscience, that is in the application of the law of nature when the common law was defective.

Although some debts were recoverable at common law, it was inevitable that the Chancery should become the forum for mercantile disputes once its credentials as a court of equity were established. The law merchant, like the maritime law, comprised time-honoured local custom interpreted in the light of universal principles provided by the law of nature.[41] Initially, this law was ministered in the localities in a variety of customary courts. At each fair, for example, the attendant merchants would constitute a court in which they themselves declared the law and acted as judges. Moreover, in each borough the mayor and aldermen presided over a customary court. These borough courts seem often to have been indistinguishable from piedpowder courts,[42] as the market tribunals were called. One important difference, however, was that alien merchants invariably sued in piedpowder rather than borough courts.[43] This was because the principle was early established that foreign merchants were subject to no law, but the natural law of nations. Thus, a statute promulgated in 1353 decreed that alien merchants were to be ruled not by the common law of the land or the usage of the boroughs but by their own universal laws.[44]

An increasingly large proportion of mercantile cases were brought before the chancellor as the fifteenth century progressed. These, for the most part, took two forms: appeals from lower courts and causes involving aliens. Both were evidence of a desire in the mercantile community to be judged by a distinct judicial process founded on conscience and the law of nature. As to the first category, the fact that, in line with continental usage, the jurisdiction of a mercantile court was limited to the duration of the fair itself meant that many cases were not brought to a satisfactory conclusion. Litigants petitioned the Chancery claiming that the judges of a provincial mercantile court had failed to do justice for reason of lack of time, incompetence or simple corruption.[45] It is possible to date the growth of such petitions with some confidence. Bundle C 1/27 which originates from the last three years of the reign of Henry VI and the first two of his successor contains 508 petitions, many of which arise from debt, and yet none of them seek to overturn the sentences of lower mercantile courts. Yet bundle C 1/66 contains 472 petitions from about the year 1483. There is roughly the same proportion of debt to other causes, but now no fewer than 51 of them were petitions against sentences given according to common law or borough usage in the commercial courts. So, this type of case seems to have become common at exactly the same time as authorities such as Stillington were unequivocally describing the Chancery as a court of conscience. When petitioners complained to the chancellor the inadequacy of the commercial courts, they did not request him to see the common law or borough usage better enforced. Rather they claimed a right in conscience. When, for instance, Alexander Portnay petitioned Chancellor John Russell for the reversal of a sentence given in the Southampton piedpowder court, he requested him to do as 'right and conscience require'.[46] In other words, he was treating conscience as the ultimate authority in a matter of mercantile debt. To do that is but a short step from explicitly stating that commercial matters were to be determined on grounds of conscience. This step was taken under the Tudors when the new court of requests and other burgeoning local courts for small debts, such as that established at the Guildhall in 1518, were known as courts of conscience.[47]

Secondly, during the fifteenth century, it was decreed that the Chancery was the only court in which alien merchants could properly sue for redress of their grievances. As the chancellor said in a case concerning an alien merchant in 1473, alien merchants ought to sue in the Chancery because their cases were determined not according to the law of the land but according to the law of nature.[48] The equity of the Chancery and, the law of nature and equity of the canon and civil laws all derived their ultimate authority from nature, reason in general and conscience as discovered by reason in particular.[49] Once the right of alien merchants to sue and be sued according to the law of nature was established, it was inevitable that they should ultimately seek redress in the highest court of equity in the land.

As a consequence of this growth in the mercantile role of the Chancery, the numerous local courts were tied to the centre. To illustrate, the judges of the tolset court in Bristol grew accustomed to submitting their sentences to the scrutiny of the chancellor and frequently to seeing them overturned.[50] The bundles of early Chancery petitions relating to the 1460s and 1470s are littered with supplications arising from disputed judgements in the tolset court. They invariably related to unpaid debts so small as scarcely to come within the 40s jurisdictional limit set in the fourteenth century to prevent the royal courts being flooded with personal action for trivial sums.[51] This pattern was repeated throughout the country with the result that the workings of local courts were supervised and controlled by the government in a manner that was quite new. The local customary maritime courts had fallen under the sway of the Admiralty court at Southwark in much the same way fifty years or so before. Thus, towards the end of the fourteenth century, the burgesses of Scarborough had complained about the loss of their jurisdiction over the local maritime court, held on waste ground, to the lieutenant of the king's admiral.[52] The comparison between the maritime and the mercantile courts is an apt one, for both administered a universally-applicable law founded in custom but applied by the procedural methods of the civil law.[53] Litigants soon realized that the law merchant and the law of the sea were best administered by the royal courts with sophisticated judicial machinery. It is most instructive that in the early sixteenth century the two laws were fused, and that the law merchant was brought within the compass of the court of Admiralty during the reign of Henry VIII. As Dr Sanborn wrote,

> the success and cohesion of this fusing need not surprise us, since the one and the other were essentially cut from the same cloth, even though at different places and in different times, by generations which had taught themselves through many struggles and difficulties the underlying unity of the principles involved, principles which had their bases in the universal requirements of international commerce.[54]

The growth in petitions relating to enfeoffments to use and sentences in commercial courts, therefore, established the principle that the equity side of the Chancery was entirely distinct from the common law. Thenceforth, it was accepted that, as a seventeenth-century commentator wrote, 'where there is conscience in it, the Chancery shall help by a subpoena'.[55] The development of the Chancery as a court of conscience was reflected in the phraseology of the petitions. The earliest mention of conscience in the context of the Chancery is to be found in parliamentary petitions of the year 1391 which were referred to the chancellor with the instruction that he do what good faith and conscience required.[56] A Chancery petition of 1393, moreover, requires the chancellor's assistance 'in accordance with the demands of loyalty good faith and conscience and in way of charity'.[57] This appeal to conscience was, however, an isolated harbinger of later developments. Even as late as the mid-years of the reign of Henry VI it was still usual for petitions to end with the phrase , 'for Godde's sake and in way of charitee'.[58] By the early years of the reign of Edward IV, however, when the Chancery was fully established as a court of conscience, the petitioner invariably claimed a specific right in conscience. The formula most commonly employed by the petitioner was that he sought redress 'as right and conscience requireth'. This development coincided with the infiltration of the Chancery secretariat by civilian lawyers who soon came to dominate it. In the 1450s, Richard Welton DCL became the first master in Chancery not to have risen through the ranks. Welton was appointed to the office of master in 1448. He had previously been the principal of the civil law school at Oxford, a royal commissioner in appeals arising from the court of Admiralty, and a diplomat who had treated with the ambassadors of the Duke of Burgundy.[59] Moreover, in 1472, Dr John Morton was the first civilian to be appointed master of the rolls. Morton had cut his legal teeth in the court of the chancellor of Oxford University where he had served as the official of George Neville.[60] From 1464 onwards, he had combined a career as a clerk of the rolls of Chancery with work as an advocate in the court of arches, the highest ecclesiastical court in the land.[61] Among the late fifteenth-century masters, Dr David Williams, the master of the rolls, had been dean of the arches,[62] and Dr Thomas Hutton had been the senior legal official of the Lincoln diocese.[63] It is clear that by the reign of Henry VII the senior personnel of the Chancery were largely being drawn from the elite of the civil law profession, that is the London based group of lawyers who dominated the main ecclesiastical courts, the courts of chivalry and Admiralty, the offices of the signet and privy seal, and royal diplomatic service. Such men comprised what became known as Doctors' Commons. Indeed, by the year 1515, when Thomas Wolsey was chancellor, all Chancery masters were civilians and members of Doctors' Commons.

Mr Pronay has suggested that it was the influence of these civilians on the court that led to the increase in commercial causes.[64] Given that, as was said above, judicial change is usually born of demand from below, it seems more sensible to invert Mr Pronay's suggestion and assert that, on the contrary the civilians came into the Chancery because of the growth in the numbers of suits pertaining to commercial matters and uses. After all, civil lawyers were uniquely qualified by training and experience to enforce a jurisdiction which followed romano-canonical procedure, was entirely distinct from the common law, and yet sought to compensate for its deficiencies by the application of standards provided by conscience and the law of nature. As Yelverton, a judge of the king's bench, said during the reign of Edward IV: we will now do in this case as do the civilians and canonists when a new case arises uncovered by previous law. Then they resort to the law of nature which is the foundation of all laws, and therefore what commends itself to them as most beneficial to the commonweal.[65] Or again, as a fifteenth-century civil law dictionary now deposited in the British Library states, 'where the law is silent, the law of nature which is written in men's hearts must be applied'.[66] It is intriguing that it was only after the civil lawyers had come to dominate the Chancery that complaints about its jurisdiction, made by common lawyers, start to appear regularly in the year books. In other words, the coming of the civilians marked the full development of the Chancery as a court of equity distinct from the common law and perceived by its practitioners as potentially injurious.

The influx of civilians irrevocably changed the character of the Chancery. It ceased to be an inward-looking antiquarian office and became very much a part of the vibrant London mercantile community. Moreover, it rapidly shed its ecclesiastical skin under the aegis of professional, secularly-minded masters. The Chancery clerk started to become a worldly man of business. For instance, in 1478, William Hill, a non-graduate Chancery clerk, was owed £475 as the result of a complex business deal with merchants of the staples of London and Hull.[67] Furthermore, well before the Reformation, the Chancery began to assume a character that was altogether lay. In 1523 the Chancery clerks successfully petitioned parliament for permission to marry. Revealingly, they state that it had long been the custom for their subordinates, the cursitors, to take a wife. In 1534 Thomas Cromwell became the first master of the rolls never to have been in holy orders. The laicization of the Chancery was complete before the break with Rome was enacted.

4. The Relationship between Chancery Equity and Arbitration

Some have maintained that Chancery equity was primarily a well-documented and sophisticated fount of arbitration and that consequently it was not a judicial innovation as such.[68] This is not true; for the equitable jurisdiction of the chancellor was a new and distinct form of judicial remedy. Nevertheless, Chancery equity was heir to a long tradition of legal remedies which served as alternatives to common law litigation and which rested on arbitration. The meaning of arbitration, however, needs to be defined with some exactitude if errors of legal categorization are not to be made. Above all, it is important to differentiate between mediation which was not legally binding and submission to arbitration which was. The matter is obfuscated by the fact that English law never differentiated between the two. It is first necessary therefore, to draw a distinction between those cases which had been entrusted to the mediation of an *amicabilis compositor* and those in which there had been an actual submission to arbitration. The former normally occurred when a petitioner sought the assistance of the lord of a man he felt had wronged him. The petitioner suspected that his adversary would be uninclined to disregard the mediation of his lord or to refuse to perform the award he made. Having said that, neither party was bound in law to accept the award of a mediator. This held true whether the *amicabilis compositor* was the greatest lord in the land or even the king. So, the mediator, unlike the chancellor, had no jurisdiction which he could enforce on behalf of a petitioner.

The arbitrator to whom a written submission was made, on the other hand, did have an enforceable jurisdiction. The award of an arbitrator was final in such circumstances and was a bar to further proceedings at the common law. To this extent, arbitration pursuant on written submission does resemble Chancery equity. As Dr Post's transcription and analysis of the Ladbroke manor dispute reveals,[69] it comprised a series of answers and replications, following from the initial submission and the oral examination of witnesses. The lord would commonly delegate this form of arbitration to a sort of sub-committee of his council.[70] Such sub-committees would include a number of men trained in the law, both common and romano-canonical. The statute of livery, enacted under Henry IV, makes it clear that such bodies were considered part of the lord's household and their members would include men, 'learned in one law or the other'. The arbitration they provided was founded on a pragmatic application of reason to the facts of the case.

J.B. Post has claimed that there was more than a mere resemblance between arbitration and Chancery equity.[71] He maintains that this kind of seigneurial jurisdiction was in fact equitable. He sees a parallel between the lord's delegation of the work of arbitration to a sub-committee of his council and the king's delegation of petitions to the chancellor. The Chancery, so Post asserts, was but the most sophisticated and best documented of a number of sources of arbitration. This is to claim too much. In the first place, proponents of Chancery equity as a form of arbitration make much of the fact that its procedures were much like those of canonists arbitrament which gives the same importance to oral examination of witnesses and written submission. Yet the procedure of the Chancery does not bear any closer resemblance to the arbitrament than it does to the summary and plenary procedures of the ecclesiastical courts. More significantly, the chancellor, in any cause which a petitioner brought before him, might claim jurisdiction, whether or not the parties were agreeable. In the canon law arbitrament or the arbitration of seigneurial council, however, the aggrieved party had an inalienable right to refuse to submit to the arbitrator's judgement. Undeniably causes in Chancery were sometimes referred to mediation in the search for a satisfactory solution. Mediation and litigation were always complementary rather than mutually exclusive. But Chancery equity, the arbitrament and the arbitration of the seigneurial council cannot be equated with any degree of certainty.

In as much as the Chancery was an alternative legal remedy to the common law, it did have a number of antecedents which hinged on arbitration. Such remedies, unlike the equitable justice which has been described, did not deviate from the standards of the common law. Rather they were preliminary judicial channels to be explored before litigants had recourse to the king's courts. Associations, such as guilds, which had their own rules, were particularly keen to solve their own problems by arbitration. For instance, the rules of the guild of St George at Norwich decreed that, in the event of a disagreement between members, the masters should seek to settle the matter within fifteen days and only if they failed were they to 'sue the common lawe and els nought'.[72] Sometimes however a member of a guild or trade association would consider himself unlikely to receive an impartial verdict from the company in question and would submit himself to the arbitration of respected figures in the mercantile community who were knowledgeable but unconnected with the litigants' trade. So, in 1447, John Sewale, a broderer in dispute with the Broderers' Company over their trade regulation, submitted his case to the arbitration of two leading London tradesmen, John Derby and Nicholas Wifolds.[73]. They were prosperous merchants, leading guild members, and aldermen, well-versed in the law merchant and trade regulations, yet they had no connection with the broderers. This desire for impartial yet expert arbitrators placed a premium on the services of civilians in this capacity; after all, what more useful tool did the arbitrator possess than the law of nature? Consequently, civil lawyers were ceaselessly called upon to arbitrate in disputes concerning tithes,[74] debts,[75] and property disputes.[76] One civilian, Dr John Aleyn, seems to have built a successful career out of being a professional arbitrator.[77]

The equity enforced by the Chancery fundamentally differed from this arbitration in that the *denuntiato evangelica* had endowed it with a jurisdiction and a distinct set of rules which set it apart from any of its judicial antecedents. There is, however, some evidence, albeit rather flimsy to suggest that equitable standards were beginning to be applied to arbitration in the late fifteenth century. To elucidate, in 1498, an arbitration was conducted in the Isle of Ely in a suit between Alice Bate and Richard Ronde. The four arbitrators inquired into the cause 'after their conscience'. Their award was found by the bishop, in whose register the proceedings are preserved, to be 'according to goode conscience and right'.[78] It is interesting to note that the bishop in question was Dr John Alcock, a civilian who had a long and successful career in the Chancery and who ultimately became keeper of the rolls. Moreover, one of Alcock's main associates at Ely was Robert Hutton, his diocesan register and himself a Chancery master at the time this arbitration was conducted. So there was certainly a direct channel along which equitable ideas of rights founded in conscience might have been conveyed from the Chancery at Ely. At any rate, such arbitrators' awards, made early in the fifteenth century, might make mention of 'good faith' or 'law', but never conscience. The Mancetter arbitration of 1404, preserved in the register of Bishop Burghill of Lichfield, is a case in point.[79] This remains, however, a contentious issue.

Conclusion

The development of Chancery equity served to make conscience an indispensable tool not just of litigants in the ecclesiastical courts but of *all* litigants. By the mid-fifteenth century, courts of conscience were an integral part of the legal fabric of England and it was established that they were the preserve of civil lawyers. So that when the equitable court of requests came into being under the early Tudors, to apply reason and conscience to those cases which were too small to put before the Chancery, it was staffed by the leading civilians of the court of arches, men such as William Wareham, Richard Mayhew and Thomas Jane. Among their colleagues on the bench of the court of requests was Christopher St German, whose definition of equity was the starting point for this consideration of the development of the Chancery.[80]

Notes

1. F. Pollock and F.W. Maitland, *The History of English Law* (2 vols Cambridge 1898), i. p. 124.

2. See for example, J.L. Barton, *Roman Law in England: Ius Romanum Medii Aevi* (Milan 1971), pp. 53–4.
3. *RP* iv. 84, No. 46.
4. Barton, p. 54.
5. The court of chivalry also developed in response to demand from below. Dr Keen has suggested that it was a gradual extension of the lieutenancies traditionally exercized by the constable and marshal in the king's host stimulated by the many suits about ransoms and armorial bearings during the Hundred Years War.
6. See J.F. Baldwin, *The King's Council in England during the Middle Ages* (Oxford 1913), pp. 132–3.
7. Cf. Statute 36 Edward III re-purveyance. 'If any man feeling himself aggrieved will come into the Chancery and make his complaint he shall presently there have remedy without pursuing elsewhere.'
8. C. St German, *Doctor and Student*, T.F.T. Plucknett and J.L. Barton (eds), (Selden Soc. xci 1975), 1.16; St German sought to demonstrate that English law is in accord with conscience. He utilized the concept of Epikeia, the presumed intention of the legislator founded on natural law, to further his argument.
9. Cambridge University Library, Ely Diocesan Records, D/2.1 f. 76v.
10. H. Coing, 'English Equity and the Denunciato Evangelica', *LQR* lxx (1955), pp. 223–241.
11. Antonius De Butrio, at c. quae in ecclesiarum, ex. de constitutionibus, Barton, p. 65. Bartolus uses the phrase *quotidianu est* in connection with the *Denunciato*. As he was most studied of all post-glossators, it was probably common opinion among law graduates by the late fourteenth century.
12. Skirlow joined the Chancery in 1377. An Oxford-educated lawyer, he was official of York in 1377–80. Cf. B. Wilkinson, *The Chancery under Edward III* (Manchester 1929), p. 227.
13. Clitherow became Bishop of Bangor in 1423. His role in Chancery seems to have been a diplomatic one, like a protonotary, a civil lawyer with little or no contact with the secretariat.
14. Both were protonotaries. Ronhale was possibly recruited by Chancellor Braybroke, whom he helped administer London diocese, see e.g. Guildhall Library MS 9531/3, Reg. Braybroke, ff. 317, 366v.
15. P. Chaplais, *English Royal Documents: King John to Henry VI* (Oxford 1971), pp. 20–23. Few Chancery clerks can be identified with certainty. Only senior clerks (clerks of the first form) signed Chancery writs and records. Lower grade clerks are merely denoted 'clerks of the crown' and are thus indistinguishable from household clerks.
16. Emden, *BROU*, iii. pp. 1863–4; Wilkinson, *Chancery*, p. 119.
17. J. Grassi, 'Clerical Dynasties from Howdenshire, Nottinghamshire and Lindsay' (Oxford Univ. DPhil. thesis, 1959), p. 181. Thoresby, himself a civilian, personally trained Skirlow in the mysteries of the Chancery, just as Archbishop Melton had trained him. Skirlow was also keeper of the privy seal. His career parallels the civilian masters who dominated the Tudor Chancery. He combined work as ecclesiastical lawyer, diplomat, and administrator, becoming in turn Bishop of Lichfield, Bath and Wells, and Durham.
18. e.g. John Waltham, the subject of the 1415 commons petition and joint keeper of the rolls with Skirlow, was a related to Thoresby. His cousin, another John Waltham, was official of York in 1374–80 jointly with Skirlow, cf. BI Reg. Thoresby f. 142.
19. Emden, *BROU* iii. pp. 2120–1; *CPR 1452–1461*, p. 152. Although at Oxford, Wymbush never took a degree or studied either learned law. He was a Lincolnshire man.
20. See for example, BL Hargreaves MS 219 f. 76v; E 404/29/159.
21. Grassi, p. 185.

22. For what follows, see P. Chaplais, 'John de Branketre', *Essays in Medieval Diplomacy and Administration* (1981), xxii, pp. 169–179.

23. Ibid. pp. 175–89.

24. See A.D. Hargreaves, 'Equity and the Latin Side of the Exchequer', *LQR* lxvii (1952), pp. 481–99.

25. Sturgeon was a law student at New College between 1402 and 1405, cf. New College Lib. Alb. ff. 88, 115.

26. C 1/6/135 (b).

27. See for example, M. Avery, 'The History of the Early Equitable Jurisdiction of the Chancery before 1460', *BIHR* xlii (1960).

28. C 81/1365/4.

29. C 1/15/30.

30. G.W. Sanders, *Orders of the High Court of Chancery* (1845), 7b–7d. These orders show the equity side of Chancery at its administrative culmination. It is only reasonable to assume that the machinery of 'equity' justice and its essential character developed in tandem. Under Henry V equity was but half formed. Sanders dates the orders to the reign of Henry V 'from certain intrinsic circumstances', yet concedes the *Renovacio* is defective in several places, explicitly on p. 7d (note). Hargreaves' most telling evidence is that the *Renovacio* names Henry Beaufort and Simon Gaunstede, chancellor and keeper of the rolls to Henry V. But other parts of BL Hargreaves 219 contain dating errors. On p. 78, a list of notables attributed to Edward VI's reign clearly pertains to Henry VI's. The supposed date of the *Renovacio* is inconsistent with the few known facts concerning the development of equity justice. There is no other reference to the master of the rolls hearing causes before Henry VI's reign and no other record of register books before 1545. Probably the *Renovacio* belongs to the end of Henry VIII's reign.

31. YB 9 *Edw. IV* 14 no.9. This refers to help given by masters extraordinary in the administration of equity justice. For the first conclusive reference, see *Foedera* xi. p. 507, where Richard Fryston and the civilian Richard Welton were called in to assist the master of the rolls in the administration of Chancery equity in 1463. So, the development of administrative machinery of Chancery and its acceptance as a court of conscience appear to have coincided.

32. C 1/5/89. The term 'mercantile debt' is a blanket one. My criterion here includes any suit arising from transactions between tradesmen or merchants in which the plaintiff claims to be owed money through non-fulfilment of a contract. The most striking aspect of such suits in the fifteenth century was the growth of bills to the chancellor from commercial men seeking judgement by standards other than the common law.

33. Cf. F. Metzger, 'The Development of Equitable Jurisdiction, 1450–1550', *Law, Litigants and the Legal Profession*, E.W. Ives and A.H. Manchester (ed.), (1983), p. 83. Bundle C 1/63 contains 216 cases, only fifty-five of which concern either uses or debts, but is atypical of those from the mid or late fifteenth century.

34. For the clearest statement of why uses arose see J.L. Barton, 'The Medieval Use', *LQR* lxxxi (1965), pp. 565–77.

35. Ibid. p. 568.

36. Cf. *Imperatoris Justiniani Institutionum in libri quattuor*, J.B. Moyle (ed.), (Oxford 1912), p. 189, for a discussion of this civilian principle. Unable to draw on common law precedent, chancellors had to apply, empirically, other legal standards to suits arising from uses, thus helping ultimately to establish the principle that the Chancery was run by rules distinct from common law and founded in the law of nature and conscience, the essential tools of the canonists and civilians.

37. *Calendar of Proceedings in Chancery in the Reign of Queen Elizabeth* (3 vols Record Commission, 1827–32), ii, p. xxvii; Barton *LQR* lxxxi p. 570.

38. C 1/38/51.

39. C l/38/202.
40. C l/469/15. This suit came before the chancellor under Henry VIII.
41. See F. Sanborn, 'Origins of the Early English Maritime and Commercial Law'. *American Historical Association* (1930), esp. 336–401.
42. See *Select Cases concerning the Law Merchant AD 1270–1638*, C. Gross (2 vols Selden Soc. xxiii, 1896), p. xxi: at Gloucester and Bristol the two courts appear to have been identical. See also YB 12 Edward IV, f. 9: 'A Chescun Market est incident in Court de Pypoud'. Debt cases in piedpowder courts were not merely small suits against pedlars or hawkers, but often concerned amounts of £60 or £100; cf. Sir Gurney Benham, 'Piedpowder Courts in Colchester', *Essex Review* (1938).
43. See *Monumenta Juridica: The Black Book of the Admiralty*, T. Twiss (ed.), (4 vols RS 1871–6), ii. pp. 20–25.
44. Statute 27 Edward III, St. II Ch. 8. The essence of the universal laws of the mercantile community was the law of nature, to which civilians and canonists required that all positive laws comply.
45. Such appeals against sentences from local courts in matters of debt arose from transactions between tradesmen/merchants of an altogether loftier status. Petitioners sought to be judged by standards other than those of the common law. So a humble maltman like Henry Wyn during the chancellorship of Stillington sought to reverse a judgement of the Ware piedpowder court, C l/64/1111, and *c.* 1469 Henry Cheseman, a prosperous merchant, required the chancellor to overturn a sentence of the court of Havering. Cheseman wanted the chancellor 'in conscience' to find a loan made by his adversary John Rexwolds usurious, C l/64/948.
46. C l/59/39. This case concerned a mercantile debt of £300. It is alluded to in N. Pronay, 'The Chancellor, The Civilians and the Council at the end of the Fifteenth Century', *British Government and Administration*, H. Hearder and H.R. Loyn (eds), (Cardiff 1974).
47. J.R. Tanner, *Tudor Constitutional Documents 1485–1603* (3rd edn 1951), p. 302. Such courts of conscience stole the business of the local 'small claims' courts which ran according to the common law and local usage. Before the courts of conscience developed, debts under 40s were the prerogative of a panoply of local, proprietary courts, e.g. *VCH Bucks*. iv. p. 413 on the portmote of Newport Pagnell.
48. YB 13 Edw. IV p. 9. Even before Waltham and the beginnings of equity, some aliens had sued in Chancery. The chancellor had early developed a jurisdiction in international law, see CCR 1327–1330, p. 181, which shows the great seal used for letters of reprisal in favour of Englishmen abroad. See also Barton, *Roman Law in England*, p. 51. An early instance of delegation of matters involving aliens from council to Chancery is SC l/43/11 concerning a ship off Barcelona *c.* 1380. The development of his court as a forum for aliens was, therefore, perhaps inevitable.
49. See John of Legnano, *Tractatus de Bello*, cf. 11, 'Nam Jus Civile et Jus Canonicum Non Dicunt Aliam Aequitatem Quam Sit Aequitas Jure Gentium.' Only in the sixteenth century did civilians like Benvenutio Stracclia finally standardize international practice of mercantile law by applying to it the burgeoning law of nations, itself merely an extension of the law of nature. See Benvenutio's *Tractatus de Mercatorii seu Mercatore* of 1550.
50. See, for instance, Cl/64/1106 (Robert Walsale dyer v. wool-supplier, *c.* 1473). All such local courts came under the watchful eye of the chancellor through the agency of petitioners: cf. Cl/46/156, where the merchant Stephen Shelton claims that the customary law of the mayor's court at Newcastle preclude a litigant from 'makying hys lawe' in actions of detinue and is consequently contrary to reason and conscience.
51. For the 40s jurisdictional limit, see J.S. Beckman in *Legal History Studies*, D. Jenkins (Cardiff 1975), 110–15; C l/63/188: Thomas Clerk v. Mayor of London concerns a bond of just 40s.

52. *CPR 1374–1377*, pp. 321–2.
53. See M. Keen, *The Laws of War in the Later Middle Ages* (Oxford 1965), p. 15.
54. Sanborn, p. 401.
55. BL Lansdowne MS 621 f.21.
56. *RP* iii. p. 297, petitions 1 and 2; Barton, *Roman Law in England*, p. 64. Petitions were to be determined by good faith and conscience. By 1425, petitions turned over from parliament to the council were explicitly directed to be dealt with according to conscience.
57. C 1/2/2: the plaintiff had no written evidence so could not sue at common law.
58. C1/2/33.59. Emden, *BROU* iii. pp. 2027–8.
60. Bodl. Libr. Laud Miscellany MS 28 (SC 492), ff. 89v–90. This is the record of a suit between William Hart and Peter Barbor.
61. *RP* v. 515; see Worcestershire RO Reg. Carpenter ii f. 53 for Morton's work in the court of Arches. He became dean in 1474. C47/30/10 (20) shows that in 1475 Morton was sent, as master of the rolls, with letters to the king of France.
62. See for example Queen's College, Oxford, MS 54 f. 302v.
63. Emden, *BRCU*, pp. 323–4.
64. Pronay, p. 95.
65. *YB Mich. 8 Edward IV* 9. Pl 9 at f.12v.
66. BL Royal MS 10BIX f.105v.
67. Cited by Pronay, p. 95.
68. See for example J.B. Post, 'Equitable Resorts before 1450', *Law, Litigants and the Legal Profession*, p. 68.
69. *Medieval Legal Records*, R.F. Hunnisett and J. Post (eds), (1978), 290–339.
70. Ibid. p. 297; A.E. Levett, 'Baronial Councils and their Relation to Manorial Courts', *Studies in Manorial History*, H.M. Cam, M. Coate and L.S. Sutherland (eds), (Oxford 1938), pp. 21–41.
71. Post, *Medieval Legal Records*, pp. 296–8. For a legal action pursuant on a failure to observe an arbitrator's award to whom a written submission had been made, see BL Royal MS 11AXV f.155v. Unlike the chancellor the arbiter could not subpoena a reluctant defendant to submit to the process in the first place.
72. *English Guilds: The Original Ordinances*, J. and L. Toulmin Smith (eds), (Early English Text Society xl, 1870), pp. 450–451.
73. BL Royal MS 17BXLVII f.38.
74. See for example *The Register of Robert Hallum, Bishop of Salisbury 1407–11*, J.M. Horn (ed.), (Canterbury and York Society clxv, 1984), p. 134.
75. Exeter Cathedral Library MS 3498 (26): arbitration of Christopher Cook DCL in a debt case between the chapter and Richard Hobbs.
76. Dr Philip Morgan frequently arbitrated land disputes, mainly involving grandees, cf. *CCR 1422–1429*, 62, 72, 122, 472.
77. For Allen's early career, see R.J. Mitchell, 'English Law Students at Bologna in the Fifteenth Century', *English Historical Review* li (1936), p. 273.
78. Cambridge University Library, EDR/G/1/6/, Reg. Alcock, pp. 131–2.
79. Lichfield Joint Record Office B/A/1/7, Reg. Burghill, ff. 128–140.
80. See *Select Cases in the Court of Requests*, I. Leadam (ed.), (Selden Soc. xii, 1898), pp. cx–cxiv. A sixteenth-century Chancery petition C 3/78/55 shows the close connections of Chancery and court of arches. The plaintiff appealed against the judges of the Arches: Yale, Weston and Lewes, all current Chancery masters.

7

The Profits of the Law and the 'Rise' of the Scropes: Henry Scrope (d. 1336) and Geoffrey Scrope (d. 1340), Chief Justices to Edward II and Edward III

Brigette Vale
Postgraduate Officer, Loughborough University of Technology

> A sergeant of the Lawe, war and wys, . . .
> Justice he was ful often in assise
> By patente and by pleyn commissoun.
> For his science and for his high renoun,
> Of fees and robes hadde he many oon.
> So greet a purchasour was nowher noon;
> Al was fee simple to hym in effect.[1]

Insofar as Geoffrey Chaucer's portrait of the man of law can be said to indicate a contemporary view of lawyers, it was a view which embodied great wealth and corruption. Edward I's dismissal of the majority of his justices in 1290 for misconduct and the very large fines of £20,000 which the justices paid goes some way towards explaining this attitude. Indeed there can be no doubt that medieval lawyers were considered to be very wealthy, for in the poll tax assessments of 1379 the royal justices were assessed at the same rate as the baronage. This paper seeks to examine the opportunities for enrichment and advancement, which the legal profession could offer. Detailed consideration will be given to the careers of two remarkable brothers Henry Scrope (d. 1336) and Geoffrey Scrope (d. 1340) and the contribution that their careers made to their family's future prominence.

The late K.B. McFarlane considered that the well-known success of the families of the Scropes of Bolton and of Masham was based on the profits of the legal careers of the two brothers.[2] In brief the success of the two branches of the family by 1400 lay in their establishment of considerable landed estates in the North Riding and their elevation to major political and administrative positions including the treasurership, chancellorship, the primacy of York and the earldom of Wiltshire. The career of Geoffrey Scrope and in particular the legal administration over which he presided was examined in detail by Professor Lionel Stones, but that of his elder brother Henry Scrope has not hitherto received any attention.[3] Moreover the precise relationship between the activities of the lawyer brothers and the success of future generations has never been fully established and put in the general context that is the purpose of this paper.

The assumption that the practice of the law transformed the position of the Scrope family has tended to obscure the fact that well before 1300 the Scropes were an established North Riding family belonging to the knightly stratum of society. Indeed the origins of the family can be traced back, if not to the conquest as was the boast of some noble families, at least to 1166 when a certain Robert Scrope held a knight's fee in Flotmanby in the East Riding and Barton in Lincolnshire.[4] At the same time members of the family were members of the household of the Earl of Lincoln, Gilbert de Gant.[5] In the first half of the thirteenth century the family acquired land in the manor of Wensley in the North Riding. By the end of the century William Scrope, father of the two lawyers, held property in two additional manors and had acted as bailiff to the Earl of Richmond.[6] As bailiff, William must have had some rudimentary legal training and it may have been this which suggested the law as an appropriate occupation for his sons. Indeed William's ambitions for his sons were reported in 1385, when a witness in the famous dispute over the Scrope arms explained that Henry Scrope 'fuist par assent de cez parentes mys al le ley'.[7]

Much of the personal history of the two brothers Henry and Geoffrey inevitably remains hidden. No record of Henry's date of birth survives, but it probably occurred about 1267–70. This is based on the assumption that he was at least of age in 1288, when he received a grant of land in the 'Westhall' fee of Wensley. This is the earliest known reference to him; and he was thus many years older than his brother Geoffrey, who was born about 1285. Both men married into local knightly families. The identity of Henry's wife remains unknown. She is variously said to be either a daughter of Lord Roos or Lord FitzWalter, but neither candidate can be confirmed. Henry may, in any case, have married late in life, since his eldest son William was only sixteen on his death in 1336. Margaret, Henry's widow, remarried a certain Hugh Mortimer, and survived Henry by twenty-two years. Geoffrey Scrope's marriage presents fewer problems, for he certainly married Ivetta, daughter of William Roos of Ingmanthorpe, who had probably predeceased Geoffrey by the time of his death in 1340.[8] It is not possible to say whether the two brothers acquired cash or property through their marriages.

Precisely how the two brothers came to enter the legal profession is, however, a mystery. Although in the fifteenth century it may have been customary for sons of knightly families to gain some legal training at the inns of court, these institutions were still in their infancy at the beginning of the fourteenth century. It seems unlikely that William would have had the resources to provide his sons with the training necessary for both of them in the course of their careers to hold the most important legal positions in the country. It seems more likely that the brothers attracted the patronage of some important figure, whose identity remains unknown.

The first reference to Henry Scrope as a lawyer appears in 1292, when he was a pleader in the court of common pleas at Westminster. He was still a pleader in 1303–4, when the courts had moved to York. It is at this stage that his brother Geoffrey also appears as pleader, presumably attracted by the proximity of the courts and of his brother.[9] In the course of his career, Henry was to serve many masters. By 1305, at least, he was being employed as counsel by Henry de Lacy, Earl of Lincoln. A single entry in the surviving accounts for 1304–5 reveals a payment to Henry and to William de Norry of 70s 10d for four days' work at Ightenhill, the caput of the Clitheroe honour and the stronghold of the earl. This probably represents a payment for routine administrative work. William de Norry had been employed by the earl since at least 1296, when one of his duties was the auditing of accounts. When Scrope began working for the earl is impossible to determine; perhaps, like Norry, he had been employed for the last eight years. It is quite a striking coincidence that the family should appear again in the service of an Earl of Lincoln. Lincoln himself employed several lawyers to conduct his affairs. In 1295–6 he paid £1 2s to pleaders and clerks to conduct his business in Cheshire; and in 1304 he paid Richard Starky £7 6s 8d for pleadings and retained a certain William de Midgeley, counsel, for 13s 4d per annum.[10]

Unfortunately only two years of accounts for the Earl of Lincoln have survived and no further payments to Scrope have been recorded. Nevertheless, the connection between Henry Scrope and Lincoln seems to have been a close and lasting one. On the earl's death, Henry Scrope was appointed one of his executors. As such he was immediately put under pressure to loan the crown 4,000 marks for a forthcoming Scottish expedition. In 1333 Henry Scrope also gave St Agatha's Abbey, Easby, £200 in order that they should provide a canon to say mass for himself and his family every day in the church of Wensley. Among those to be remembered was Henry de Lacy, Scrope's former patron. Finally in 1385 a deponent recalled that Henry had been permitted to add to his arms, as a special mark of favour, a purple lion, the device of the Earl of Lincoln. This associated Henry very closely with the earl and perhaps the use of this symbol performed much the same function as the granting of livery and badges in the later part of the century.[11]

Close though the ties between Henry Scrope and Lacy were, Scrope was able to offer his services to others too. According to its internal accounts,

Henry was employed by Durham cathedral priory as early as 1300–1, when he was in receipt of an annual pension of 20s.[12]. This relatively small sum perhaps gave the priory an 'option' on Scrope's advice and legal skills, since it seems unlikely to have been enough to buy them. Nor did this pension prevent Henry's possible involvement in the disputes of the cathedral priory with Anthony Bek, the Bishop of Durham. In 1302, following the confiscation of the liberties of Durham, the royal justice William de Ormesby held an assize to hear complaints against the prelate. Among the plaintiffs was the prior of Durham, who had been at loggerheads with the bishop for some time. Henry Scrope, however, acted as mainpernor for the bishop's justices, Guichard de Charon and Peter de Thoresby. Although the bishop is not recorded as having retained the services of Henry Scrope, nevertheless all the other mainpernors were members of Bek's council, which contained several lawyers. Bek may well have had an eye for talented young lawyers since among them were Walter de Friskeney, later chief justice of common pleas, and Hugh de Louther, later a king's serjeant.

There are other connections that suggest that Henry had an association with Bek. The other knightly members of Bek's council were all men with Richmondshire connections. Two of the most prominent of the bishop's officials were Guichard de Charon and Peter de Thoresby, justices of the bishop. Charon's father had been steward to the Earl of Richmond and both men, together with a third member of the council, witnessed at least one charter copied into the Scrope of Bolton cartulary.[13] Other Richmondshire knights on the bishop's council included Brian FitzAlan, lord of the Bedale fee, and Sir Thomas de Richmond, who may be identified with the Sir Thomas who sold the Constable's fee to the Scropes of Masham. Although there is no firm evidence that Henry Scrope was in Bek's service, it would be surprising if no link existed, given Bek's connections with Richmondshire knights and demand for legal talent.[14] On 19 January 1309 Henry Spigurnel and Henry Scrope were appointed as justices of oyer and terminer to investigate the raid by Bek's officers on Middleton-in-Teesdale. The suit, brought by the Earl of Warwick, was never heard because the bishop's officials failed to appear. It may be no coincidence that Henry Scrope was a justice in this case.[15]

In the case of Geoffrey Scrope, however, there is no evidence relating to his early service. As a pleader at the court of common pleas, he was particularly active from 1311 onwards. He first entered royal service at Easter 1315, when he became one of the royal serjeants. Geoffrey's promotion was in fact much quicker and more direct than that of his brother, perhaps because he was more talented or because his brother's success had made his own career easier. It is only in Geoffrey's later career that evidence of his other employers emerges. He was, for example, in receipt of a pension from Westminster Abbey of £2 a year. He was also in receipt of a pension from Durham cathedral priory until his death in 1340. The receipt of such pensions was by no means unusual and most of Scrope's contemporaries on the bench received similar retaining fees. Nor is the assumption that such pensions inevitably led to corruption necessarily correct. However, there were attempts to outlaw the granting of gifts and fees to royal justices and Scrope's later pensions were probably in breach of these regulations. Nevertheless the practice persisted into the following century. It seems certain that, had the records of more potential employers survived, there would be much greater evidence of the feeing of justices.[16]

One aspect of the careers of the two brothers which merits consideration is their long service on the bench throughout the upheavals of Edward II's reign. Henry Scrope's first recorded royal appointment as a judge came on 26 May 1306, when he was appointed to a commission of oyer and terminer at Durham. On 27 November 1308 he was appointed justice of the King's bench and was one of six judges of the common bench appointed at Langley on 18 September 1309. The appointment of these six justices was apparently encouraged by the number of pleas 'now greater than ever'. From May 1306 to September 1309 Henry was appointed to eleven more commissions of oyer and terminer.[17] Henry Scrope's appointment to the bench was fairly rapid, though he had been a prominent lawyer for many years. Comparison with the careers of his fellow justices reveals that they had had to wait rather longer for their promotion. Harvey de Stanton, Lambert de Trickingham, and William de Bereford, for example, all served long apprenticeships. Geoffrey Scrope was one of the first serjeants-at-law to be appointed a king's serjeant in 1315 and his promotion to the bench soon followed.[18]

Henry Scrope's promotion to the bench came when he was still presumably in the service of the Earl of Lincoln and it may well be that the latter's political influence at the start of Edward II's reign helped Scrope's career. On at least two occasions in 1309 Henry was involved in hearing cases which concerned the earl. On 15 June 1309 he was on the commission to discover whether the earl's *nativi* had rights of common on one of his Oxfordshire manors. On 2 October 1309 Scrope was a member of a commission of oyer and terminer to investigate a complaint by the earl about a breach of his park at Canford. Scrope's appearance on these commissions may represent concessions to the earl's political prominence.[19] The same could be said of Henry Scrope's appointment to the bench on 9 September 1309. Thereafter until 15 June 1317, when he was made chief justice of the King's bench, Henry was continually active on commissions of oyer and terminer. The majority of the commissions were in the north of England and frequently involved Scrope's neighbours. On

12 February 1310 he was ordered to investigate the attack by Maria de Neville and her men on St Mary's Abbey. On 19 December he was on a commission to investigate the burning of the house and deeds of Thomas de Richmond at Burton Constable. Similarly, on 24 October he was a member of a commission to inquire into the burning of John de Insula's mill at Thornton Steward. This John may have been Henry's fellow justice of the same name.[20] After the death of the Earl of Lincoln, Henry is not known to have been closely associated with any great magnate. In fact the remainder of Henry Scrope's career indicates that he was consistently loyal to Edward II.

Henry Scrope did not go to London with Edward in 1311, but remained attendant on the Earl of Gloucester. He was excused attendance on the general eyre as he was elsewhere. He was, however, active during the King's absence. On 23 January 1312 at York he received the custody of the lands of John de Grey of Rotherfield, worth £12 12s 1d per annum in lieu of 40 marks due for his fee and 20 marks expenses for going 'divers places'.[21] On 8 March also at York he was appointed to correct any of the Ordinances harmful to the King and he is first described as a knight on this occasion.[22] Another favour which Henry Scrope received was exemption for life from granting livery to the King's marshals and ministers with respect to his houses on Bishophill, York. Mobility between Westminster and York seems to have been a necessity during this period of the Scottish wars. And when Henry Scrope was replaced by Harvey de Stanton on the King's bench on 8 July 1323, he was unable to hand over all the rolls as some were in London and some were in York. Sir Henry Scrope's service to the crown was rewarded in 1317 when he was appointed chief justice of the King's bench. His tenure of office coincided with a period of political and economic instability, and that this affected the administration of justice is suggested by an order of 22 November 1317 to all judges not to deny doing justice.[23]

As chief justice Henry Scrope was too valuable a figure to be dispensed with, even during the political ascendancy of Thomas of Lancaster, this was surely appreciated by Lancaster himself, who in 1318–19 distributed furs to William de Bereford, chief justice of the common pleas, and to Henry Scrope. These gifts do not necessarily indicate Henry Scrope's personal political sympathies. Nor does it seem likely that the importance attached to these offices in the *Modus Tenendi Parliamentorum* reflects Bereford's and Scrope's sympathy for the Lancastrian cause, a sympathy of which there seems to be no other evidence.[24] Henry Scrope was himself a target for attack in 1322 when on 3 April he obtained a licence to recover his horses and corn appropriated by the contrariants. On 8 July 1322 Henry Scrope was appointed with Bereford to deliver the Marshalsea gaol of 'those who were at war with the king'.[25]

Henry Scrope's political position during the Despensers' regime is rather more ambiguous. He continued on the King's bench for about a year. He was summoned to York as part of the council on 15 May 1323 and remained there until removed from office. From July to September 1323 Scrope received no appointments, but then, on 10 September, he was appointed keeper of the forests north of the Trent. On 18 August 1324 he was appointed justice of the forest north of Trent and chief keeper and surveyor of the King's parks.[26] According to Tout, the 'justice or keeper of the forests had great authority. It was an office held by men of great position'.[27] Indeed Piers Gaveston had held the post in 1310. Nevertheless Henry Scrope seems a strange choice for the post, especially since no other royal justice had ever been appointed to it. Yet there seems to be no evidence that Sir Henry was in disgrace prior to his removal from the bench. On 4 March 1323 he received a life grant of the manors of Uckerby and Caldwell, forfeited by Andrew Harclay, and on 9 March this was extended to include all the corn growing there. On 3 July, five days before his removal, the grant was extended to include his heirs.[28] There may, however, have developed a certain coolness between Scrope and the Despensers. Scrope was never again as active in legal affairs. He exercised the keepership of the forest in person and was still acting as justice of the forest on 7 April 1326. During these years he was a member of only a very few commissions. On 8 November 1324 he was appointed to a commission to make a final peace with Robert Bruce and in December he was on a commission to survey weirs. In 1325, however, he was not appointed to any commission at all.[29]

Henry Scrope was probably not entirely at ease with the new regime of Isabella and Mortimer. Some months after their arrival in England, on 5 February 1327, Scrope was appointed second justice of the bench, an apparently novel post. Scrope had previously refused the office of chief justice, because he alleged that he felt unequal to the labours of the office.[30] It is possible that this was a diplomatic response on Scrope's part, although admittedly he was nearly sixty years of age by this time. Scrope, however, renewed his participation on commissions at least until December 1330. He was treated favourably in that year, when in response to his petition the King remitted Scrope's services on his manor of Bayford, from 20s 2d to 1d per annum. Shortly after Mortimer's arrest on 19 December 1330 Scrope was made chief baron of the Exchequer. This promotion was what could be expected by most senior justices towards the end of their careers. After 1330 Scrope appeared on no more commissions, although he occasionally acted as chief justice during the absence of his brother Geoffrey. On 18 November 1333 Scrope was referred to as chief justice, but on the next day was again baron of the Exchequer. This may have been a clerical error, or perhaps there were attempts to promote him against his will. Less and less is known of Scrope in the final years of his life. In 1334 he acquired property from the Bishop of Ely in Holborn, which then became known as Scrope's Inn. Two years later he died and was buried at St Agatha's, Easby.[31]

Geoffrey Scrope survived his brother by only six years, exhausted perhaps by a very active career. Politically Geoffrey Scrope had been much more partisan and pragmatic than his brother. He was closely associated with Edward II, conducting the hated eyre of London in 1320, for which, in 1326, the Londoners were said to have wanted to kill him. He also tried the rebels who were captured after Boroughbridge in 1322 (including Thomas of Lancaster himself); received many grants from the Despensers; and was knighted in 1323, the year in which Mortimer is said to have wanted him dead. Yet in 1326, when Mortimer and Isabella returned to England, Geoffrey Scrope remained perfectly secure and continued in office as chief justice. Likewise he remained in office after Edward III assumed power in 1330, continuing as chief justice until his death in 1340. The stability of his position can be explained in terms of the indispensability of professional lawyers. Geoffrey's position seems to have been more secure than Henry's, who may have been less of a 'trimmer'. Henry was certainly less successful under the Despensers and Isabella and Mortimer than Geoffrey, which perhaps indicates that family ties do not always dictate political choices.[32]

The opportunity for receiving fees and gifts was one important aspect of the potential profit to be made from a legal career. Nevertheless none of these payments seem to have been particularly large. In cash terms it has been estimated that the profits from royal service were not huge either. Geoffrey Scrope is said to have earned on average, between 1315 and 1340, about £80 a year from the crown for all services.[33] It is doubtful that Henry earned much more. There was less money to be made at the King's bench, where Henry was appointed chief justice in 1317, than in the common pleas, where Geoffrey was briefly appointed in 1323. On the whole salaries for justices have been described by G.O. Sayles as 'absurdly low'. Henry received, for example, £20 4s on 28 October 1328 and £40 on 17 November 1330 as his annual salary.[34] He did receive expenses for diplomatic missions, but it is doubtful that these were very profitable. In fact, considering the amount of work royal justices were expected to undertake, they do seem to have been underpaid. Geoffrey Scrope, for example, in the period from 1315 to 1340, besides being chief justice of King's bench most of the time, also undertook twenty diplomatic missions to Scotland and overseas. Henry Scrope was less active, yet in 1310–11 sat on fifteen commissions of oyer and terminer. Both men were expected to be diplomats as well as legal experts. They also found time to be militarily active and Geoffrey in particular was said to have participated in tournaments.

The evidence of low salaries does not however accord well with general impressions of the wealth of late-medieval lawyers. Moreover it is certain that both Henry and Geoffrey had earned substantial sums early in their careers. On 20 September 1314 Henry Scrope was granted a licence to crenellate his manor of Kirkby Fleetham and the same year to enclose his park at Little Bolton.[35] At that date he was clearly assuming the outward trappings of a major county family. In 1312, before he had entered royal service, Geoffrey had acquired the manor of Clifton on Ure, which five years earlier he had made the family seat, and obtained a licence to crenellate there.[36] Presumably for a skilful pleader there was also money to be made at the bar. Apart from cash rewards, the crown also had land at its disposal with which to enrich its servants. Some land grants came the way of the Scrope brothers. Henry was given the forfeited land of Andrew Harclay in Uckerby, in the North Riding, and also land in Medbourne, Leicestershire, and Bayford in Hertfordshire.[37] Geoffrey Scrope acquired a sizeable amount of land by royal grant. This included several East Riding manors and Great Bowden and Market Harborough in Leicestershire.[38] It is noticeable that the royal grants of land did not consolidate the Scropes' hold on the North Riding. Nevertheless the Leicestershire manors in particular were valued by the family and retained by them. In both cases the advowsons were acquired and provided family livings.

Although the cash sums earned by the Scropes seem relatively low, they must have been sufficient to enable them to build up the vast estates that they left their heirs. It may be that the economic circumstances of the fourteenth century were to their advantage. There is some evidence to show that both brothers took advantage of their neighbours' financial difficulties to acquire their estates. Professor Stones noted that Geoffrey frequently advanced money to his North Riding neighbours on the security of their lands. He also noted a complaint against Geoffrey's unjust seizure of property and his abuse of his own position to prevent a legal inquiry.[39] Henry Scrope ultimately acquired the remainder of the manor of Wensley through a series of mortgages, which James de Wensley was unable to redeem.[40] Several Yorkshire gentry were noted as owing Henry Scrope money. Roald de Richmond owed him 100 marks; George Salvayn owed him £10; and Sir Thomas Sheffield owed him £5.[41] There is insufficient evidence to suggest how widespread were the activities of the brothers as loan and mortgage brokers, yet this might explain their relentlessly successful acquisition of property in a very compact and well-defined area, suggesting a certain ruthless design on the estates of their neighbours. This type of activity may well explain the unpopularity which medieval lawyers enjoyed, as indicated by the hostility towards them during the Peasants Revolt. Henry Scrope himself experienced an attack on his property in 1317, when his manor of Hendon in Middlesex was attacked and his corn was taken from there.[42] Since, however, this occurred in a year of famine, it is perhaps not necessarily indicative of any sentiment towards lawyers.

The careers of Henry and Geoffrey Scrope accordingly indicate the extent to which it was possible for members of the laity to advance themselves through the study of the law. The legal profession was indeed the 'growth industry' of the late-thirteenth and fourteenth centuries. It had proved an extremely shrewd step for both brothers to exploit this new avenue of advancement in the interests of themselves and their family. If Chaucer had been writing a century earlier, his portrait of the man of law would scarcely have been recognizable. Until the mid-thirteenth century most courts had been staffed largely by ecclesiastics. Litigants had either represented themselves or were represented by their attorneys, who were often friends, relatives or officials such as bailiffs. The expansion of statute law and the increasing complexity of writs encouraged the growth of a professional lawyer class. The sums that the Earl of Lincoln paid in 1304–5 for counsel and pleading indicate the demand that existed for legal expertise. Most magnates and ecclesiastical institutions seem to have needed expert legal advice for the management of their affairs. The two Scrope brothers, then, developed skills, which were in demand at exactly the right time for their family fortunes. William Scrope can only have bequeathed his sons a limited territorial inheritance, namely property in the three manors of Yafforth, East Bolton, and Wensley. Evidence from the Scrope of Bolton cartulary indicates that during his own lifetime Henry acquired property in an additional fifty locations in the North riding and the county palatine of Durham. Geoffrey Scrope had obtained property in a comparable number of locations in the North and East Ridings, in York itself, and in the Midlands and southern counties.[43] They were not the only families to do so: the Bourgchiers counted a lawyer among their early successful ancestors; the Stonor estates were accumulated from the profits of a legal career; and the Pastons owed much of their later prominence to their legal expertise. Indeed, as Professor Ives has recently argued, for a later period, the 'family which could afford to send the heir to be trained as a lawyer was placing its money where it could yield the most rapid and considerable social dividend'.[44]

There were however drawbacks for those who entered and prospered in the legal profession. It has already been argued that lawyers were likely to encounter resentment, largely because of their wealth. Socially the lawyer's position remained ambiguous. It may be that he gained some kudos by being closely associated with a noble household and by entering royal service. Yet contemporaries regarded lawyers as socially inferior. This is quite simply stated in the Scrope v Grosvenor case, when Richard Scrope was taunted with the rebuke that he could not be a gentleman (gentilhomme) because his father was a lawyer.[45] It was not until the fifteenth century that lawyers were accorded the title of gentlemen. This may indeed indicate partly why no other members of the family entered the same profession. Despite their success, it must be recognized that Henry and Geoffrey were unable to secure the family's immediate promotion into the ranks of the nobility. As the de la Poles were to demonstrate it was involvement in trade or more particularly finance, which could bring the most exceptional advancement. It was not until the next generation that the family were to enter the ranks of the lower nobility. While Henry and Geoffrey had provided the means to establish a noble dynasty, it was up to their sons to effect it.

Notes

1. Chaucer's *Works*, p. 20.
2. McFarlane, *Nobility*, p. 12.
3. E.L.G. Stones, 'Sir Geoffrey le Scrope, Chief Justice of King's Bench, 1324–38' (Glasgow PhD 1950); idem, 'Sir Geoffrey le Scrope, *c*. 1280–1340, Chief Justice of the King's Bench', *EHR* lxix (1954), pp. 1–18.
4. *Early Yorkshire Charters*, ii, W. Farrer (ed.), (1915), p. 430.
5. Ibid. ii, No. 1148.
6. A.S. Ellis, 'Yorkshire Deeds', *YAJ* xiii (1895), p. 46.
7. *The Controversy between Sir Richard Scrope and Sir Robert Grosvenor in the Court of Chivalry*, N.H. Nicolas (ed.), (1832), i. p. 142: deposition of Sir William Aton.
8. Cheshire CRO, Scrope of Bolton cartulary, DCH/X/15/1 f.15. A calendar of the cartulary has been prepared and submitted as volume two of my PhD thesis. Entry numbers to the calendar will henceforth be given in brackets after the folio number. *CIPM* viii, No. 43; *GEC* xi. 538; *DNB* li.138.
9. *YB 20 Edward I*, p. 360; *YB 30 & 31 Edward I*, p. 307; *YB 32 & 33 Edward I*, pp. 58, 231; Stones, *EHR* lxix. pp. 1–18.
10. *De Lacy Compoti 1296 and 1305*, P.A. Lyons (ed.), (Chetham Society cxii, 1884), pp. 113, 147, 152, 154.
11. *CCR 1307–13*, p. 304; Scrope cartulary ff.68–v (No. 267); *Scrope v. Grosvenor*, i. p. 98.
12. This reference was given in a letter by Dr C.M. Fraser appended to E.L.G. Stones' thesis on Geoffrey Scrope, Durham Cathedral Archives misc. ch. 4668. Henry Scrope continued to be paid by Durham priory throughout his career, receiving fees and robes from the prior in 1324 and in 1333, Durham Cathedral Archives, misc. ch. 4927, 4510.
13. Scrope cartulary ff.63v, 78v–79 (Nos. 253, 299).
14. C.M. Fraser, *A History of Antony Bek* (Oxford 1957), pp. 101, 184n.
15. Ibid. p. 221; *CPR 1307–13*, pp. 169, 170.
16. Stones, *EHR* lxix. 1–5; Durham Cathedral Arch, misc. ch. 3746, 4694, 4005; J.R. Maddicott, *Law and Lordship: Royal Justices as Retainers in Thirteenth and Fourteenth Century England* (Past and Present Supplement 4, 1978). In 1317–18 Henry Scrope received £66 8d in fees from Ely cathedral priory: Cambridge University Library, EDC 5/13/2. I am grateful to Dr Nigel Ramsay for this reference. For the continued retaining of royal justices, see M.A. Hicks, 'Restraint, Mediation and Private Justice: George,

Duke of Clarence as 'Good Lord', *of Legal History* iv (1983), pp. 68 & n. 38.

17. *CPR 1301–7*, pp. 474, 539, 541, 545; *1307–13*, pp. 125, 126, 131, 147, 166, 169, 173, 231.

18. E. Foss, *Judges of England* (1851; repr. New York 1966), iii. pp. 231–7, 239–40, 300–6, 533–4; T.F. Tout, *The Place of Edward II in English History* (Manchester 1914), p. 370; J.H. Baker, *The Order of Serjeants at Law* (Selden Society, Supplementary Series, v, 1984), p. 24. I am grateful to Dr Nigel Ramsay for drawing this to my attention.

19. *CPR 1307–13*, pp. 131, 243.

20. Ibid. pp. 244, 252, 36.

21. Ibid. pp. 337, 350, 413.

22. Ibid. p. 437.

23. Ibid. *1313–17*, p. 166; *CCR 1323–7*, p. 2; *1313–18*, p. 514.

24. J.R.Maddicott, *Thomas of Lancaster 1307–22* (Oxford 1970), p. 49, 290–1. Lancaster also feed Geoffrey Scrope in 1313–14, ibid. p. 49.

25. *CPR 1321–4*, p. 88; *CFR 1319–27*, p. 152.

26. *CCR 1318–23*, p. 712; *CPR 1324–7*, p. 14.

27. Tout, *Edward II*, p. 359.

28. *CPR 1321–4*, pp. 248, 262, 305.

29. E 101/130/8 & 9; *CCR 1323–7*, pp. 246, 302, 569, 625, 652; *CPR 1324–7*, pp. 46, 74, 256, 287, 289.

30. *CPR 1327–30*, p. 7. On 1 March 1327 Scrope's appointment was confirmed in this manner: Henry Scrope, Chief Justice of King's Bench, 'has represented that he is no longer equal to such labours . . . the king is not willing yet to lose his service, has appointed him second justice in the same court. Lest this lowering of rank should give rise to suspicion, it is notified that the change has been made for the king's advantage, for the benefit of the people of his realm, and to spare his labours, and for no other reason', ibid. p. 25.

31. Scrope did act as chief justice of King's bench, 28 Oct. – 19 Dec. 1330, during the absence of his brother, *DNB*; SC 8/242/12087; *CPR 1327–30*, p. 495; *1330–34*, pp. 29, 477, 482; J. Lehmann, *Holborn* (1970), p. 321.

32. Stones, *EHR* lxix. pp. 1–18.

33. Ibid. p. 13. In contrast the early fifteenth-century salaries for royal justices seem to have been in the region of £250, Ives, *Common Lawyers*, p. 323.

34. *Select Cases in the Court of King's Bench*, iv, G.O. Sayles (ed.), (Selden Society lxxiv, 1955), p. xxi.

35. *CPR 1313–17*, pp. 80, 175.

36. Stones, *EHR* lxix. p. 1.

37. *CPR 1321–4*, pp. 248, 262, 305; Foss, *Judges*, iii. p. 499.

38. Stones, thesis, p. 248.

39. Stones, *EHR* lxix. p. 16.

40. Scrope cartulary ff. 14v–18v (Nos. 64–85).

41. *CCR 1318–23*, p. 24, 566; *CCR 1323–7*, p. 128.

42. *CPR 1317–21*, p. 89.

43. Scrope cartulary f. 47v (no.192); Stones, thesis, pp. 248–52.

44. T.F.T. Plucknett, *A Concise History of the Common Law* (5th edn 1956), p. 217. For a discussion of lawyers and the development of the legal profession, see also ibid. pp. 215–31; A. Harding, *The Law Courts of Medieval England* (1973) pp. 75–8; Ives, *Common Lawyers*, p. 32.

45. *Scrope v. Grosvenor*, i, p. 181; A. Wagner, *English Genealogy* (Oxford 1960), p. 189.

8

John Holland, Duke of Exeter and Earl of Huntingdon (d. 1447) and the Costs of the Hundred Years War

Michael Stansfield
Research Archivist, Canterbury Cathedral Archives

The debate over the costs and profits of the Hundred Years War has now produced a considerable amount of specific evidence to set against the more general conclusions of such as the late K.B. McFarlane and Professor Postan. The points of their disputes have often been rehearsed, investigating the profitability of the nobility's involvement in the prolonged, intermittent warfare between England and France in the fourteenth and fifteenth centuries on the one hand, and considering how deep a scar this warfare left on the medieval community as a whole on the other. These premises tend to accept war as the costly, destructive, peculiar state it is today, which is the attitude Bridbury tries to dispel. War was an integral, continuous part of medieval society, as much as religion, and soldiering was the very fulfilment of the medieval aristocracy's purpose; it is vital to remember this precept when considering the career of John Holland.[1]

Case studies exist which itemize the costs of war for particular noblemen, producing conflicting conclusions: Fastolf was an undoubted beneficiary from the fighting in France; the Hungerford family were losers. Ralph Lord Cromwell opted out of a military career in France to pursue a profitable political one in England. John Cornwall Lord Fanhope, John Holland's stepfather, similarly fought little in France during Henry VI's reign, going only to Calais in 1436, yet he remained an active financier in the ransom market and did not neglect such potential war profits. It is only really A.J. Pollard's John Talbot that has provided us with a full picture of the consequences and benefits of a lifetime in military service, mostly in France, in the Hundred Years War.[2] John Holland remained similarly committed to the English cause and it is the profits and costs of this commitment which this paper will make some attempt to examine. It will also try to go beyond such largely financial consequences and illustrate to what extent Holland's political career in England, his local territorial influence, and his family's future were affected by his involvement in France. Bridbury shows us that it would be wrong to see the Hundred Years War as a peculiar event, without which Holland's career would have developed very differently, so it is vital to consider the depth and extent of the impact of such warfare on this late medieval aristocrat, reputedly bred for just such an environment.

The starting point for such an investigation needs to be the financial, landed background in England at both the outset and culmination of Holland's career. Having said that, it should however be stressed that in this case land was not the vital financial or political element that it was for some other magnate families. The Hollands were, throughout their ascendancy, curialist rather than territorial in their interests and inclinations. This will be demonstrated by an outline of Holland's military career up to 1421, his capture and ransom, and its effects, good and bad, on his subsequent career, culminating in some overall assessment of the results for himself, and for the future Hollands.

When Holland began his military career in France in 1415, he was still a minor, though only just, and so very short of independent resources. The inheritance he was due to come into, concentrated in the south-west,[3] had by then endured a minority of over fifteen years. Of even greater consequence, and detriment, to the inheritance was the fact that Holland's father had died in rebellion against Henry IV in 1400, and so his lands had suffered the taint of forfeiture. Henry IV had retained some of them in royal hands, but some went to resurgent rival claimants, dormant during the ascendancy of Holland's father. The insecurity of Richard II's policy of passing on to Holland's father estates where the legal title had not been watertight was now fully exposed.[4] Holland was fortunate in that his mother Elizabeth was Henry IV's sister, and so she was allowed to pursue her considerable and, in many cases, successful efforts to reassemble much of her former husband's inheritance.[5] Yet her efforts had drawbacks for her Holland son and heir. She had remarried in 1400 to Sir John Cornwall, and he came to have a more than detached interest in his wife's estates, some of which they held jointly. Elizabeth, as King's sister, was also very much a lady of the court, and she did not obviously share the enthusiasm of Holland's father for the south-west, where the majority of his estates had been. So, what influence and power Holland's father had built up there was allowed to dissipate, making Holland very much a stranger when he was finally able to visit his tenants in person on his release from captivity in 1425, a quarter of a century after his father's demise.

In 1415 then, with Holland's restoration to title and lands imminent, his landed prospects were not quite as bright as they might have been, being clouded by his mother's longevity, his stepfather's interest and the decline of Holland local power in the south-west, his natural area of influence. He would certainly not be restored to the inheritance his father had held at the height of his ascendancy in the summer of 1399, when he had had titular command of massive resources from Gaunt, Arundel, Mortimer, and duchy of Cornwall lands, as well as those strictly his own, with a potential income of thousands of pounds. In 1415, Holland's financial expectations on restoration must have been less than £1,000 : (the majority of his brother Richard's inheritance was extended at under £600 in 1416).[6]

After his restoration, his landed position steadily improved as he benefited from a similar familial situation to that of his cousin Henry VI: relations died out heirless and he spawned little family of his own, at least not for a while. His last brother Edward, Count of Mortain, died in 1418, unmarried, as did Sir John Cornwall, the only son of his mother and stepfather, in 1421. Both were victims of the French campaign, at Rouen and Meaux respectively. Holland made no recorded gains of estates thereby and their deaths only removed potential, rather than actual, drains on his inheritance.[7] Of more positive benefit was the death of his mother Elizabeth in November 1425, bringing him estates, most of them extended for about £130, in the south-west, with some duchy of Cornwall lands still being retained by his stepfather. In 1437 Holland's sister Constance, Countess Marshal, died, and he gained four more scattered manors. Finally, his stepfather John Cornwall's death in 1444 allowed Henry VI to pass on to Holland some duchy of Cornwall manors his father had held some forty-four years before.[8]

To set against this gradual concentration of estates from deceased relatives in his hands, Holland did have progeny of his own: a legitimate son and daughter from his first wife, as well as possibly three or four illegitimate sons. His daughter Anne was betrothed as a child bride to John Neville, son and heir of the Earl of Westmorland, in 1441. Holland may have provided a cash dowry, but the estates settled on the couple all came from the Nevilles.[9] Holland did provide estates for his son Henry's marriage in 1445 to Anne of York. Despite this, the marriage ought to have benefited Holland financially as it cost York some 5,000 marks. This sum was to be paid in instalments; the 1,000 marks due at the wedding was paid, then York defaulted.[10] The price of this marriage is some indication that, despite what was an apparently continually improving landed income, Holland had perhaps deliberately sold his son to the highest possible bid. This, compounded by York's failure to pay up, is but one sign that, at the time of his death, and after a lifetime of soldiering, Holland's financial position was by no means as healthy as it might have been.

Further indication of this comes from Holland's will, where this sum owing from York was assigned to pay the Holland servants' wage arrears, and some of Holland's enfeoffed lands were assigned to pay other debts. Detailed enfeoffments of much of his estates shortly before his death, the granting of London property to the Duke of Suffolk in return for assistance in claiming wage arrears and his son's violent, perhaps aggrieved, efforts to seize some of Sir John Cornwall's inheritance in 1453, all enhance this impression that Holland's soldiering did not leave a strong financial position for his son.[11]   One final testimony to this is an inventory of Holland's London household valuables and effects, drawn up in November 1450. Under the direction of the Dean of St Martin-le-Grand, Richard Caudray, the local goldsmith community valued some 66 lb of gold, 226 lb of gilt, and 166 lb of silver at nearly £2,035; a further 178 lb of similar plate was worth £1,134, and still more was unvalued. The plate was inventoried in some detail, decorated with precious stones, heraldic devices and coats of arms, yet none of it was obviously French in origin. Also listed, though unfortunately not valued, was a magnificent variety of tapestries and hangings, chapel fittings, bedding and clothing, and horse furniture.[12] Again, nothing was self-evidently the former property of some French noble or townsman.

In spite of this lack of obvious booty, the great extent and value of these possessions would seem to indicate that Holland died a wealthy man, having made a considerable profit from his French service. This, however, only partly appreciates Caudray's purpose. He was having the plate valued to use it to satisfy Holland's creditors, many of them London tradesmen and merchants, who were owed detailed sums totalling £3,300, with some of the plate assigned as a pledge for a £1,000 loan. A further unspecified sum owed to the Archbishop of Canterbury, the dukes of Buckingham and Suffolk, the Bishop of Carlisle and Lord Say, and the incompleteness of the document, mean that it can in no way be taken as a full statement of Holland's financial position at his death. It does show that he had spent lavishly, and beyond his means, on the ostentatious display of wealth, so expected of his ilk in that age. Overall, if precise details are wanting, it can at least be said that Henry Holland did not inherit a very satisfactory financial, and landed, situation. A consequence of his father's involvement in France, it was compounded by the fact that Holland's benefits from war service had either been in France, and so would soon be extinguished, or had been for his lifetime, and so were already lost to his son. It now remains to examine something of that involvement in France, and assess in more depth its consequences for Holland's career and for the future Hollands.

In 1415 Holland embarked for France with his prospects at least hopeful. Henry V bore him no grudge for his father's transgressions and he had been uninvolved in any of the turbulence of Henry IV's reign. Henry V and Holland were, after all, cousins, and the affinity was real as well as theoretical. Holland was knighted at Henry V's accession and received early military responsibility from Henry. He had the honour of being first ashore at Harfleur and served with distinction in the subsequent campaigns of 1415 and 1417–20. He was even more impressively involved in several naval engagements 1415–17, his greatest success coming on 29 July 1417, when he captured four Genoese carracks, the French commander (the Bastard of Bourbon) and the cash for the French payroll for one quarter.[13] This haul of prizes, ransoms and booty cannot have been the only such profits Holland reaped during these campaigns, both on land and sea.[14] He must have benefited further from the surrender of towns to his command, such as Coutances in March 1418, from the captaincies he was awarded, such as Gournay and Pontoise in 1419, and from the Norman estates he was granted by Henry V, chiefly in the Cotentin, in 1418 and 1419.[15]

Apart from these French lands, Holland's inheritance was not directly augmented because of his French service. No English lands were bought and none were awarded him by Henry V.[16] Holland had been restored to his inheritance and his title, Earl of Huntingdon, before he left for France in 1417, but this was not without constrictions. His mother Elizabeth kept the estates she had held jointly with Holland's father and also those she was entitled to in dower. Furthermore, the restoration took time to take effect, as it was disputed by the abbey of St Mary Graces by the Tower and by Holland's sister, the widowed Countess Marshal, and writs of livery for some estates were only issued as late as 14 December 1418.[17] Overall, it was evident that Henry V had no intention of building up Holland as the great magnate that his father had been. He received none of the duchy of Cornwall estates his father had held and his father's title of 'duke of Exeter' had already been awarded to Henry IV's half-brother Thomas Beaufort.[18] So the increase in Holland's influence and income in England was not as great as he might perhaps have hoped for and, fighting in France, he had little chance to oversee his English interests personally.

Holland's plight did not improve with the outcome of the battle of Baugé in March 1421. This skirmish of otherwise limited importance cost the English heavily in terms of casualties. Henry V lost his brother Clarence, killed, and his kinsmen John and Thomas Beaufort and John Holland, captured. Holland initially fell into the hands of the Scottish knight Sir John Sibbald. Like the Beauforts, his subsequent ransom would involve complex negotiations and exchanges, all giving witness to his financial power, or poverty, and his deemed value to the English cause.[19]

In fact, Holland had little family to help his own cause, being wifeless, and, by now, brotherless. It was thus left to his stepfather, Sir John Cornwall, to undertake much of the negotiating and gathering of his ransom, a task he was well-suited for, being a pretty active financier in the prisoner and ransom market 1404–40.[20]

However, for over two years little is heard of efforts to secure Holland's release as he languished in Anjou. No contacts are recorded with England, though Sibbald may have been reluctant to allow Holland home on parole to sort out a ransom, given his record of not always honourable conduct.[21]

It was then, in 1423, that Sir John Cornwall returned to England from serving in France. After some agitation, his claim to the person and ransom of Louis de Bourbon, Count of Vendome, was recognized in November, and he was also licensed to grant Vendome safe-conducts to return to France to sort out the financing of his liberation.[22] Cornwall took immediate advantage of this and Vendome returned to France in November. It was probably then that Vendome bought Holland from his Scottish captor.[23] There is no indication that Sibbald had made any headway before then with his captive's ransom, a measure perhaps of Holland's lack of financial resources, and so he may have been quite ready to receive some return for his capture and sell out to Vendome, though for how much is not known. The purchase price greatly enhanced Vendome's own hopes for release as it meant an exchange deal could now be set up with Holland. It also meant Holland was effectively negotiating with his stepfather Cornwall over his ransom. Yet Cornwall was not likely to let his stepson off lightly as he had already been put to some trouble and expense over Vendome's ransom, having originally captured him at Agincourt and then had him claimed by the crown.[24] For his part, Holland was not the most attractive investment on the prisoner market, as some indication now comes to light of the costs of his loyal military service to Henry V. In the February 1424 parliament, Holland detailed his financial claims on the crown as £8,157 14s 11d in war wages, 2,000 marks (£1,333 13s 4d) bequeathed to him in Henry V's will of June 1421, and £1,000 promised prize money for Genoese carracks captured in 1417. In return for Holland dropping 3,500 marks (£2,333 13s 4d) of these claims, the crown handed over to Cornwall the prisoners Sire de Gaucourt and Sire d'Estouteville as a contribution to the ransom.[25] The pace of negotiations now accelerated.

Holland petitioned the May 1425 parliament for permission for the Duke of Exeter to be allowed to treat with the two French lords over their ransoms and for them to be allowed home to sort out raising the money. The dukes of Orleans and Bourbon and the Count of Eu were to act as pledges. All this was allowed and the reimbursement of Cornwall for his ransom expenses from the Arundel wardship was also reiterated.[26] Agreement was reached for the two Frenchmen to be ransomed together for 5,000 marks (£3,333 13s 4d). All appeared settled when Holland signed a deed on 6 July detailing the breakdown of ransom payments and, at the same time, safe conducts were issued for Vendome and others to bring Holland back into English territory, while others were settling the financial details. Gaucourt was also allowed back to France with authority from Estouteville to sell off land to help realize his part of the ransom.[27] Yet negotiations still dragged. Holland confirmed the July agreement on 2 August, and Denis Rogier, a servant of Vendome's brother the Duke of Bourbon, travelled to England in the same month to finalize his release. However, Holland was still at Loudon in Anjou on 28 October writing a covering letter for the two ransom deeds. These documents were only produced in London just before Christmas and this was probably about the time when he was finally released, though he does not re-emerge in England before the spring of 1426.[28]

The July deed detailed the breakdown of the ransom, but laid down no timetable for payment, nor any penalties for default. At that stage Vendome owed Cornwall 11,665 marks for his ransom. Out of consideration for his stepson's financial straits, and no doubt also out of family amity, Cornwall agreed to remit 2,665 marks of that. Whether or not Holland paid anything to Vendome above this final figure of 9,000 marks (£6,000) is not known.[29] Holland was able to raise the majority of the 9,000 marks from the ransoms of the French lords Gaucourt and Estouteville (5,000 marks). A further 1,750 marks came from the Arundel wardship and 1,150 marks was pledged by friends and associates of Holland,[30] who himself only directly contributed 500 marks from his estate revenues and 450 marks from his pay as constable of the Tower. 150 marks had no source specified.[31] All this was probably actually paid in full. Gaucourt paid up the whole of his and Estouteville's ransom and was still chasing Estouteville's son for repayment some years later. Cornwall received Holland's Tower pay in full just three days after the July agreement was signed and he was also being assigned various payments made into the Exchequer from the Arundel wardship.[32]

At first glance, Holland appears to have been greatly assisted by the crown over his ransom, with no great financial contribution being required from himself. That ignores the 1424 accommodation. Holland had claimed some 15,376 marks of arrears from the crown. He had accepted two French lords in satisfaction of 3,500 marks of these debts and then ransomed them for 5,000 marks, so apparently making a profit. That still left outstanding nearly 12,000 marks (£8,000), which he must now have had a diminishing hope of ever seeing.[33] Furthermore, in the parliament of January 1431, he claimed his ransom had cost him 20,000 marks.[34] The variance between this and the sum he agreed to pay in 1425 can probably be explained by unknown payments made to his initial Scottish captor and, mostly, by the costs of his detention in France for nearly five years and the expenses of communication with England to secure his release. He might also have included in that figure the loss of income he might otherwise have expected to gain from his estates and through royal service. He was not just detailing the actual costs of his freedom, but the figure represented the total cost of nearly five years' captivity.[35]

Moreover, the effects of his capture and ransom went far beyond the mere financial cost. He returned to England for probably the first time in eight years in 1425. He was now aged over thirty, was still unmarried and heirless, and he had had no chance to view his estates since his majority, or to establish his authority in government, either at Westminster or in the south-west. This prolonged absence from affairs in England first as a soldier and then as a captive was to condition his political stance and attitudes for the rest of his life. He was never really to show any great concern for his influence in the south-west and he had none of his father's fondness for the magnificent mansion of Dartington. Instead, he remained close to the court in London,[36] though even here he was not often to be a vital figure in political events. He was remained committed to the English cause in France, yet even in this sphere his service was often constricted by financial considerations. He was characteristically employed on short-term relief expeditions, in 1433, 1436, and 1438, and he never really built up a career in France by collecting captaincies and holding area commands. When he did seem to be becoming established in France, in 1430 in Normandy and in 1439 in Gascony, he was home sooner than might have been anticipated.[37] Other English commanders would also claim wage arrears for French service, but it did not prevent them from continuing to serve in France. Such as the dukes of York and Buckingham and Lord Talbot were able to sustain their military effort from their own resources if need be; Holland could not.[38]

Indeed, after his release from captivity in 1425, it was to be nearly five years before he would return to France. This was a period of some financial and personal recuperation necessitated directly by his war costs, and indirectly by his absence in France from domestic affairs. Nothing more is heard of his ransom payments after the agreements of 1425 and they may well all have been paid at once then. This was helped by the augmentations his inheritance now received. Firstly, his mother's dower estates fell in to him on her death in November 1425, except, that is, for those duchy of Cornwall manors retained by Holland's stepfather Sir John Cornwall.[39] Holland also received considerable indirect compensation for his war costs in the form of the dower brought by his wife. Sometime in the late summer of 1426, he married Anne Stafford, widow of Edmund Mortimer, last Earl of March. Her lands extended into some seventeen counties of England and much of Wales, as well as Ireland. Despite problems over actually gaining seisin of them, and the cost of the fine Holland had to pay for the marriage (1,200 marks),[40] the hand of such an important widow must have been some compensation for his financial problems. It was a pattern that was to be repeated. On Anne's death, Holland remarried in 1433, with compensation for French service specifically cited, Beatrice of Portugal, Countess of Arundel, who had by then been a widow for eighteen years.[41] This elderly and wealthy dowager was most obviously an indirect contribution to Holland's war expenses, and, on her death, another well-dowered widow was found for Holland. In 1442 he married Anne Montagu, widow of both Sir Richard Hankford and Sir John Lewis, who brought more directly significant estates for Holland in the south-west.[42]

Holland clearly needed the short-term, assured wealth of dowagers rather than the long-term, if only potential, wealth of heiresses. He entered married life late, aged over thirty in 1426, and none of his brides was young. The possibilities of producing a large family were not great and the survival of his line might be at risk. In fact, he only produced one son, Henry, thirty-five years his junior, and one daughter, Anne, both by his first wife. Henry would die heirless in 1475, and so his father's failure to produce a large family, compounded by Henry's own political vicissitudes which saw him estranged from his wife, and, for long periods, in prison and in exile, resulted in the extinction of the Holland line.

The financial benefits that Holland's marriages brought are hard to quantify, other than that they must have been considerable. Even so, his reputed taxable income from land in 1436, when he was married to Beatrice Countess of Arundel, was only £1,002, the lowest comital income except for that of the Earl of Somerset. Of this, probably around one third was provided from FitzAlan sources, to judge from the appended lists of annuitants charged on the Holland and FitzAlan estates respectively.[43] This shows that Holland's landed income was not great. That he was able to take the second largest retinue after the Earl Marshal to France in 1430 may well owe something to the recruiting potential of the Mortimer estates of his first wife.[44]

These marriages may have contributed much to Holland's financial position, but they also had a considerable bearing on his political outlook. Such large influxes of estates meant that the make-up and concentration of his landed holdings was frequently changing. The administration of his estates had to be adapted to accommodate a series of officials first of his mother, then Mortimer, then FitzAlan, then Hankford and John. The basis of the purely Holland estates may have been in Devon, but a great proportion of income was coming in now from the Welsh Marches and Essex, then from Sussex, and neither of his first two wives brought any augmentation to his interests in Devon.[45] These shifts in the weight and focus of his estates helped to distract Holland from showing a great deal of interest in local politics in Devon and encouraged his residence in London.

So the Huntingdon inheritance was much augmented, albeit in the short-term, but the theme of compensation for French war costs also extended beyond the sphere of lands. Though it may have become something of an official formula, and other reasons are often cited as well, it was perpetuated in a series of financial awards for Holland, for whom it no doubt continued to be highly meaningful. For instance, an Exchequer annuity of £123 6s 8d was awarded to him in March 1428 specifically to offset his ransom, as well as to compensate him for the duchy of Cornwall estates formerly in Holland hands and now held by the King.[46] The financial sacrifice he was making for the English cause in France was a view he was doubtless keen to foster. His claim in the 1431 parliament that his ransom had cost him 20,000 marks would have been the maximum bid he could have put up, but his expeditions to France were probably not a source of great profit. His siege of Compiègne in 1430 was reputedly broken up because the Anglo-Burgundian force was not prepared to continue serving any longer without pay. In 1433, Holland had to be awarded a 1,300-mark (£866 13s 4d) regard out of consideration for past service to induce him to return to France and he returned early from Gascony in 1440 because of a lack of financial support. He had to enlist Suffolk's support in claiming around half a year's wage arrears from Gascony, and he was in fact awarded a 500-mark (£333 13s 4d) annuity on the customs in July 1441 to compensate for his losses because of France. He even indented to serve as captain of Calais in 1443, but that post's poor financial record must have influenced his decision not to serve.[47]

As well as the landed and financial inducements and compensation that Holland received in England, he was also directly rewarded in France for his commitment there. Having missed out on the great bonanza of Verneuil, he was awarded the Norman county of Ivry in 1427, though this failed to induce him to return to France before the coronation expedition of 1430. The only indication of income from his Norman estates comes after his death, in 1448, when the Duke of York, guardian of the young Henry Holland, received £200 from the Norman Exchequer for his charge's estates there. Landed grants also enhanced Holland's interest in Aquitaine, where the lordship of Lesparre was awarded him in 1440, a place he was to use as his base for much of the period of his lieutenantcy there.[48]

So, Holland's commitment to France had thus brought him a considerable patrimony there, comprising a county, a lordship and other Norman estates.[49] The direct profitability of such estates, with their heavy concomitant defence responsibilities, has been a matter for some debate.[50] For Holland, at least Lesparre also brought with it a valuable trade in wine from the important Medoc region, well-protected from French forays into Gascony.[51]

In fact, income from trade overall is another vital factor in this consideration of the effect of the French war on Holland's prosperity, though it is hard to assess precisely. He had early established a reputation as a naval commander and he eventually acceded to the post of admiral of England, Ireland, and Aquitaine on the Duke of Bedford's death in 1435.[52] He was a significant owner of shipping, some of which traded into the Mediterranean,[53] and he was a considerable importer of wine through Southampton. His authority as admiral, his west country contacts, and his command of the approaches to London as constable of the Tower must have helped his trading interests in a time of such turmoil, and have facilitated an indulgence in a little profitable piracy when legitimate commerce was not so beneficial. The Admiralty also brought its own potentially profitable perks from court proceeds and rights to a share of the spoils of the sea. Though such rights were difficult to enforce,[54] they were an area where increased activity on and off the sea in a time of war could have raised income.

In addition, the post of constable of the Tower, granted to Holland by Henry V in 1420, brought in another annuity from the Exchequer of £100, of which three years' worth contributed towards his ransom. This was when he had not actually done anything to earn it, having been a captive all that time. One of the post's perks was being paid for the custody of important prisoners, and the French war obviously brought an increased traffic in these, and, thereby, an increased potential for profit from such inmates as the Count of Eu.[55]

Holland's appointment to these highly significant posts of admiral and constable of the Tower must have owed much to the military reputation he had built up through the French war, though it was also influenced by his royal kinship. This stemmed from his grandfather Thomas Holland's marriage in the 1330s to Joan of Kent, granddaughter of Edward I and mother of Richard II, and was enhanced by his father John's marriage to Henry IV's sister Elizabeth. Holland's precise position within the royal circle is uncertain, yet the granting of these two posts to him and his son in survivorship in 1446, and his tenure of the post of marshal during Mowbray's minority [56] from 1432 shows that his status was higher than his often moderate political influence might otherwise suggest.

This status meant that his favour became worth cultivating, and this is increasingly apparent in the 1440s, when he was involved in several grants of goods and property by people otherwise unconnected with him.[57] His status is also evident in the retinues he took to France.[58] Around a fifth of those identifiable, largely from enrolled protections, came from the south-west, yet the largest proportion, around a half, came from the south-east. The areas of his estates were significant, but not overwhelming, providers of recruits: many more must have been attracted for other reasons, such as the military reputation he had gained before he even had control of his estates.

None of this has provided any firm figure for the effect of the French war on Holland's income, yet it does provide some idea of the indirect consequences of the war and some balance to the sums claimed as wage arrears or costs of ransoms. It might further be pertinent to reflect that Holland made none of the great investment in land of Sir John Fastolf. Holland was of course in rather a different category: he was already of comital status and, besides, his marriages brought him great tracts of land. These, however, were only of short-term benefit for his inheritance, which saw little permanent expansion during his lifetime, either by purchase or by royal grant. This would cause problems for his son, but it both reflected and conditioned Holland's own attitude to his inheritance. The Hollands had always been a curialist rather than a territorial noble family; offices and services had as much significance for them as their landed holdings, and one of the overriding effects of the French war was that this was perpetuated for Holland. His service militated against a concerted effort to build up his local power based on his south-western estates. [59] By contrast, the war augmented the significance of his posts of constable of the Tower and admiral and encouraged his residence in and interests around London. This facilitated his attendance at councils planning the expeditions of himself [60] and others to France and the augmentation of his property interests in the area: he acquired London property by his stepfather's will in 1444, Berkhamsted Castle from the King in 1443, and St Albans property at some date, and he showed, curiously, considerable concern for his duties as J.P. in Bedfordshire in the late 1420s. [61]

Indeed, whatever the costs of his military service and whatever the debts he may have left, the fact is that these did not prevent Holland from making a major and continuous contribution to the French campaign. The inventory of his plate and personal effects [62] illustrates the purchasing power, or at least credit, he possessed, and such items demonstrated to contemporaries the stature he had gained through military service. His royal kinship, his Gascon lieutenantcy and English offices, his respected position as a political moderate and tried councillor, and his son's marriage are all reflected in the inventory of his luxurious goods. Whatever may have been the detailed cost of his service, known, however precisely, to Holland, he came out of his commitment to France with much personal credit.

This personal position must be set against the overall impression that Holland's landed and financial position suffered as a consequence of his commitment to the English cause in France. The war kept him away from England and his inheritance for considerable periods of time, especially in the formative years of his early childhood. His father had perforce been a curialist through his close familial links with his half-brother Richard II. Holland continued in the same vein, earning respect and status by his long service in France, but not really a great deal of power either in London or the south-west.[63] Testimony to this is the legacy he bequeathed to his son. Henry Holland was provided with a wife, Anne, who brought a cash dowry and close links to the Duke of York; Henry, in the event, gained little from either. He gained less from the wealthy dowagers that his father had married and, furthermore, he had to provide his stepmother with her dower entitlement from his own estates.[64] He thus suffered from the short-term compensation that his father had received from the French war and from the neglect of his natural south-western power-base this had induced. He was further deprived by his father's arrangements to provide cover for his debts from his estates, and any income from his French estates soon disappeared in the 1450s. Henry Holland may have inherited the dukedom of Exeter, [65] but he inherited little of the concomitant power that a ducal title should have implied. It was to be his sense of grievance at this, combined with his naturally irrational temperament, that would impel him to a tempestuous career to seek lands and power, often in opposition to his father-in-law the Duke of York and often far away from the expected area of his natural influence, in Bedfordshire and the south-west.

The case of John Holland illustrates that assessing the profits and costs of the Hundred Years War to the English nobility is by no means a simple task, and extends far beyond a purely financial appraisal. Holland undoubtedly felt and exhibited a deep commitment to the English cause in France and Henry V's ambitions there. The war was not really something he could detach himself from just because it was proving too costly. It affected his whole career and personal life and thereby left a lasting legacy for the Holland future. What this paper has tried to do is to set John Holland's career within the context of the French war and to show what a dominating and conditioning factor the war was for him. The profits and costs are what we can now attempt to measure, but John Holland was not always so calculating about his commitment, and so neither should we be in our assessment of his success.

Notes

1. McFarlane, *Nobility*; M.M. Postan, *Essays on Medieval Agriculture and General Problems of the Medieval Economy* (Cambridge 1973), pp. 63–80; A.R. Bridbury, 'The Hundred Years War: Costs and Profits', *Trade, Government and Economy in Pre-Industrial England*, D.C. Coleman and A.H. John (eds), (1976), pp. 80–95. I am deeply indebted to the comments of the editor and M.H. Keen for helping to formulate this paper.

2. K.B. McFarlane, 'The Investment of Sir John Fastolf's Profits of War', *TRHS* 5th ser. vii (1957), pp. 91–116; M.A. Hicks, 'Counting the Cost of War: The Moleyns Ransom and the Hungerford Land-Sales 1453–87', *Southern History* viii (1986), pp. 11–31; R.L. Friedrichs, 'The Career and Influence of Ralph, Lord Cromwell,

1393–1456' (Columbia Univ. PhD thesis, 1974); A.C. Reeves, *Lancastrian Englishmen* (Washington, DC, 1981), pp. 139–84; A.J. Pollard, *John Talbot and the War in France 1427–53* (1983).

3. The majority of the estates were in Devon, with some in Cornwall and Somerset, and there were scattered manors in Wiltshire, Berkshire, Bedfordshire, Cheshire, Flintshire and Pembrokeshire and property in London.

4. John Windsor now disputed Manorbier and Penally in Wales and the abbey of St Mary Graces by the Tower pressed its claim to various south-western manors: D.J.C. King and J.C. Perks, 'Manorbier Castle, Pembrokeshire', *Archaeologia Cambrensis* cxix (1970), pp. 84–93; CPR *1399–1401*, p. 274; E 328/380, /381.

5. She was initially granted dower of 1,000 marks from the customs in 1400, until she was provided with sufficient lands. By 1410 she only needed to draw £73 of her annuity: CPR *1399–1401*, p. 201; *1408–13*, p. 189.

6. E 149/107/3.

7. *DKR* xli. p. 717; E. Hall, *Chronicle*, H. Ellis (ed.), (1809), p. 108.

8. C 139/24/32; CIPM *(RC)* iv. pp. 185–6; CFR *1422–30*, pp. 126, 212; CPR *1441–6*, p. 267.

9. CIPM *Henry VII*, i. p. 101.

10. *A Collection of Royal Wills*, J. Nichols (ed.), (1780), pp. 282–9.

11. Idem; E 149/184/5; E 152/544; P.Norman, 'Sir John de Pulteney and his two residences in London', *Archaeologia* lvii (1900), p. 267; M.G.A. Vale, *English Gascony 1399–1453* (Oxford 1970), p. 109.

12. WAM 6643.

13. J.H. Wylie, *The Reign of King Henry the Fifth*, i (Cambridge 1914), p. 3; *Gesta Henrici Quinti*, F. Taylor and J.S. Roskell (eds), (Oxford 1975), p. 23; M.H. Keen, *Chivalry* (1984), p. 170; GEC v. pp. 205–11; *The Boke of Noblesse*, J.G. Nichols (ed.), (Roxburghe Club, 1860), p. 16; C.L. Kingsford, 'An Historical Collection of the Fifteenth Century', *EHR* xxix (1914), p. 512.

14. He should also have gleaned a third share from ransoms and booty won by his soldiers: *Rotuli Normaniae in Turri Londoniensi Asservati*, T.D. Hardy (ed.), (1835), pp. 286–7. He did not gain much from Agincourt, but was present at the profitable engagement at Frésnay in 1420: N.H. Nicolas, *The Battle of Agincourt* (2nd edn 1832), appendix, pp. 61–3; T. Walsingham, *Historia Anglicana*, ii, H.T. Riley (ed.), (RS 1864), p. 331.

15. *Foedera* ix. pp. 553, 556; Archives Nationales, Dom Lenoir Collection xxvi, No. 23267; *DKR* xli. pp. 680, 730, 781, 791.

16. Henry V's only English award to Holland was the wardship of William Zouche's heir in 1416: CPR *1413–16*, p. 394; E 101/406/26 m.6.

17. *RP* iv. pp. 100–1, 110; C 1/9/357–61; *Calendar of Signet Letters of Henry IV and Henry V (1399–1422)*, J.L. Kirby (ed.), (1978), pp. 167, 172; CCR *1413–19*, pp. 483–6; DKR xxxvii. p. 393.

18. Though Earl of Dorset and Duke of Exeter, Thomas Beaufort was not a great territorial power in the south-west: CIPM *(RC)* iv. pp. 111–13.

19. M.K. Jones, 'The Beaufort Family and the War in France 1421–1450' (Bristol Univ. PhD thesis 1982), pp. 20–56; idem, 'Henry VIII, Lady Margaret Beaufort, and the Orleans Ransom', *Kings and Nobles in the Later Middle Ages. A Tribute to Charles Ross*, R.A. Griffiths and J.W. Sherborne (eds), (Gloucester 1986), pp. 254–73.

20. Reeves, *Lancastrian Englishmen*, pp. 168–72.

21. The Holland trait of hot-headedness had shown itself in incidents at Breteuil, Pontoise, and Roye in 1419: *La Chronique d'Enguerrand de Monstrelet*, iii, L. Douet-d'Arcq (S(ociété de l')H(istoire de) F(rance) 1860), pp. 336, 368–71; Walsingham, ii. p. 330; *Mémoires de Pierre de Fenin*, L.M-E. Dupont (ed.), (SHF 1837), pp. 122–4; *Oeuvres de Georges Chastellain*, i, K. de Lettenhove (ed.), (Brussels 1863), pp. 98–101.

22. *POPC* iii. pp. 108–110, 122–3; *CPR 1422–9*, p. 142.

23. Safe-conducts were issued for Vendome going to France on 28 November 1423 and for returning to England on 15 July 1424: *DKR* xlviii. pp. 229, 231; *Calendar of Select Pleas and Memoranda of the City of London 1413–37*, A.H. Thomas (ed.), (Cambridge 1943), p. 184.

24. For ransom agreements, bonds provided and expenses claimed by Cornwall, see: *Foedera* ix. pp. 442–5, 450, 529; *POPC* ii. p. 342; *CPR 1416–22*, p. 89; Steel, *Receipt*, p. 156; E.F. Jacob, *The Fifteenth Century* (Oxford 1961), pp. 222–3; A.D. Carr, 'Sir Lewis John – A Medieval London Welshman', *BBCS* xxii (1967), p. 268.

25. *RP* iv. p. 247; SC 8/85/4229; P. Strong and F. Strong, 'The Last Will and Codicils of Henry V', *EHR* xcvi (1981), p. 95. Gaucourt and Estouteville had been captured at Harfleur in 1415.

26. *RP* iv. pp. 283–4.

27. *London Plea & Memoranda Rolls 1413–37*, pp. 182–7; *DKR* xlviii. p. 238; Nicolas, *Agincourt*, appendix, pp. 25–8.

28. *London Plea & Memoranda Rolls 1413–37*, pp. 182–7; *DKR* xlviii. p. 239. He was appointed a councillor on 20 March 1426: E 404/43/164.

29. Ransoms were theoretically fixed at a year's expected income. Holland's importance meant that he was charged with a sum well in excess of this. Vendome, though unable to raise his ransom of 1417, was not thereby impoverished, offering to let the Duke of Orleans raise cash on his estates two years later: M.H. Keen, *The Laws of War in the Late Middle Ages* (1965), pp. 158–9; E. McLeod, *Charles of Orleans* (1969), p. 152; *Foedera* ix. pp. 442–5.

30. The Earls of Northumberland and Stafford and Richard Neville (650 marks); Justice John Hals and William Allington (200 marks); William Halle serjeant-at-law; William Yerde, John Mason clerk and Richard Ketford saddler (100 marks).

31. *London Plea & Memoranda Rolls 1413–37*, pp. 182–7.

32. Nicolas, *Agincourt*, appendix, pp. 25–8. Gaucourt was back in France as governor of Orleans in 1425: McLeod, *Charles of Orleans*, p. 174; E 403/671 m.11 (the warrant was issued on 1 June, E 404/41/327); E 401/712,/713.

33. *RP* iv. p. 247.

34. Ibid. iv. p. 385.

35. John Beaufort claimed his captivity cost him £24,000 in total: Jones, thesis, pp. 20–56. For a similar claim, see Hicks, *Southern History* viii. pp. 12–31.

36. There is little evidence of building work at Dartington dating from Holland's time: A. Emery, *Dartington Hall* (Oxford 1970), pp. 139–225. He showed some interest in the London property market: *London Plea & Memoranda Rolls 1413–37*, p. 196; *1437–57*, pp. 47, 49.

37. Vale, *Gascony*, p. 116. Even his promising 1433 expedition was probably curtailed through lack of cash: H.L. Ratcliffe, 'The Military Expenditure of the English Crown 1422–35' (Oxford Univ. MLitt thesis 1979), pp. 84–8.

38. P.A. Johnson, 'The Political Careeer of Richard, Duke of York, to 1456' (Oxford DPhil thesis 1981), pp. 94–106; C. Rawcliffe, *The Staffords, Earls of Stafford and Dukes of Buckingham 1394–1521* (Cambridge 1978), pp. 117–18; Pollard, *John Talbot*, pp. 103–112.

39. C 139/24/32; *CCR 1422–9*, pp. 283–5.

40. *CCR 1422–9*, pp. 218–19, 222–3, 248–56, 273–4, 408, 415–16, 436–7; *1429–35*, pp. 5–6, 146–7; *CFR 1430–7*, p. 102; *CIPM (RC)* iv. pp. 140–5; C 139/67/51; *CPR 1422–9*, p. 414; *POPC* iii. pp. 252–3.

41. *CPR 1429–36*, p. 250; E 28/53/22. This marriage cost Holland 500 marks.

42. C 139/170/41.

43. H.L. Gray, 'Incomes from Land in England in 1436', *EHR* xlix (1934), p. 607; E 163/7/31/2/30.

44. A total of 320 men, E 404/46/243.

45. *CIPM (RC)* iv. pp. 140–5, 197–9. Holland was appointed a JP in Essex, Bedfordshire, Huntingdonshire, Hertfordshire and Herefordshire, as well as Devon, Cornwall, and Somerset, in July 1426: *CPR 1422–9*, pp. 559–69.

46. Ibid. p. 465; SC 8/117/5839, /5841, /5842.

47. *Letters and Papers Illustrative of the Wars of the English in France*, ii(1), J. Stevenson (RS 1864), pp. 156–160; E 404/49/34, /147; E 404/50/117; Vale, *Gascony*, p. 116; Norman, *Archaeologia* lvii. p. 267; *CPR 1436–41*, p. 565; E 101/71/4/915.

48. Archives Nationales, Dom Lenoir Collection xxii, No. 5251; BL Add. Ch. 1511; E 28/63/23; C 61/129, /130.

49. Henry Holland continued to use his French titles after he had lost the land: Pierpoint Morgan Library, New York, R of E Box I (a 1454 order).

50. For other English magnates' French incomes, see Johnson, thesis, pp. 31–3; L.S. Woodger, 'Henry Bourgchier, Earl of Essex, and his Family (1408–83)', (Oxford DPhil thesis 1974), pp. 13–14; C.T. Allmand, *Lancastrian Normandy 1415–50* (Oxford 1983), pp. 70–1; R. Massey, 'The Land Settlement in Lancastrian Normandy', *Property and Politics: Essays in Later Medieval English History*, A.J. Pollard (ed.), (Gloucester 1984), p. 79.

51. E 101/195/19 ff.14v, 16, 23v, 24, 28, 41 (shipments by his son in the autumn of 1448); *The Brokage Book of Southampton 1443–1444*, ii, O. Coleman (ed.), (Southampton Record Series vi, 1961), pp. 202–5 (carriage of wine from Southampton to London for Holland in May 1444).

52. *CPR 1429–36*, p. 488.

53. *CCR 1447–54*, pp. 169, 174 (a Holland barge in Barcelona in 1449). See also *CPR 1436–41*, p. 310; E 28/69/71; C 1/68/40.

54. See instances of his right to the wreck of the sea in *The Black Book of the Admiralty*, i, T. Twiss (ed.), (RS 1871), pp. 266, 271–2; Exeter Dean and Chapter MSS 934, 2330.

55. *DKR* xlii. p. 383; E 403/671 m.11. 1430 and 1432 accounts of his Tower lieutenants are in E 101/531/32; E 101/51/11.

56. *CPR 1441–6*, p. 405; *1446–52*, p. 32; *1429–36*, p. 242. Another military post he held was warden of the Marches towards Scotland in 1435: *Rotuli Scotiae in Turri Londiniensis*, ii (Record Commission 1819), p. 291; E 404/51/350.

57. *CCR 1435–41*, pp. 426, 452, 454–5; *1441–7*, pp. 270, 274–5, 351–2.

58. Expedition musters are in E 101/45/7 (1415); E 101/51/2 (1417); E 101/53/22 (1439). Protections are in: *DKR* xli, xliv, xlviii; C 61/129, /130.

59. For a measure of his transient influence there, see the infrequent grants of wine to him from the city of Exeter in Devon CRO, Exeter City Receivers' Rolls, 4–25 Henry VI.

60. Such as in the spring of 1430: E 28/51.

61. *CPR 1441–6*, pp. 228, 230; C 139/127/25; R.E. Archer, 'The Mowbrays, Earls of Nottingham and Dukes of Norfolk, to 1432' (Oxford Univ. DPhil thesis 1984), pp. 258–62. His only Bedfordshire manor, Stevington, was heavily charged with annuitants, including the locally eminent John Enderby and Thomas Gray: E 163/7/31/2/30.

62. WAM 6643.

63. Holland appears little in M. Cherry, 'The Crown and the Political Community in Devonshire 1377–1461' (Univ. of Wales (Swansea) PhD thesis 1981), pp. 218–73.

64. He even tried to get her to alter the dower arrangements to his benefit in 1452: Devon CRO, Exeter Diocesan Records, Chanter catalogue 12 part 1 (Bishop Neville's Register) ff.76v–77v.

65. Restored to Holland early in 1444: *Calendar of Charter Rolls 1427–1516*, p. 39.

9

The Benefits and Burdens of Office: Henry Bourgchier (1408–83), Viscount Bourgchier and Earl of Essex, and the Treasurership of the Exchequer

Linda Clark
History of Parliament Trust

On 29 May 1455, just one week after the victory of his brother-in-law, Richard, Duke of York, at the battle of St Albans, Henry Viscount Bourgchier was made treasurer of England for the first time.[1] One of his younger brothers, Thomas, Archbishop of Canterbury, was already chancellor, having been appointed on 7 March, so these two, placed in control of the great government departments, effectively dominated the administration until October 1456, when they were 'sodeynly discharged' in favour of men who enjoyed the confidence of the Queen, Margaret of Anjou.[2] Viscount Bourgchier's second term of office began in July 1460, within three weeks of his having marshalled his followers in support of the Yorkist earls at the battle of Northampton and helped to escort the captive King Henry VI into London. Edward IV, nephew of Bourgchier's wife Isabel, confirmed him in office in March 1461, created him Earl of Essex at his coronation, and kept him as treasurer until 14 April 1462.[3] Nine years later Essex, his brothers and his sons all provided invaluable services to King Edward in facilitating his return from exile and the recovery of his throne.[4] As a consequence, on 22 April 1471, immediately after the collapse of the Lancastrian cause, the earl was re-appointed as treasurer. He was then retained in the post for the rest of his life and of Edward's reign: as it turned out a period of almost twelve years, for he died on 4 April 1483, just five days before the King.[5] Altogether, Bourgchier spent as long as fifteen years and two months as treasurer of the Exchequer; longer than any other person during the fifteenth century, when the average length of tenure was little more than three years. Only two others came close to him in terms of duration of service: Ralph, Lord Cromwell (1433–43) and John, Lord Dynham (1486–1501).

It is widely accepted that offices were competitively sought after in the Middle Ages because they were a sure path to preferment, honour, additional wealth and prestige. They were a long established means of founding or confirming a family's fortune; indeed, it had been mainly the proceeds of royal service that had enabled the Bourgchier family to rise in the fourteenth century and to purchase estates sizeable enough to support its entry into the baronage. Yet an investigation of the treasurership in the mid-fifteenth century must call this generalization into question. Despite the prospect of high rewards, this particular office was not necessarily one which men desired. On the contrary, it may well have been the case that substantial incentives had to be offered in order to persuade competent public figures to devote their energies to difficult tasks of government during that period of extreme financial and political crisis. The rewards would need to be worthwhile to encourage able men to place themselves at risk of personal attack and vilification.

Exactly how much financial advantage did Henry Bourgchier derive from his three terms of treasurer? When first appointed he was allocated, in unspecific terms, 'the usual fees, profits, wages and rewards' pertaining to the office, but it is not easy to discover precisely what this phrase meant. It may even be suspected that the vague wording of the grant was designed to facilitate undue disbursements in the treasurer's favour. The treasurer's fee itself was established at 100 marks (£66 13s 4d) per annum, as authorized by regular writs of *liberate* in portions of 50 marks each for payment in the Easter and Michaelmas terms.[6] However, the issue rolls reveal that Bourgchier took out of the Exchequer considerably more than this fixed sum. In the Easter term of 1455 he received £90 6s 8d; in the Michaelmas term of 1455–6 £195 13s 4d; in April 1456 £48 15s 1d; and in July following a further £291 15s. This made a total of £625 10s 1d for his 'wages, fees and reward' as treasurer for his first term of office, which lasted seventeen months in all.[7] Regrettably, these figures cannot be taken simply as they stand. An investigation of Bourgchier's receipts as treasurer is somewhat hampered by the fact that, according to the rolls, this sum also included payment of his salary as a member of the King's council. He had been officially sworn as a royal councillor on 15 April 1454, during the Duke of York's first protectorate, when regular wages for attendance at the rate of £116 13s 4d a year had been authorized for him. The scale of fees for councillors was dependent upon estate and rank,[8] and in Bourgchier's case a viscount was considered to rank mid-way between an earl (who received £133 6s 8d) and a baron (£100); later, on his appointment as treasurer, his salary as a councillor was adjusted to the equivalent of an earl's. Payment for his services on the council from April 1454 onwards was not officially warranted under the privy seal until 9 July 1456, and a week later he duly took out of the Exchequer £100 of the £131 0s 2d deemed due unto him for the period April 1454 to 30 May 1455.[9] Since Bourgchier's salary as councillor from then until July 1456 had not been paid separately from his fees and rewards as treasurer, we need to deduct about £155 10s as being his due for fourteen months' work on the council while treasurer, leaving him with £471 as his remuneration for the office alone. This was some £371 more than the fees for which specific authorization by warrant survives. The abrupt political changes of the autumn of 1456 are reason enough for the absence of further reward for his services after July of that year, and it is clear from the many large payments Bourgchier received in July, both directly connected with his treasurership and otherwise, that he foresaw his dismissal.

In the period 1460–2 the Exchequer again apparently paid out more to the treasurer than was his official due: at Michaelmas 1460 for his fees and attendance at the Exchequer Bourgchier took out £100; in the first term of Edward IV's reign as much as £424 19s 5d; and at Michaelmas term 1461–2 no less than £595 8s 5d,[10] making an overall total of £1,120 7s 10d for a period of office lasting just twenty months. This time his services as a royal councillor were not expressly mentioned on the issue rolls, but it may be assumed that a reward for such was tacitly included. During Bourgchier's final twelve years as treasurer evidence for the amounts paid out to him as his official emoluments is incomplete, because several of the issue rolls are missing and the tellers' rolls, on which we are forced to rely, provide insufficient information.[11] Full totals for the period 1471–83 are no longer available (records for seven Exchequer terms are missing), but from the details surviving it appears that on average the earl received £155 a term (that is £310 a year), for over seventeen terms his official income from the Exchequer came to £2,636 7s.[12] Throughout this last treasurership payments are described as being for his fees, rewards, diet and attendance on the king's council. In all three periods of office payments to Bourgchier were nearly always made in ready money and only rarely by assignment on crown revenues. This was obviously a great advantage, and one that few other of the crown's creditors enjoyed. Also, on occasion in the 1470s the sums were deducted from the customs duties Bourgchier himself owed as an outcome of his ambitious mercantile ventures.[13] All in all, Bourgchier received substantial remuneration for his services; sometimes as much as 25 per cent of the annual income that he could expect from his landed estates.

It will not have passed notice that Bourgchier appears to have received considerably less during his final term in office than during his first two treasurerships. Some of the reasons for this will emerge later. Of more immediate interest is the fact that, save in the period of his second treasurership (1460–2), he took less from the Exchequer than did other treasurers of the 1450s and 1460s. A few examples will suffice to exonerate him from the charge of greed beyond the acceptable norm. In 1447, at the height of a crisis of grave proportions in funding at the Exchequer, Marmaduke Lumley, Bishop of Carlisle had taken out as much as £895 in cash for himself, disregarding the many other pressing claims on the crown's revenues. In the nine months from November 1453 the then treasurer John Tiptoft, Earl of Worcester received about £607; and his successor James Butler, Earl of Wiltshire, who was treasurer for just ten weeks from March to May 1455, was handed £102 14s 8d in cash the day before his dismissal. In his first term of office in the autumn of 1456 John Talbot, Earl of Shrewsbury took out from the Exchequer over £387, to which, shortly after his discharge in November 1458, the King added a special gift of £800 as his reward for his 'costes, charge and attendaunce', as well as for his success in 'chevysshing of goode withoute losse' for the expenses of the royal household.[14] Most notable of all, during his treasurership of 1466–8 the King's father-in-law Richard Wydeville, Earl Rivers was paid 200 marks a year for his attendance on the royal council, £500 for his 'diettes' and 1,000 marks a year 'for his reward for his diligent occupation and executing of the said office', making an annual total of as much as £1,300. Even more surprisingly, payment of these excessive sums to Rivers was warranted on 26 March 1467 expressly to 'encorage hym to contynue' as treasurer.[15] In the cases of Shrewsbury and Rivers there were specific warrants of authorization from the King for the large sums paid out by the Exchequer; but, as no such warrants survive for the majority of the sums fifteenth-century treasurers received, it must be assumed that payments were usually made on the verbal authority of the treasurer himself. On at least one occasion the treasurer went too far: Edmund Lord Grey of Ruthin (treasurer 1463–4) took out of the Exchequer for his 'diettes, wages and attendance' £139 17s 7d more than was considered acceptable; an action which earned him a reprimand from King Edward, who told him that the money 'shuld be set upon you as a apprest without oure special grace be showed unto you in this behalve', but then, relenting, granted it to him 'by weye of reward'.[16] It was evidently not unusual for the treasurer to help himself; whether he was ever admonished for doing so depended on his current personal relationship with the King.

There was undoubtedly a correlation between the size of loans which individual treasurers offered to the crown and the comparative amounts that they took out of the Exchequer, ostensibly as wages and rewards for their services. Several years ago Anthony Steel commented on the practice that seemed to pertain in the latter half of Henry VI's reign of appointing rich men as treasurers 'so that they could tide the Exchequer over any pressing emergency out of their own resources'. He estimated that from 1452 to 1475 the huge loans to the crown made by successive treasurers amounted to nearly £50,000.[17] After the first battle of St Albans in May 1455 it was loans coming from the Duke of York's supporters that kept the government functioning; the new treasurer, Bourgchier, lent £1,100 immediately and a further £500 two months later.[18] Similarly, at the beginning of his second treasurership, on the first day of Michaelmas term of 1460, Bourgchier made a loan of £2,538 and in January 1462 he advanced a further £1,333 6s 8d.[19] During his third term of office, in 1473, he lent £1,010, and two years later £1,000.[20] Bourgchier's total individual lending thus amounted to £7,481 6s 8d: more than that of any other treasurer of the period, with the exception of that of Earl Rivers during his short treasurership of 1466–8, which amounted to an enormous £12,259. There has been considerable debate among historians as to whether concealed interest was paid on loans of this sort,[21] and so far as the official evidence goes there is no documented proof that Bourgchier's loans were anything other than interest-free. But then, those treasurers who were prepared to make substantial loans were the very same as those who received from the Exchequer the highest 'wages and rewards', and in Bourgchier's case as the scale of his lending diminished, so too did the size of his official emoluments. The possibility that interest on loans was concealed in this manner should not be discounted. Furthermore, there was, of course, little risk attached to the making of such loans. The treasurer was in a privileged position, enjoyed by only the most influential of those who lent to the crown. He was virtually guaranteed full and speedy repayment, in so far as assignments of revenues were made in his favour promptly and on reliable sources, such as parliamentary subsidies.

The treasurer was also well-placed to receive quick and full payment for any extraneous services he performed. Thus, a journey to Maidstone on royal business, which Bourgchier undertook in company with the Earl of Warwick, earned him £20, as warranted in July 1456, and a special reward of £100 in ready money was authorized for him by the King in September 1461 after he had accompanied Edward on his royal progress through the marches of Wales.[22] In July 1471 he received £33 6s 8d in cash for having served on an important commission of oyer and terminer to restore order in Essex (even though it was extremely rare for a nobleman appointed to such a commission to be rewarded in this way); and in 1475 when he supervised the musters of the royal army about to embark for France he was promptly paid £20 for his labour.[23] Then, too, the treasurer's salary was not meant to cover the cost of his royal livery: in 1473 Bourgchier personally handed over, from the Exchequer to the clerk of the wardrobe, the very large sum of £30 for the making of splendid new robes for himself.[24] We may speculate that the treasurer's income would also have been considerably augmented by 'rewards' offered him by the crown's creditors, hoping to influence the process of the Exchequer in their own interests. Many payments to officials which would be condemned nowadays as bribes were then reckoned to be permissible perquisites of office. Over the long period of Bourgchier's captaincy of Le Crotoy (Picardy) in the 1440s, he himself had seen fit to allocate to the treasurer of England 'for the reward' as much as £200 (3 per cent of his nominal salary for the post) in order to expedite disbursements from the Exchequer. He no doubt expected and received similar gratuities when he himself came to hold the office. An example of such expectations may be taken from 1461, when John Paston pestered Bourgchier to intervene with the King in the interest of his father. The treasurer's servant pointedly told Paston that the father 'must nedys do sumwhate fore my lord and hys', drawing attention to the fact that 'ther was a lytyl mony be-twyxe (Paston senior) and a jantylman of Estsexe called Dyrward, seyyng that ther is as myche be-twejn my seyd lord and the seyd jantyilman of the wyche mony he desieryth (Paston's) part'.[25]

One of the many advantages to be derived from the treasurership was the opportunity presented to its holder to secure payment for past services undertaken on the crown's behalf for which remuneration had been inadequate or wanting. Now he had the authority to obtain replacements for old tallies which for one reason or another had failed to be honoured by collectors of revenue, or, better by far, to make sure that outstanding debts were paid off in cash. Thus, during his treasurership Bishop Lumley had cashed tallies for £1,018 which he had held since surrendering the West March in 1443. As far back as the summer of 1439 Bourgchier, on his first diplomatic assignment, had spent four months at Calais attending the peace conference between England and France. Payment for his services at the rate of £2 a day, as befitted one of his rank, had been authorized before his departure, and he was given an advance of £133 6s 8d. On his return to London, after spending 122 days away, the Exchequer officials were instructed to audit his accounts for his expenses and assess the amount still due to him.[26] It was then that Bourgchier, doubtless regarding his rank as a French comte (of Eu) as equivalent to that of an English earl, and expecting an earl's remuneration accordingly, instructed his attorney to claim 5 marks (£3 6s 8d) a day, only to find that his excessive demands resulted in delays in payment of the £110 13s 4d, which the barons of the Exchequer deemed to be his full entitlement.[27] Although he received small sums by assignment in the 1440s as part payment of this debt, it was not until he became treasurer that it was finally cleared: in July 1456 (seventeen years after the embassy) he took out £40 in cash to do so.[28]

There were even larger debts to be considered. For seven years from October 1441 Bourgchier had served as captain of the important fortress of Le Crotoy, for which he was promised wages at the rate of £1,000 a year for himself and the garrison.[29] But during the 1440s, while he was actually serving in France, a full year's salary was rarely disbursed by the

Exchequer, or, if it was, then the payments were for the most part made by assignment of tallies, which not infrequently Bourgchier found himself unable to exchange for ready money. The question of these 'bad' tallies and Bourgchier's failure to obtain full remuneration for his war services still rankled as late as 1455, long after Le Crotoy had fallen to the French. That April, shortly before he was appointed treasurer for the first time (and no doubt taking advantage of his brother's position as chancellor), Bourgchier secured a royal warrant which, after referring to the 'grete costes and charges' that he had suffered as captain of Le Crotoy and the difficulties which he had experienced in converting many of the tallies issued by the Exchequer into cash, instructed the officials of the Receipt to re-examine his accounts, scrutinize all assignments made to him and cancel all returned tallies, making immediate payment of any part of the £7,000 still owing to him. When the account was formally presented the treasurer was none other than himself,[30] and there is good reason to believe that he had let it be known that his acceptance of the treasurership was conditional upon full acknowledgement of the crown's indebtedness to him. The amount still owed was found to be £1,258 13s 11d. Instead of now receiving a direct payment, the following year, on 5 July 1456, he obtained a royal licence to export wool without paying the subsidy due, until he had saved the sum of £1,200.[31] In the meantime, two months earlier, he had obtained at the Exchequer £200 in cash in return for four 'bad' tallies worth that amount, which had originally been issued in 1446. Indeed, in the course of his treasurership of 1455–6 Bourgchier was able to secure the large total of £635 in cash for old tallies, as well as a further £65 in fresh assignments.[32]

It would be mistaken to suppose that the King was personally respon-sible for every appointment to every office or for the disposal of every wardship or lease coming into the crown's possession. Control over the bulk of routine patronage, in which the crown's interest was mainly financial, was in the hands of the treasurer. He was responsible for granting numerous offices that were connected with the financial admin-istration: by his bill Bourgchier warranted several types of appointment, most notable among them the customs' officials and alnagers.[33] The full-scale replacement of about seventy officials of this sort at the beginning of the new reign in 1461 confirms that there was a political element in the granting of such posts, and the treasurer's control over appointments indicates that the function of these offices in providing security for creditors, or for putting a break on assignments, was fully appreciated and worthy of his careful attention. During Bourgchier's third treasurership his powers of patronage in this respect were somewhat curtailed, for reasons to be discussed later, although he did nominate several of the surveyors of customs whose untoward efficiency in parting merchants from their money excited contemporary comment.[34] That on occasion he signed bills personally is suggestive of his interest in, and close attention to, this particular aspect of his work.[35] It is not hard to guess one of the reasons for this: Bourgchier was making considerable use of his powers of patronage to reward his own retainers and associates. Indeed, it is possible to compile a list of no fewer than twenty instances where offices in his gift were bestowed on such followers. To take but one example: in 1474 Robert Plomer, receiver-general of the Earl of Essex's estates, was given a profitable customership in London.[36] Clearly, Bourgchier could in this way effectively demonstrate his 'good lordship' without suffering any loss to his own pocket, while at the same time endeavouring to assert greater control over the collection of revenues by introducing a certain level of personal supervision. Among the offices which fell to the treasurer's gift were lucrative posts at the Exchequer itself, most notable among them being that of his deputy, the under-treasurer. Bourgchier employed only four under-treasurers in his fifteen years of office, and all of them were connected with him personally. For instance, with one of them, Sir John Say, he formed in the 1470s a highly successful trading partnership for their own profit; and another, William Essex, could state in 1478 that he had been appointed as a member of the King's council expressly so as to assist his kinsman the Earl of Essex as his clerk.[37]

Viscount Bourgchier's main sphere of influence over royal patronage, in particular during his first term of office, came from his control over the grant of wardships and custodies of lands coming temporarily into the crown's possession. To obtain perquisites of this nature the grantee either had to pay a lump sum of money or else negotiate with the treasurer as to terms regarding rent and the duration of the lease.[38] Bourgchier could not resist the opportunity presented by such arrangements to pass on profitable leases to his retainers, and, more important, to feather the nests of members of his own family. His appointment to the treasurership heralded a spate of offices and leases granted to his sons and brothers by the authority of his warrant. The viscount's younger sons profited most. In June 1455, just ten days after Bourgchier first took over at the Exchequer, his son John was named alnager of Norfolk, Suffolk and Essex: a lucrative office entitling him to a moiety of the forfeitures arising from his surveillance. Moreover, in November 1460, when his father was treasurer again, John was able to obtain a royal pardon for losses allegedly sustained through robberies, and to have this pardon specially enrolled among the Exchequer memoranda.[39] On 4 March 1456 Viscount Bourgchier made provision for his second son, Henry, by authorizing a grant to him of a twenty-year lease of land in the lordship of Castle Rising. Nor was this all. Just over a week later, on 13 March (although the business was not to be finalized until May), young Henry negotiated with his father for a share in the wardship and marriage of a Somerset heiress. The very same day he received a ten-year lease of certain properties in Essex, and two days later he was given custody of a mansion near Baynard's Castle, which had once belonged to the late Duke of Gloucester (whose effects were currently being administered by his father and uncle Archbishop Bourgchier as authorized by parliament).[40] During his second treasurership, apart from securing a profitable wardship for his eldest son William, Bourgchier concentrated mainly on increasing the already substantial income of his third son Humphrey, Lord Cromwell. Thus in November 1460 Humphrey was able to take over the custody of the Lincolnshire estates of Henry Tudor for the duration of Tudor's minority; and in July 1461 he obtained a number of leases, all of them for as long as twenty years, most important among them being that of the royal manor of Eltham. Not long afterwards, Humphrey's younger brother, now *Sir* John, obtained custody, initially for seven years (though later altered to ten), of a manor in Suffolk, and finally, in 1477, the Earl of Essex's fifth son, Sir Thomas Bourgchier (who had been constable of Leeds Castle in Kent since 1469), was granted custody of the manor of Leeds for twenty years.[41] Nor were the treasurer's brothers overlooked when he doled out the royal bounty: both Thomas, Archbishop of Canterbury and John, Lord Berners received important wardships,[42] and he himself, in association with the archbishop, obtained in February 1462 the keeping of certain properties in Leicestershire.[43] It will be noted that with few exceptions the leases granted to the Bourgchiers were excessively long ones by Exchequer standards and were not infrequently made on unusually advantageous terms.

Of course, the advantages of being treasurer were not restricted to the tangible material rewards. The post brought with it political power, with ready access to the King and unlimited opportunity to influence royal policy and patronage. The treasurer naturally enjoyed a prominent place as a member of the royal council; indeed, the oath as taken by the treasurers of the 1480s specifically included the requirement that 'ye shalle councille the King and his counselle ye shalle layne & kepe'.[44] It is clear from such evidence of the composition of the council as survives that when in office as treasurer Bourgchier was assiduous in his attendance. For example, records of meetings in December 1455, when a good deal of important work was being done by the councillors (who had re-adopted the practice of signing warrants during the Duke of York's second protectorate), show him and his brother the chancellor as being always present.[45] And these two continued to be leading members of the council long after the return to 'normal' government under the monarch the following year.[46] Very few details are available for the composition of the council in 1460–1, but nevertheless, where records do survive, Bourgchier and one or other of his brothers were nearly always in attendance, and made appearances on Edward IV's council within days of his accession.[47] The prominence of certain councillors may be seen in the attempts by suitors to gain their attention. Most revealing in this respect is the letter, already referred to, in which John Paston wrote to his father in August 1461 regarding his failure to report about 'the materys that ye sent to me fore'. In exoneration he explained that 'I laboryd dayly my lord Estsexe, tresere of Ynglond, to have mevyd the Kyng . . . everye mornyng ore he went to the Kyng, and often tymys jnquieryd of hym and he had mevyd the Kyng in these materys'; but it had taken some considerable time to persuade Essex to raise the issue with Edward and bring back an answer to the suitor.[48] The earl's enjoyment of a regular morning audience with the King is indicative of his highly influential position at the centre of government. Immediately after his re-appointment as treasurer in 1471, Essex took his place again in the council and such evidence as there is for conciliar attendance during the following twelve years confirms that he retained this prominence. The council in the 1470s was greatly concerned with financial problems, so that it is not surprising to find the treasurer, rather than the chancellor, most often presiding over meetings in the King's absence. Furthermore, he was one of the very few councillors paid a regular salary in this period. [49]

There can be no doubt of the treasurer's power, in particular in his role in deciding which of the crown's many creditors should be accorded preferential treatment at the Exchequer.[50] The highly political nature of such decisions is evident from the immediate contrast between the warrants acted upon by the Exchequer in the winter of 1459–60, when urgent payment was required to such staunch loyalists as the dukes of Somerset and Exeter, the Earl of Wiltshire, and lords Rivers and Roos, expressly to pay for arms and soldiers to defeat the Yorkist rebels,[51] and the payments which Bourgchier made in July 1460 as soon as he became treasurer, for among those were large sums handed to the earls of March and Salisbury, and £1,000 forwarded to the Duke of York himself for artillery, gunpowder and 'habilements of werre'.[52]

Manifold then were the benefits of holding office as treasurer of the Exchequer: recorded fees and rewards, gratuities from creditors, the opportunity to exercise patronage on a large scale, and the enjoyment of political power with untold effects on the fortunes of self and family. But while examining such obvious advantages, we should not overlook certain distinct drawbacks, which might outweigh even such incentives as these. Most important for the faint-hearted was the knowledge that, not so very long before, in Richard II's reign, two treasurers had lost their heads as a consequence of unpopular policies for which they were held responsible, and even more fresh in the memory must have been the murder by the mob of James Fiennes, Lord Saye and Sele, within days of his enforced retirement from the treasurership in 1450. While it is now debatable to what extent financial policies were the treasurer's own, and how far he could act on his own initiative, contemporary opinion, wary of the treasonable consequences of criticizing the King himself, rested the responsibility for any financial crisis firmly on his shoulders. This burden of responsibility should not be underestimated, in particular in the difficult (and often impossible) task of dealing fairly with the crown's creditors. In 1433, more than twenty years before Bourgchier first took up office, Ralph, Lord Cromwell had told the young King Henry VI in parliament about his constant headache:

> Daily many warantis come to me of paimentz . . . of much more than all youre revenuz wold come to, thowe they wer not assigned afore . . . the which warrantes yf I shuld paye hem, youre Household, chambre and warderope and your werkes shuld be unservid and unpaide, and yf I paye hem not, I renne in grete indignation of my lordes and grete sclander, noyse and maugre of all youre peple.[53]

Every medieval treasurer was faced with the same dilemma. When it was impossible to pay all creditors, it was clearly important to pay those to whom the crown looked for financial and political support. And if this had been a pressing problem in Cromwell's day, it was considerably more so in the 1450s, for the burden of royal debt had mounted enormously in the meantime, and, as Dr Harriss has recently shown, there was little that even a treasurer determined to bring expenditure under a strict rein could do to correct the by then major disparity between royal revenue still available for disbursement at the Exchequer and the increased requirements of household and government. Although the treasurer retained the initiative over assignments and issues, in deciding whether payment should be in cash and who should be accorded preferential treatment, and he might discriminate between debts which had to be paid speedily and others which might be deferred or ignored altogether without untoward consequences, to a certain extent his hands were tied. A masterful treasurer like Bishop Lumley might well promote a coherent policy for dealing with financial crises (including the imposition of a moratorium of several weeks on assignments at the Exchequer, and the systematic replacement of collectors of customs so as to invalidate all tallies issued in the names of their predecessors), yet all the while he had to battle against individual pressures for exemption, his task seriously compounded by Henry VI's feckless authorization of warrants expressly designed to over-ride the treasurer's restrictions. During his second treasurership, Bourgchier was confronted with an especially delicate political task: since tallies were invalidated by a change of monarch whose name was carved on them, at the beginning of Edward IV's reign the treasurer had to examine all tallies brought back to the Exchequer inscribed with Henry VI's name and decide which of them should be re-assigned. It provided him with an opportunity to address the problem of royal debt from a fresh standpoint, unhampered by the deposed King's heedless generosity, yet even then the political pressures brought to bear by the supporters of the Yorkist cause seeking their reward rendered his task no easy one.[54]

Not surprisingly, the liabilities of the office prompted Bourgchier on occasion to seek some protection against prosecution for losses. On 31 March 1462, just before the completion of his second term of office, he petitioned the King for letters officially exonerating him from liability for specified sums of money issued from the Exchequer. Doubtless he had in mind the kind of discrepancy which came to light just two months later, when he received a warrant requiring him to enter up in the Exchequer's 'booke of appele' certain sums amounting to £457, which he had issued in response to verbal royal instructions, but had failed to see properly recorded.[55] There was always a danger that he might be held accountable for errors arising from carelessness on his own or his subordinates' part. Similarly, royal pardons were granted to him and his under-treasurer in August 1474 and June 1475 to cover all debts, accounts, issues and arrears. It may be that these were intended specifically to exonerate them from mistakes made in the course of the financial preparations for the King's expedition to France; but nevertheless such pardons draw attention to the treasurer's constant feelings of insecurity.[56]

It is often tacitly assumed that fifteenth-century noblemen rarely filled their offices in person, and that they took up posts merely for the money and prestige afforded by them.[57] But it is dangerous to generalize. The evidence suggests that while Bourgchier may have regarded those minor offices he held merely as a painless way to supplement his income from land, he brought to the treasurership and to his other important posts a marked degree of professionalism, conscientiously carried out the duties involved, and readily devoted time and energy to serving the crown to his full ability. During a critical period of government he actively sought solutions to the major problems of administration and finance: problems exacerbated by decreasing crown revenues, years of high expenditure on foreign warfare, an enforced dependency on borrowing, and a King only too willing to give away his inheritance. That Bourgchier was by no means unique in this period is clear from the examples of Ralph, Lord Cromwell and Marmaduke, Bishop of Carlisle, whom he followed by tackling his duties with zeal and competence.

Bourgchier was undoubtedly interested in financial matters and fast made himself an expert in the monetary problems facing the crown. In this he may have enjoyed an advantage over many of his peers; for when he first came to the treasurership he brought some useful experience in dealing with fiscal concerns, learned through his involvement in the affairs of Calais, which dated from as far back as 1439. This had made him conversant with a difficult area of government, which combined to a marked degree the overwhelming problems of enormous debt, political instability, and continuous dependence upon vast government loans. Significant in the development of this expertise had been his mission to Calais of 1454, involving as it did complex and delicate negotiations between the crown, the merchants of the Staple and the mutinous soldiers of the garrison. On that occasion he had been sent across the Channel to have 'speche and communicacion with the souldeours for the safety of the town', taking with him 6,000 marks with which to bargain on the government's behalf. On 28 May the council (of which he was himself a member) formally issued instructions as to how he should conduct the negotiations: no easy matter, for the soldiers were demanding 4,000 marks in cash immediately, 16,000 more at midsummer, and a further amount at Christmas. Bourgchier's brief was to offer them 3,000 marks at once, to persuade them to 'depart fro their askinge' with regard to the 16,000, and to offer up to 8,000 marks more before the New Year. The mission was one of the highest importance both for the future stability of Calais and the political standing of the Duke of York. The sensitive situation demanded careful handling, along with a rare ability to influence and persuade, to drive a bargain and above all to conciliate a potentially violent group of men. Bourgchier's talks with the garrison were a success: by July reports from Calais were suggesting that his proposals had won over the mutineers.[58] The experience stood him in good stead following his appointment as treasurer of England less than a year later, for the payment of the garrison of Calais long continued to be a major concern to the government. Bourgchier became skilled in negotiation with the merchants of the Staple for loans, and when the subject of Calais came up for discussion in the parliament of 1461, the new Earl of Essex was naturally one of those assigned to have talks with the Staplers. In 1463 he headed a commission sent to Calais, whose work culminated in a thorough and efficient report investigating the full extent of the Lancastrian debt and recommending extensive reforms to make the English stronghold economically viable in a way it had never been before.[59]

According to Dr Wolffe's carefully expounded reading of the records, Bourgchier's second treasurership saw the introduction of new policies with regard to the management of crown estates coming temporarily into the King's possession, which themselves prompted far-reaching administrative changes in the central government under Edward IV.[60] In his view, one of the earliest innovations, made at the beginning of 1462, was the

omission from the summons of the Pipe of all demands for farms and
fee-farms worth more than £2 annually, and the treasurer's appointment of
new officials, named receivers and approvers, to collect these dues from
eight regions and devote them solely to the expenses of the household,
there having been no precedent for such a general supervision of the
Exchequer farms by special salaried officers since the thirteenth century.[61]
Yet we should hesitate before giving credit to the young and inexperienced
King, or even to his middle-aged and seasoned treasurer, for innovations
in government practice, since there was, in fact, the germ of a precedent
for such an arrangement, and one from as recently as 1459–60, which
Wolffe apparently overlooked. Then, following the attainder of the Duke
of York and his allies, the bulk of their forfeited estates had been assigned
to royally-appointed stewards and receivers to be exploited for the crown's
benefit, the intention being most likely that the revenues would be paid
into Henry VI's chamber rather than into the Exchequer (although since
the Lancastrian defeat at the battle of Northampton precluded any of
these officials rendering account at the end of the financial year at
Michaelmas 1460, the evidence for this is lacking).[62] So, Bourgchier
would appear to have been less of an innovator than an adaptor of
experiments already partly tried out. From a survey of lands coming into
the crown's possession after 1461, it looks as if Bourgchier and his
colleagues were seeking to develop a system of royal estate management
modelled on methods employed on private estates. At the beginning
appointments of receivers and special auditors (for example, officers to
administer those estates forfeited by attainted Lancastrians), were all made
by the treasurer, Bourgchier.[63] Some wards' lands received the same new
treatment, but not all estates were placed under such skilled professional
control right from the start. Several, according to previous practice,
continued to be let out to farm to individual persons for lump sums. So in
the early stages of this development Bourgchier continued to negotiate
leases and handle wardships as before.[64] One eventual effect of this policy
was, however, to diminish the amount of work the Exchequer, and
therefore the treasurer, had to do, for it was intended that the King should
be provided with a substantial and reliable income independent of that
received by the Exchequer. The proceeds of estates dealt with in the new
way began to be paid directly into the King's own coffers, and from soon
after the beginning of his reign Edward IV received sums of money directly
into his chamber from all manner of sources, without the intervention of
any Exchequer process.

Earl Henry's third treasurership thus saw two major changes already
more or less fully put into effect: the chamber had taken the place of the
Lower Exchequer as the principal treasury; and the Upper Exchequer had
lost its power to hold audits for the officers administering the King's land

revenues. In the 1470s the treasurer had the responsibility of appointing only a few of the new receivers and auditors of crown lands, the remainder of the appointments being made by the King personally. Nevertheless, as one of the largest groups of counties was placed under the supervision of Robert Plomer, the Earl of Essex's most trusted retainer, it is clear that the treasurer was by no means excluded from consultation as to the suitability of candidates for such offices.[65] The practice of leasing lands out by the Exchequer was by then being used only rarely, and the increasing employment of special 'foreign' auditors also decreased the treasurer's work. But the treasurer had not necessarily relinquished all his powers in this respect: Essex continued to grant the custody of some wardships,[66] and his control over revenues from certain major sources, including customs and subsidies and parliamentary taxation, remained unaffected. In the extensive financial organization necessary for the military expedition to France of 1475 the Exchequer played at least as important a part as the chamber. The special tenth on incomes granted by the lords in parliament was in the event handed over to the Earl of Essex rather than to a special receiver as had originally been intended, and certain contributions by benevolence, supposed to be recorded in sealed 'billes' to be forwarded to the King and *not* 'delevered unto the eschequier nor to any other courte of record', nevertheless found their way to him also. The treasurer not only paid the wages of a number of indentured soldiers and others concerned with the organization of the expedition, but also received a personal allowance of £950 a year to pay the expenses of the household and royal family during the King's absence overseas.[67] While his scope had undoubtedly been narrowed since his earlier treasurerships, it should not be assumed that Bourgchier ever retired completely; indeed, he seems to have remained active right up to his death at the age of about 75.[68]

The treasurership was no sinecure. In the mid-fifteenth century there can have been few more thankless tasks. The treasurer was constantly beset by creditors, plagued by suitors, subject to vilification by the commonalty, and blamed by his peers for any financial crisis. During Henry VI's reign he was denied any intelligent support from the monarch for attempts to reverse the headlong slide into debt – indeed, his policies might even be actively undermined – and at the same time he was expected to help the Exchequer out with substantial loans from his own pocket. An explanation for the fact that so large a number of men occupied the treasurership for relatively short periods of time is that few wished to undertake the office for long; it involved too many responsibilities. The reluctance of competent public figures to serve in the Exchequer needed to be overcome by increasingly substantial incentives, which reached their apogee when it proved necessary to offer Earl Rivers the inducement of an annual salary of as much as £1,300 to persuade him to stay in office. Far from actively seeking participation in government, many of Bourgchier's peers invented excuses to be let off such a responsibility. Nor was he himself particularly willing. In 1454 when Henry VI's mental illness required that a group of noblemen should form a council to take control of the government under the Duke of York, 'the Vyescount Bourchyer for diverse reasons and specyallye for he thowght hymselfe unable desired he might be excused but fynally he graunted he wold do as other with that he might be sene to aftyr his eastate as other aftyr theires'.[69] Bourgchier's modesty (whether feigned or real) in doubting his ability to master the problems of administration was here mixed with evident determination that if he were to take on the task it would only be with adequate financial compensation. The same attitude persisted at least during his first and second treasurerships: there would be no question of self-denial, nor any intention of allowing the crown's debt to him for past services to be overlooked. If he was to shoulder the burden of responsibility, then he would make certain that he received his just rewards. It is worth remarking that as, under Edward IV, the state of royal finances improved and new administrative practices introduced at the Exchequer shifted some of this burden, so the direct rewards of office fell and opportunities for the treasurer to exercise royal patronage in his own interests diminished. Yet it was only then that magnates (Bourgchier in his third term, from 1471 to 1483, and Lord Dynham serving under Henry VII from 1486 to 1501) were prepared to occupy the treasurership for very long periods at a stretch. To these two, at least, comparative freedom from the stress of repeated financial crises, in the service of monarchs able themselves to address the problems of solvency with some maturity of vision, proved to be a greater incentive to stay in office than the excessive inducements offered in earlier times.

Notes

1. *CPR 1452–61*, p. 242. My thanks are due to Dr Carole Rawcliffe for her perceptive comments on this paper.
2. *Paston L&P* ii. p. 165.
3. PSO 1/20/778; *CPR 1461–7*, pp. 9, 182.
4. *Historie of the Arrivall of Edward IV in England*, J.Bruce (ed.), (CS i, 1836), pp. 10, 36–7; J.Warkworth, *A Chronicle of the First Thirteen Years of the Reign of Edward IV*, J.O.Halliwell (ed.), (CS x, 1844), p. 15.
5. *CPR 1467–77*, p. 258; C 141/3/31.
6. e.g. for his first term's fees: E 404/70/3/11, 54; E 404/74/1/20.
7. E 403/802 15 July, /806 1 Dec., 26 Jan., 12 Feb., /807 29 Apr., 10, 12, 15 July.
8. The example had been set in 1424 during the King's minority: *POPC* iii. p. 154.
9. E 404/70/3/80–1; E 403/807 17 July. It is interesting to note that Bourgchier had received no salary whatsoever actually during York's first protectorate, nor indeed did so

until he became treasurer and therefore controlled disbursements at the Exchequer. Furthermore, although sums were then still owing to seven other councillors as well, it was only he and his under-treasurer John Say who obtained payments.

10. E 403/820 31 Oct., /823 23 May, 9, 22 June, 2, 17 July, 7 Aug., /824 3, 20, 30 Oct., 7, 12, 26 Nov., 7 Dec., 30 Jan., 18, 22, 25 Feb.
11. This was mainly because the tellers were intended to keep track of movements of cash, not to make full records of issues.
12. See table in my thesis: L. Woodger, 'Henry Bourgchier, Earl of Essex and his Family (1408–83)', (Oxford D.Phil. thesis 1974), p. 157, based on E 403/845, /848, /850; E 405/54–6, /58–60, /62–71, /80.
13. e.g. E 405/70 m.8d.
14. G.L. Harriss, 'Marmaduke Lumley and the Exchequer Crisis of 1446–9', *Aspects of Government and Society in Late Medieval England. Essays in Honour of J.R. Lander*, J.G.Rowe (ed.), (Toronto 1986), p. 156; E 403/795, /798, /800, /801, /809; E 404/71/3/36.
15. E 404/73/3/2, quoted by C.L. Scofield in *Life and Reign of Edward IV* (2 vols 1923), i. p. 398.
16. E 404/72/4/71.
17. Steel, *Receipt*, pp. 330–1.
18. E 401/844 31 May, 15 June; and for repayments: E 403/801 4 June, /806 16 Oct.
19. E 401/873 8 Oct. Repayments: E 403/820 15 Oct., /824 18 Feb.
20. E 405/57 m.1d, /60 m.8d.
21. Fully summarized and discussed by G.L. Harriss in 'Aids, Loans and Benevolences', *HJ* vi (1963), pp. 18–19, and in 'Cardinal Beaufort – Patriot or Usurer?', *TRHS* 5th ser. xx (1970), pp. 129–48.
22. E 404/70/3/83, /72/1, 37; E 403/807 15 July, /824 25 Feb.
23. E 403/844; E 404/76/1/31.
24. E 405/56 m.1d.
25. E 101/53/40; *Paston L&P* i. pp. 390–2.
26. Harriss, 'Lumley', p. 156; E 404/55/270, /56/313; E 403/734 18 May; E 101/323/14; E 364/74.
27. E 101/323/15 m.15. Significantly, when using the English form of his French title, he called himself 'earl of Ewe': E 101/53/40.
28. E 403/807 17 July.
29. BL Lansdowne MS. 810 f.40.
30. E 404/70/2/56; E 101/53/35; E 364/88 m. G.
31. Longleat MS 181; C 76/138 m.6.
32. E 403/807; E 401/794, /796.
33. For examples from his first treasurership, see C 81/1621, /1622, enrolled in CFR 1452–61, pp. 104–11, 136–7, 140, 148–9, 160; CPR 1452–61, pp. 202, 214, 246, 248, 274–5.
34. C 81/1636/10, 70; C 81/1637/3; CPR 1467–77, pp. 391–2; CFR 1471–85, Nos. 60, 115; *The Crowland Chronicle Continuations 1454–1486*, N. Pronay and J.C. Cox (eds), (Richard III & Yorkist History Trust, 1986), p. 138.
35. e.g. C 81/1636/107, dated December 1472.
36. See Woodger, pp. 294–5.
37. Ibid. pp. 239–40; J.L. Kirby, 'The Rise of the Under-Treasurer of the Exchequer', *EHR* lxxii (1957), pp. 666–77; E 403/845.
38. There is ample evidence of Bourgchier's activities in this respect. His 'concordats' are frequently recorded, e.g. E 368/234 recorda Hil.1 Edw.IV m.8; E 368/235 Easter 2 Edw.IV m.54.
39. C 81/1621/67; CFR 1452–61, p. 104; CPR 1452–61, p. 631; E 368/233 recorda Mich.39 Hen.VI m.9d.
40. C 81/1622/62, 69, 74, 85; CPR 1452–61, p. 285; CFR 1452–61, pp. 129, 152, 159;

E 368/236 recorda Hil.36 Hen.VI m.3; *RP* v. p. 339.

41. *CPR 1461–7*, p. 19; C 81/1626/32; C 81/1628/88, 90, 91; C 81 /1629/40; C 81 /1638/75; *CFR 1452–61*, p. 294; *1461–71*, pp. 26–27, 35, 76; *1471–85*, p. 423.
42. The archbishop became in October 1460 co-grantee of the custody of some of the estates of their late half-brother Humphrey Duke of Buckingham (C 81/1628/32; C 81/1629/19, 93; *CFR 1452–61*, p. 284; *1461–71*, pp. 11–12; E 159/243 brevia Mich. m.26), and Berners obtained a long lease of certain forfeited estates (C 81/1628/112, 113; *CFR 1461–71*, pp. 36–7; *CPR 1461–7*, p. 180).
43. *CFR 1461–71*, pp. 67–8, 75. The warranting authority for this particular grant is not stated.
44. *British Library Harleian Manuscript 433*, R.E. Horrox and P.W. Hammond (eds), (4 vols Upminster 1980–4), iii. p. 174.
45. E 28/87/3, 7–10, 12–14, 16–18, 20, 23–9, 32, 33; POPC vi. pp. 267, 272, 275, 279, 285. R. Virgoe in 'The Composition of the King's Council 1437–61' *BIHR* xliii (1970), p. 159, amalgamates the attendance figures for the two protectorates and thus obscures the differences in personnel in the two periods.
46. E 28/87; C 81/1546/110; *Paston L&P* ii. p. 148.
47. *POPC* vi. pp. 304–10; *CSPM* i. 36; *Foedera* xi. p. 473.
48. *Paston L&P* i. pp. 390–2.
49. C 81/1502/22; C 81/1574/10; E 28/90 25 May; Woodger, pp. 118–19; J.R. Lander, 'Council, Administration and Councillors 1461–85', *BIHR* xxxii (1959), p. 151; E 405/80 mm.28–32.
50. A subject explored fully by G.L. Harriss in 'Preference at the Medieval Exchequer', *BIHR* xxx (1957), pp. 17–40.
51. E 404/71/4/18, 24, 30, 33, 34, 36.
52. E 404/71/5/2, 3, 5, 34, 35, 38.
53. *RP* iv. p. 439. Cf. J.L. Kirby, 'Issues of the Lancastrian Exchequer and Lord Cromwell's Estimates of 1433', *BIHR* xxiv (1951), pp. 121–51.
54. Harriss, 'Lumley', pp. 143–78, esp. 152–6; G.L. Harriss, 'Fictitious Loans', *EcHR* 2nd ser.viii (1955), pp. 189, 196.
55. E 28/89 31 Mar.; E 404/72/2/24.
56. C 81/1508/3; *CPR 1467–77*, pp. 466, 531, 541.
57. e.g. by G.R. Elton, *Tudor Revolution in Government* (Cambridge 1953), p. 22.
58. E 28/84/25, 27; E 404/70/1/57; *Paston L&P* ii. p. 95.
59. *The Fane Fragment of the 1461 Lords' Journals*, W.H. Dunham (ed.), (Yale Hist. Pubs, New Haven, Conn., 1935), p. 20; Lander, pp. 141–3; C 81/1547/5; C 76/147 m.3; C 47/2/50.
60. As first expounded in his 'The Management of the English Royal Estates under the Yorkist Kings', *EHR* l (1956), pp. 1–2, and amplified in *The Royal Demesne in English History* (1971), pp. 158–80.
61. B.P. Wolffe, *The Crown Lands 1461–1536* (1970), p. 96; C 81/1629/99; *CPR 1461–7*, pp. 110–11.
62. R.A. Griffiths, *The Reign of Henry VI 1422–61* (1981), pp. 826–7.
63. C 81/1628/35, 68, 80, 83, 89, 104; C 81/1629/2–6, 76; enrolled in *CPR 1461–7*, pp. 12, 19, 26, 94, 129–30; *CFR 1461–71*, p. 37.
64. e.g. C 81/1626/29–30; *CPR 1461–7*, p. 95.
65. C 81/1635/52; C 81/1637/46, 47, 66; *CPR 1467–77*, p. 329.
66. e.g. C 81/1637/68; C 81/1638/90. The former is a grant of wardship of his own great-nephew John, Lord Berners.
67. *RP* vi. p. 42; E 405/60; *CPR 1467–77*, p. 528.
68. PSO 1/51/260A.
69. R.A. Griffiths, 'The King's Council and the First Protectorate of the Duke of York, 1453–4', *EHR* xcix (1986), pp. 80–1.

10

From Caitiff and Villain to Pater Patriae: Reynold Bray and the Profits of Office[1]

Margaret Condon
Assistant Keeper, Public Record Office

Two main themes emerge from a study of the estates of Reynold Bray, chancellor of the duchy of Lancaster (1485–1503), treasurer of England (1486) and sworn councillor of the King (1485–1503). The first is so familiar as almost to be a platitude: the profit of office and power was visible wealth. New riches encouraged investment in land, whence came an increase in profit and diversification in the sources of income, bringing, in turn, yet further acquisitions of real estate. The second theme is of some historiographical significance, and is inherent within the range of sources available to the would-be chronicler of Bray's career. The restrictions imposed by the nature of the record material present a recurrent challenge. The solutions adopted have a relevance and application beyond the subject of Bray alone and an essay on Bray's estates can be read as a study in the uses of evidence. For there are no receivers'-general accounts, no general surveys or valors to list, summarize or value Bray's property; no family tradition or pattern of inheritance within Reynold's immediate history to flesh out the skeleton, to explain the dynamics of the expansion and management of the estates, or to preserve his archive as a coherent collection; no surviving inquisitions *post mortem* to provide a comprehensive and retrospective overview. Despite the interminable length of Bray's will, it, too, is woefully inadequate in the information it provides, and the alienation of parcels of the accumulated lands began almost immediately after Bray's death. The historian must look elsewhere: to the records of the courts at Westminster, and in dark and sometimes unexpected corners for documents held in disparate, but publicly accessible, collections. A secondary theme is the way in which Bray's past and continuing service to Margaret Beaufort (d. 1509) informed and at times assisted the pattern and the process of his acquisitions, the further consolidation of his estates, and his choice of feoffees and estate officers. It has also, coincidentally, preserved for us some of the most intimate records of his activities.

Reynold Bray was already a mature adult, when he first appears as receiver-general of Sir Henry Stafford (son of the first Duke of Buckingham) and his wife, Margaret Beaufort. Bray's father, Richard, and a brother, John, enjoyed lesser offices within the same service.[2] Reynold is commonly thought to be the eldest son of his father's second marriage.[3] His minimal endowment reflects that order of precedence, although neither father nor son seem to have possessed lands in themselves sufficient to support their status as gentlemen. Forty years later Bray's position had altered beyond all recognition. The battle of Bosworth transformed his career. By his death on 5 August 1503 Bray was one of the most influential men in England, one of the most prominent of all Henry VII's councillors, and one of the few with ready access to the person and mind of the King himself. To juxtapose the descriptions of two contemporaries, one a critic, the other an admirer, and both polemical, the 'caitiff and villain of simple birth' had been transformed into 'pater patriae'.[4] In less than two decades Reynold built up an estate sufficient to qualify his heirs for two peerages, Bray and Sandys. Ten of Edmund Bray's eleven children were female and thus that peerage fell into abeyance in 1557 on the premature death of his son John Lord Bray.[5] Bray's lands were scattered through eighteen counties at their greatest extent, although there had been some consolidation before Bray's death. Writs for inquisitions *post mortem* issued into eight counties, but not a single return now survives.[6] Reynold Bray had no heir of his own body to inherit his estates and the eventual settlement did not accurately reflect his wishes.[7]

Before 1485 Bray's salary as receiver-general was probably augmented by the fees of other offices within Henry Stafford's gift. The expenses of his peripatetic life were met largely by his lord. He was a frequent and welcome guest at Henry and Margaret's table, and in their company he dwelled within the household.[8] His patrimony may have been merely a house and some land in the parish of St John in Bedwardine, Worcestershire, where he was born.[9] He bought a tenement in Wells, convenient for his periodic visits to Somerset as receiver-general, and added in 1483 the Hampshire manor of Flood.[10] More substantial were his acquisitions by marriage (probably between 1475 and 1478) to the much younger Katherine, daughter and co-heir of Nicholas Hussey, a former victualler of Calais.[11] Bray's initial gains are by no means clear, and the full potential of his investment may not have been realized until his own accession to power after 1485. Katherine thus brought him claims to the manors of South Moreton in Berkshire and Freefolk in Hampshire, where, for a night in November 1497, Henry VII was to enjoy Bray's hospitality in the course of their victorious return from Exeter.[12] They may have obtained more immediate entry into other lands. The formal division of Hussey's estates between the co-parcenors occurred in 1478, although the complexity of the arrangements made to define and secure title in the lands that were to pass to Reynold and Katherine suggests that the settlement was not straightforward. Bray and his wife were to have Standen Huse (in Hungerford, Berkshire) and 40 marks of land from the newly dismembered manor of Harting, formerly the *caput* of Nicholas Hussey's lands. The manor, and the bulk of the Sussex estates, passed to Katherine's elder sister, Constance, and her husband, Henry Lovell. Yet despite ambiguous evidence of receipts from Harting in 1475 and, more clearly, the citation of Harting as an alternative *alias* in his pardon of 1484, by 1489 Bray was petitioning John Morton as chancellor that the feoffees appointed in 1478 should give him seisin. Judgement was then swiftly given in his favour.[13]

For twenty years before Bosworth Bray was the trusted servant of Margaret Beaufort and her husbands Henry Stafford and Thomas, Lord Stanley. Stafford's first will reveals him bound in substantial sums on his master's behalf. Margaret was Stafford's sole executrix, but Bray was to play a prominent part in the settlement of her estates and, in Stafford's final will, of 1471, Bray was the sole legatee (appropriately, of a grizzled horse) outside the immediate family.[14] It is unclear when Bray first became armigerous and later tradition assigned to his father the same arms, but it is more likely that they belong to 1485 and Henry VII's coronation, when he was knighted and his arms recorded by the heralds. In his one contemporary portrait, the eagle's foot erased 'a cuise' of the house of Stanley is the most prominent charge on the surcoat depicting his own arms.[15]

Bray's part in the revolution of 1485 is well known. He was probably not at Bosworth and may initially have remained with Margaret Beaufort, who assigned him rooms at Coldharbour, the victory gift given her by her son, and now refurbished for her use.[16] But on 13 September 1485 he was appointed chancellor of the duchy of Lancaster for life, with a fee of 100 marks p.a., by mid-October he was acting as under-treasurer in the Exchequer, he was knighted at the coronation, and on 28 February 1486, in an appointment with few precedents for a commoner, he became treasurer of England.[17] Although he held this great office only briefly, lasting only until 10 July, he did so at a politically critical time. Lord Treasurer Bray and his under-treasurer Avery Cornburgh each lent the crown over £1,600 and made assignments to repay over £3,500 advanced largely by the merchant community shortly before they took office. As King's councillor, Bray had earlier himself fronted Henry's urgent request for short term loans to support his infant regime. In later years Reynold's lent from his own resources and a rolling cycle of loan, repayment in cash, and new loan, but in 1486 it seems more probable that he was a front man for money provided from elsewhere.[18] Even after Lord Dynham became treasurer in July, Bray continued to act closely with him in the Exchequer for the rest of the century. The story of Bray's public career is to be told elsewhere;[19] it is the way in which public office helped him to private profit that concerns us here.

Bray's long service had earned Henry VII's gratitude and laid the foundation of an enduring special relationship. Offices, major and minor, worth well over £130 p.a. even without the treasurership, acknowledged his loyalty, his services and his abilities.[20] His patents and knighthood were his reward and a mark of public honour and thanks. He was not granted lands, but patronage, political manipulation and the process of the law combined with a timely and well-targeted opportunism enabled Bray to secure his fortunes by entering the property market.

Bray's first purchase is significant for more than the quality of his investment. The manor of Chelsea he acquired in the summer of 1486 was to form one of the principal endowments for Katherine Bray's widowhood[21] and was sufficiently attractive for Henry VIII to force an exchange on William Sandys, to whom it had descended, in 1535.[22] Behind the ordered language of the writ of right pleaded to secure Bray's title, a complex of forces were at work. In Chelsea, as elsewhere, some may only be deduced or suspected. Of others we have more certain knowledge because Bray, as an experienced searcher for evidence for Margaret Beaufort's disputes, frequently had his own deeds enrolled in Chancery or common pleas, obtained exemplifications of the legal processes which secured his possession, and of copies of documents, public or private, and historical matter pertinent to his title.

The entry on the *De Banco* roll proclaims only the customary legal fictions necessary to convey Chelsea to Bray; a related action placed the vendor's title on record. But the charters enrolled reveal the vendor as Robert Shorditch esquire, whose son George was required to give additional warranty.[23] Is it entirely coincidence that that same Trinity term 1486, also Bray's final term as treasurer, one Robert Shorditch, former clerk of the spicery of Edward IV, was allowed to plead his pardon for a debt of £6 17s 3d on his account?[24] An indenture between Reynold and Robert specifically safeguarded Bray against execution for debt and Robert's other land sales suggest financial embarrassment. Even allowing for improvements and additions by Bray, the purchase price was no more than 10–12 times its annual value, well below the common market rate of 18–20 years' purchase.[25] As in some other purchases, political pressure is hinted at, for the sale was made, not directly to Bray, but to Elizabeth, Dowager-Duchess of Norfolk. Bray was ultimate beneficiary, the duchess being reimbursed (or, rather, Robert paid) with 700 marks of the 'goodys of . . . Sir Reynold'. The *eminence grise* behind this extraordinary and obscure arrangement was Margaret Beaufort, at whose 'speciall desire, instance and requeste' the duchess acted. Elizabeth was also induced to sell to Bray an additional house and 40 acres of land, which 'late were Richard Beauchamp, late bishop of Sarisbury' and had, presumably, come to her by inheritance.[26] These transactions raise more questions than can easily be answered, but clearly all is not what it seems.

Chelsea also introduces another recurrent theme: Bray's reconstruction of a history, real or supposed, for himself and its concrete expression through a necessarily interrupted title to, and association with, land. Thus we find that Chelsea was held legitimately, but for a finite term, by one John Bray of Chiswick under Richard II. This John held the manor by virtue of a contingent remainder; after his death it passed to William Atwater, mentioned by name in the legal processes of 1486. A deposition by John Shorditch, father of Robert, recording this descent, is now among the archives of Westminster Abbey, a location suggesting that the document was part of the legal brief for Bray's acquisition of Chelsea, and that he was well acquainted with its contents.[27] This same awareness of pedigree, status, and self-image perhaps prompted Bray's purchase in 1502 of an interest in East Haddon (Northants.). A connection between it and the name of Bray could be traced to the thirteenth century, in the accessible source known as Kirkby's Quest, and from 1497 Bray quartered (by grant of the heralds) the arms of the ancient, knightly, Northamptonshire family of Bray with his own.[28] Quasi-historicism also passes fleetingly through the history of Great Rissington Manor (Glos.) and may explain his purchase in 1498 of land in a county in which he had no other material interest. But land in Great Rissington had been held at the turn of the fourteenth century by Henry Hussey, from whom Katherine was lineally descended, and through whom she was connected, in the cadet line, with the minor baronial family of that name. Its mid-fifteenth-century alienation may have lain within living memory.[29] Moreover, it was clearly Reynold Bray's intention that the Hussey inheritance, divided between Katherine and her sister, should be again united through the marriages of Katherine's heirs general, the daughters of her elder sister, to males of his own name and lineage, although their prospects might have commanded a greater match.[30] Consistent in spirit were the dubious claims to inheritance pleaded by Bray for South Moreton (Berks.), of which Katherine's great-grandfather had died seised in 1409, and Freefolk in Hampshire. In both cases, despite conflicting evidence offered by puzzled jurors, the courts gave judgement for Bray. In South Moreton there may have been genuine confusion, for Henry Hussey appears to have alienated the manor by way of mortgage. But clients of

Margaret Beaufort who witnessed subsequent charters and enfeoffments could have supplied Bray with pertinent information, and the final stages of the conveyance to Reynold are certainly fictitious, with a supposed default by the Duke of Suffolk on a bond of statute merchant.[31] Bray's claims to Freefolk were disputed in earnest, but after the case remained unsettled at the Winchester assizes, the defendants seem to have bowed to *force majeure* and reached a compromise which gave Bray possession. An uneasy conscience is suggested by the separation by his will of Freefolk from the main estate in favour of his nephew Richard Andrewes, husband of Elizabeth Rogers, one of the two co-parceners dispossessed in 1487–8.[32] Nor were Reynold's heirs entirely free from the taint of the self-made man: Brays of the sixteenth century and beyond concocted an illustrious genealogy for themselves.[33]

The second major acquisition of 1486 cemented more personal links. Woking (Surrey) was a favourite house of Margaret Beaufort and thus a principal residence of Bray (also the estate's steward), and was frequently visited by Henry VII before and after his mother gave it to him in 1503.[34] Bray had forged enduring ties with its bailiff, John Bigge, and with several burgesses of nearby Guildford, in whose friary his mother was buried.[35] Bray was appointed parker of Guildford by Henry VII, without account and with issues, from 5 September 1485, perhaps the occasion of their first post Bosworth-meeting. When the grant was renewed and augmented in October 1486, confirming wages of £18 5s p.a. and adding the keepership of Claygate park, the original letters patent (now lost) were cited with a date of 5 September.[36] This background makes the life grant to Bray by Thomas Butler, Earl of Ormond, 28 January 1486, of the manor of Shere, about five miles east of Guildford, a particularly graceful one. Henry's first parliament reversed Ormond's attainder and confirmed his title to the lands of his inheritance including Shere, granted by Edward IV to Lord Audley. Audley's political light was dimmed, but not extinguished, and he sat with Ormond on Henry VII's council. Despite Ormond's new honours, his elevation to the peerage, and his appointment as chamberlain of Elizabeth of York, he may still have felt in need of friends. Diplomacy was necessary to profit immediately from his restoration, while his Irish title left his revenues vulnerable to the continuance of the king's favour.[37] Similar insecurity may have moved the restored Ricardian Lord Dynham to grant Horley (Oxon.) to Bray for life.[38] Ormond's initial gift, too, was a life tenancy, reserving rights of hunting and hospitality, but in 1495 Bray purchased Shere outright.[39] Audley also bid for Bray's friendship with a £10 annuity from Somerset (in practice drawn in part from Audley's Surrey estates) and the life-grant of the lands he had added to Shere manor during his occupation. This grant was confirmed by his son James, who sold Bray these extramanorial lands in 1497, and Henry VII continued the

annuity after James's attainder.[40] Bray's legal title to the Audley lands in
Cranley and Shere was ultimately accepted, for they passed, in time, to
Edmund Bray.[41] Reynold continued to improve and expand Shere and
drew produce from Claygate for his household at Shere.[42] And is it
without significance that in 1500 Shere church possessed 'a suit of red
damask, with greyhounds', when a greyhound was one of the two principal
supporters of Henry VII's royal arms?[43]

Until about 1492 Bray expanded his estates by drawing on his growing
wealth, power and royal favour to exploit the political pressures, private
ambitions and the instinct for self-preservation of the several parties
concerned. The names of Bray's feoffees testify to the continuing strength
of his Beaufort connections: [44] indeed, he remained Margaret's receiver-
general, although increasingly conducting routine by deputy. His wife did
not wholly forsake her place in Margaret's household even after joining
the queen's.[45] But it was Henry VII who authorized the single most
important addition to Bray's estates, supplying them with a focus that
engrossed Bray for the rest of his life.

In July 1486 Henry VII had made Bray steward, receiver and surveyor of
the Bedfordshire manors of Eaton, Houghton Regis and Totternhoe, with
Ledburn and Mentmore in Buckinghamshire, forfeited by Lord Zouche.
Customarily a single administrative unit, they were leased to Bray in June
1488 for life at 100 marks p.a. The timing is significant. The grant
confirms Bray's influence and authority at a time when Henry VII was
reviewing his moral debts and allegiances, and withdrawing or extending
still generous grants of grace in the considered light of judgement and
kingly experience. Bray may never have paid the 100 mark farm. In April
1488 he was said to have taken the issues since 1485; the (very defective)
receipt rolls record no payments by him; and in 1490 the lease was
exchanged for a grant in tail male, at an annual rent of a pair of spurs. This
grant included the issues from 21 August 1485. In June 1492, perhaps in
view of the French expedition and Bray's childlessness, the grant in tail
was amended to Bray, his heirs and assigns, in fee simple.[46]

Bray's acquisition of Eaton demonstrates, perhaps more clearly than any
other transaction, the profits, tangible and intangible, to be gained from
royal office. The 1486 grant that gave Bray the most senior offices within
the Eaton condominium was part of a general distribution of patronage
after Bosworth, but it also came only two days after the King warranted a
pardon for Lord Zouche (former lord of Eaton) and on the same day that
letters were signed and sealed for the transfer of the treasurership to Lord
Dynham. Similarly the 1488 lease followed within a month of the
commission to Bray and others to let crown lands to farm. It was a

commercial lease based on the full rate of the extent, although only about two-thirds of the true value of the lands, but the rent may never have been exacted and Bray was well placed to secure subsequent grants on ever more favourable terms. Thus far is not extraordinary, and the inferences drawn are based at best on circumstantial evidence. Then follows the agreement of 23 November 1495 between Bray and Zouche. For £1,000 – a purchase price after the rate of fifteen years according to the extent, but in practice little more than Bray's probable receipts of the preceding decade – Lord Zouche, now finally restored in blood and with qualified expectations for the full restoration of his inheritance including Eaton, confirmed Bray's tenure. He conveyed to Bray full title to the Eaton complex 'for asmoche as the seid John Zouche knyght hath by the especiall labour, assistens and meanes of the seid Sir Reignold atteyned the singuler favour and the especiall grace of our . . . Soverayne lord . . . [and has been] restorid to his estate, dignite and preeminence . . . ', with restoration also, under conditions, of his lands. As a naked expression of Bray's influence, of the intangible profits of office and power, he could hardly have been more explicit.[47]

Thereafter Eaton stood testimony to conspicuous wealth. Bray built so lavishly there that the receivership of John Cutte (receiver-general of the duchy and, from 1505, under-treasurer of the Exchequer) was continually and substantially overspent. By 1501 Reynold had spent more than £1,800 on the works at Eaton and had large stocks of building material there at his death. He was aided by a gift of stone, at the cost of carriage, from the 'rector of Assherugg' (his old friend Christopher Urswick, dean of Windsor, to whose chapel Bray himself contributed so largely). The stone was probably for dressings, for the accounts suggest that the substance of the house was brick. Eaton might have compared well with Lord Cromwell's Tattershall or with Hanwell, built by William Cope, Henry VII's cofferer, Margaret Beaufort's servant, and Bray's life-long colleague, servant and friend.[48]

Eaton was the most significant land grant from Henry VII to Bray and it is entirely fitting that the parish is now distinguished by the 'feudal addition' of Bray.[49] Later grants from the King fit either into the logic of expansion of his estates, significant only against the background of the reduced liberality of Henry VII's later years, or depend on the identity of interest of King and councillor and on Bray's major office of chancellor of the duchy. Steane and Hinton in Northamptonshire, in royal hands by the death without heirs in 1489 of Lord Morley, and Ilmington, in Warwickshire, forfeited by Sir Simon Mountford, were granted to Bray in 1495–6. Next year Bray bought out Anthony Fetiplace's substantial annuity in Steane and Hinton and thus realized the full value of lands extended at over £50 p.a. While Ilmington was granted at Bray's petition, even this, by the addition over an erasure of assigns as well as heirs as a contingent remainder, indicates the symbiotic relationship between King and minister. The altered petition was not rewritten, but in a clerical intervention that was by this date unusual, Henry VII has written 'We allow the rasyng that is in this bill'.[50] By 1500 Bray was farming Pipehall in Erdington, complementing his own purchase of the other Erdington manor. Both have their origin in the murky dealings of Henry VII with the Countess of Warwick: but the grant of the farm can have come only from the crown.[51]

Grants of office continued throughout the 1490s, although the pattern changes. Many administrative tasks and local commissions carried no reward and embodied merely what was expected of a senior councillor. But local office did enhance his patronage, his status and the authority of the King. Thus Bray was regularly appointed to the bench in nine counties, though he sat habitually only in Middlesex and Surrey; the ninth county, Derby, reflects his standing within the Stanley household rather than his landholding, for he held no land in Derbyshire. His name was included in twenty-three of the thirty-one commissions issued in 1493, the major omissions being the marches (dominated by the prince's council) and the counties of the south-west.[52] Of his land offices, some, such as the stewardships of Grantham, Stamford, Ascot, Deddington and Kenilworth, the parkership of Potterspury, and the forestership of Salcey, were almost certainly granted at Bray's instance, in his own particular interests or that of a friend or protegé with whom he shared the office and the fees.[53] Others, more prestigious, were direct placements by the crown, asserting its authority through powers delegated to Bray. Clearly Bray could not exercise all these offices in person, nor could Henry long spare him from his chamber and council. The chancellorship of the duchy also called for frequent attendance in the duchy chamber at Westminster.[54] Some offices were soon regranted; in others Bray continued to devolve authority further through his use of deputies, while retaining the right to intervene if necessary and unimpaired powers of patronage.[55]

We cannot estimate the value of such offices to Bray. Custody of Carisbrooke was of some military significance, but the farm of the King's lands within the Isle of Wight officially brought Bray little above the improvements he made, for his was at the whole rate of a realistic extent. However, an inquiry in 1504 into the extortions of his deputy and his successor demonstrates the scope for illegitimate enrichment. Although Bray's patent dates only from 1495, by the King's 'speciall commaundement' he had enjoyed office and revenues since 1488, paying the farm directly to the King in his chamber.[56] In Sutton and Potton Bray received the whole of his small fee of four marks; whereas in the duchy honours of Tutbury and Bolingbroke his deputies divided the whole of his wages between themselves.[57] But profit cannot be measured by fees alone. Quite apart from the hidden douceurs that oiled the wheels of society in general, patronage equalled power, and in major offices Bray's own interests were inseparably identified with those of the King, without diminution of his own authority. In general deficiencies in the evidence render it impossible to evaluate precisely the benefit to either Reynold or his royal master. A single instance must serve to illuminate the whole. An anguished letter to Bray from Lancelot Lowther, concerning the balance of authority within the lordships of Bromfield and Yale, and the importance of maintaining tight control over appointments to offices there, well illustrates the unquantifiable benefits which could be derived by master and servant alike.[58] But office could initiate profit even at the most humble level. For example, John Etton, receiver of Bolingbroke, where Bray was steward, made Bray the supervisor of his will, with five marks 'for his labour'.[59] Moreover, where the King led, others followed, including the canons of Windsor and of Wells, the Countess of Warwick, the executors of William Trussell, or the University of Oxford, which, in 1494, appointed Bray steward for life.[60] Annuities and fees were but another expression of the same relationship, honouring the grantee as much as the donor, and bidding for a patronage which ultimately depended on Bray's major offices and standing with the King.[61] Interlinked, but more unpredictable, and at times based on a purely private and personal relationship, were his appointments as overseer or supervisor of wills. Requests to act, such as those made by the London merchants Thomas Windeout and Richard Hill, recall old friendships; Viscount Lisle spoke of Bray with warmth, but also asked for his mediation with the King; such a request, in Lisle's case, or the testamentary appointments of Bray made by Edward Story, Bishop of Chichester, or Thomas Langton, Bishop of Winchester, may well be an extension beyond the grave of the system of retaining by fee in the interests of the grantor. Whatever the origin of such requests, they provided Bray with a steady, if fluctuating, income of both specie and plate.[62] Spiritual profit enhanced Bray's earthly glories. He was, for example, granted confraternity with the monks of Durham, Canterbury and Westminster, and with the chapter of Lincoln: in the latter case, as a specific 'recompense' for his 'blessed and charitabil disposicion' in a decree made before him in the duchy chamber. Bray shared with Henry VII the benefit of prayers at St Martin in the Fields. After his death he was remembered in perpetual prayer by the wills of both Nicholas Compton and John Cutte, whom he had materially assisted in the advancement of their careers. Office as profit to the soul is most strikingly expressed in the *Magnificat* window at Great Malvern and in Bray's own chantry chapel at

Windsor, but almost his first act as lord of Eaton was to establish a chantry there, and in Bath he cooperated in similar vein with Oliver King (formerly the King's secretary), where the wealth of both and their association with Henry VII gave them access to the finest materials and workmanship and the necessary royal licence.[63]

Politically his most important casual grant, which Bray can only have accepted with the tacit approval of Henry VII himself, was his pension from the French King after 1492. Bray was treasurer of war and a signatory to the petition advising the King to make peace,[64] but his pension originates in his most ill-defined capacity, that of councillor to the King. The oft-recited words of the Milanese ambassador of 1497 express this relationship better than any modern pen may do: 'The French . . . [with Henry VII's] knowledge and consent . . . give provision to the leading men of the realm, to wit, the Lord Chamberlain, Master Braiset, Master Lovel, and as these leading satraps are very rich the provision has to be very large'.[65]

The French pension and wages of particular appointments were certainly profits of office. But no less intimately connected were the private investments for which office provided the means and, on occasion, the opportunity.

Senior office holders were well placed to bid for casualties in the King's gift, or for those grants of grace that ran 'of course' in return for the payment of a fee. Bray's two most substantial wardships belong to the early years of the reign. His patent for that of Robert Wintershill has its roots in the household of Margaret Beaufort, and the lands were administered with Bray's manor of Shere.[66] The wardship of John Writell was shared with the goldsmiths Edmund and John Shaw.[67] Bray's share of the substantial cost and profit is alike unknown, although John Shaw, whose ties to Bray were extremely close, was to marry his daughter Audrey to the ward. Bray himself came to oversee the finding and sale of the King's wards, and was in a privileged position to bid for himself and his friends.[68] His relationships with merchants encouraged investment in the shipment of wool and even shipowning. His terms as under-treasurer and treasurer reinforced a commercial dialogue pre-dating 1485. Periodically Bray obtained licences for substantial shipments of wool, and bottom in the King's own great ship, the *Sovereign*; although fragmentary evidence only of his activities now survives.[69]

But it is in relation to the active land market that the methodology adopted here has a wider application, even if here coloured by the opportunities offered to Bray. Without any major corpus of private material, the main source of information is that open to any student of late medieval land ownership: the records of the central courts at Westminster.

These are the *De Banco* rolls, the Feet of Fines, and the close rolls of Chancery, which had become primarily a register for the enrolment of private deeds.[70] Equity proceedings and 'ancient deeds', speculatively searched, produce useful sidelights. Some ground work is necessary. First, caveats must be applied to the adversarial language of the records. Land was conveyed by means of legal fictions: writs of right *precipe in capite* until about 1487–8; thereafter, for reasons still awaiting investigation, the writ almost universally used was *disseisin in le post*. Both led, by leave of the court, to a legal settlement embodied in the foot of fine. Variations from these formulae tend to indicate a genuine, rather than a collusive, suit. Second, the process is commonly obfuscated by enfeoffments to use.[71] To make progress in interpreting the records, one must first identify the feoffees commonly used by the beneficiary from charter evidence or by observing the repetition of particular groupings of names in the legal records. This is most involved in Shere, where the feoffees sued against Bray himself (as the tenant in possession) and in Barnsbury, where Reynold had seisin as a feoffee of Lord Berners. In the Shere case Bray called Ormond (the true vendor) to warranty, thus effecting the actual transfer of title; in Barnsbury the conveyance was further complicated by a suit for detinue of deeds against Thomas Bourgchier. Both times the common law fictions are clarified by charter evidence.[72] For the biographer of Bray the preliminary identification of feoffees is particularly complex. His earliest feoffees spring from his service to Margaret Beaufort before 1485 and continue sole until about 1488, when their numbers expand and the names change.[73] Yet, even though there are only two main groups of feoffees, divided in point of time, their company was not entirely constant and there are unusual features. Contrary to normal usage, the *cestui que use* was seldom given as Bray but instead as William Smith, successively clerk, Bishop of Lichfield, and, from 1495, Bishop of Lincoln. This would not matter if all fines allegedly to the use of Smith were *ipso facto* to the use of Bray: but such is not the case. Smith, like Bray, moved from the service of Margaret Beaufort to Henry VII's, maintaining his dual allegiance all his life, and even the expanded group of feoffees have a common background in Margaret's service. These variables make it difficult, at times, to distinguish when the feoffees were acting for Bray from those to the use of some other party. Fines involving John Shaw, and Margaret herself, are particular instances of a wider problem. We may wonder whether civil power combined with at times civic wealth, but speculation leaves the conundrum unresolved.

Contemporaries as well as historians were confused. Thus Remenham was included in the 1511 division of Bray's estates even though the books of Henry VII's treasurer of the chamber suggests that it was a royal purchase intended as an endowment to Westminster Abbey. This is supported by the names of the feoffees and by arrangements made by a recognizance designed to secure the transfer of title.[74] The conveyance of Wandsworth in 1502, although not to Bray's usual feoffees, was specifically said to be to his use. The circumstances suggest a political context or a mortgage, and the title to the manor was subsequently disputed between the Abbot of Westminster and William, Lord Sandys, one of Bray's lineal heirs.[75] Edmund Bray claimed Drayton in Middlesex, alienated by Reynold to Margaret Beaufort,[76] and by 1501 she held Boxworth (Cambs.), acquired in 1496 by Bray's usual feoffees afforced only by the attorney Gregory Skipwith, who also acted for Bray at Battlesden the same year.[77] The evidence for the conveyance in 1494 of Irchester (Northants.) suggests that Bray was to be the beneficiary, but by 1511 William Cope and his wife had seisin. Although the deed of sale signed in May 1490 by Lord Dudley for Shepperton (Middx) identifies Bray as purchaser, the fine was to an augmented group of Bray's feoffees, and the true use and immediate descent is uncertain. By 1505 the manor was held by the goldsmith Bartholomew Reed.[78]

The real problem in listing the lands accumulated by Bray, or by anybody whose estate came by purchase rather than inheritance, is that there are no cross-checks to serve as a controlment to the legal record. An incomplete list appears in the 1510 settlement that divided the inheritance between William Sandys and Edmund Bray consequent to litigation in the council chamber.[79] It ignores some (but not all) lands acquired before 1497, perhaps partly assigned by the terms of a will of 1497, which is now lost, as is the will made (according to Edmund Bray) in 1500.[80] Small properties may escape mention altogether. We know of a tenement in Princes Risborough only because a bill of repairs survives in Bray's correspondence: the evidence obtains circumstantial confirmation from the later distraint of Edmund Bray for suit of court.[81] Land in Suffolk is known of primarily because Bray sued in Chancery for seisin; still obscure, they are identified more closely in 1510. Again, from circumstantial evidence, we may guess that Bray's intercession for a mortmain licence formed part of the purchase price.[82] Parcels of lands added to individual manors might be too small to merit legal proceedings in the Westminster courts. Such purchases are recorded in the manorial accounts for Shere, 1485–93, and in the declared accounts for Eaton 1496–1500, but are otherwise entirely lost.[83]

Such heavy dependence on the formal record obscures mens' motives for entering the property market. Land was the most cherished and most visible status symbol in fifteenth-century society, and the land market was hedged about with legal restrictions, particularly in relation to inherited lands, yet it flourished in despite. When the sources are restricted, attempts to identify the reasons behind a particular sale rely upon circumstantial evidence open to a diversity of interpretation. Inevitably the result is compromise. Reynold Bray, with his long experience of the difficulties of conciliar arbitration, would have recognized the historian's dilemma and been the first to acknowledge that judgements based on compromise and subjective interpretation remain open to question and of doubtful longevity. But that bleak assessment need not invalidate the enterprise.

It would be tedious to provide a detailed inventory of Bray's entre-preneurial efforts. Even an abbreviated catalogue presents an awesome level of activity, suggests patterns within the expansion of the estates, and reveals quirks in the evidence. If we leave aside those investments already considered, whether by purchase or crown grant, Bray's speculations in the market in land fall into two main periods. The first, to 1495, is politically inspired. Office provided wealth, opportunity, influence and the subtle leverage to mobilize the due processes of the civil law. That element did not disappear after 1495, but there are more signs of market forces at work, and an activity that was sometimes hectic. No less than nine manors were purchased in 1499, for example, and the same number in 1502, though some were small and insignificant. And in some cases Bray trimmed his sails close, whether in genuine ignorance or in a full knowledge discounted in the arrogance of power, to the limits of legality, driving bargains for an unquiet title that in two cases at least remained to trouble or disinherit his heirs. The end product was an estate, almost all of it acquired by patent or purchase rather than inheritance, stretching along a belt fifteen miles either side of the present M1, from Cottesbrooke (Northants.) in the north through Pavenham and Bedford (Beds.), to Eaton, Ledburn and Mentmore (Beds. and Bucks.) in the south; thence along the Chilterns and the Icknield way, taking Great Milton (Oxon.) as its most westerly point until the line curved in to a group circling (can it be accident?) the queen's manor of Bray (Berks.) and found its epicentre in Windsor, the focus of Bray's last years. Estates were scattered as far west as Somerset; north to Erdington near Birmingham (Warw.); and into East Anglia in the east. There was a large, less coherent, agglomeration in Sussex and the counties of the south, houses in London, and the Surrey lands based on Shere, greatly expanded by the next generation.

Two names stand out from the first period of Bray's purchases. William Berkeley, Earl of Nottingham, Earl Marshal and, from 1489, Marquis of Berkeley, agreed sales and exchanges of land with Bray associated with, and dependent upon, his arrangements he made with Henry VII; nor, indeed, was Bray the only councillor to help pluck this self-proffered sacrificial chicken. Thomas Stillington, 'cousin' and heir of the disgraced

Bishop of Bath, may have had little option but to concur in his own disherison.[84] Both series of transactions point up the difficulties of dependence on plea roll evidence. We do not know the price or, for certain, the reasons for Nottingham's conveyance to Bray of the Bedfordshire manor of Bromham in mid-1488. Plea rolls are concerned only with the due rendering of proper legal forms, not with the human negotiations concealed by the language of the law. The indenture setting out the terms by which Stotfold and the barony of Bedford were transferred to Bray is enrolled among the charters at the rear of the *De Banco* roll, where the membranes are most vulnerable to damage. It is a fascinating and exceptionally detailed document. But water or the delicate palates of some eighteenth-century rodents have nosed out some of the most essential phrases, expunging them from the record and thus from the memory of man.[85] The parties to whom Thomas Stillington in 1491 conveyed Great Stambridge in Essex include the attorney John Berdefeld and the merchant Henry Colet in addition to Bray's usual feoffees. The true descent was to elude identification by more than one puzzled jury as well as the modern historian. The manor fitted ill within any geographical logic in Bray's estates. By 1504 it was in the possession of the London goldsmith, John Shaw, a feoffee and executor of Bray. The inquisition *post mortem* on Shaw records Bray as the vendor.[86]

When we find that the deeds for the sale of lands in Kensington and for the manor of Haynes (Beds.) were acknowledged by Berkeley in Chancery on the same day as other deeds by which Henry VII allowed him to secure property for the performance of his will, we need hardly doubt that the events were connected, particularly as the King licenced the alienation to Bray. Two terms later Bromham was added and in 1489 Mawneys (Essex), which was almost immediately exchanged, with the payment of a differential of 400 marks, for the manor of Stotfold and the more prestigious barony of Bedford: all the lands and the castle, that is, but not the title of baron nor the advowsons of abbeys, priories and nunneries thereunto appertaining.[87] Haynes and Bedford came encumbered with fees; but in Haynes Bray bought off part of his obligation, while the annuities charged on Bedford were unlikely to deter his continued interest. They were to the lawyer, John Mordaunt, a member of Bray's own estate council and his successor as chancellor of the duchy; to the king's solicitor, Andrew Dymmock, and the king's attorney, James Hobart; and to the rising lawyer and king's serjeant, John Fisher.[88] Not surprisingly in 1492 Bray sought and secured confirmation of his title from Berkeley's right heirs, Thomas, Earl of Surrey, now slowly working himself back to favour, and Maurice Berkeley, who was to suffer severely by his disinheritance. Indeed, in 1499 Maurice Berkeley, the marquis's brother, resold Mawneys to Bray at a time when he and Surrey sought from Henry livery of the Cokesay inheritance; and in July 1502 Berkeley was sufficiently desperate, or perhaps merely sufficiently perspicacious, to confirm Edmund Dudley in the reversion of the manor of Findon (purchased by Dudley from Richard Guildford, who had obtained it from the marquis) in return for a promise 'to be of his councell in all such causes and materes as the seid lord shall have a doo consernyng the lernyng of the seid Edmund without fee or reward to be had . . . but only at the plesour of the seid lord'.[89]

In Stillington's case it is perhaps not too fanciful to see Reynold Bray, Richard Fox and Robert Sherborne as the fiscal gaolers of his errant kinsman. They were identified as administrators of the bishop's possessions by juries responding to writs issued for multure and Bray's eventual discharge by the Exchequer does not prove this to be untrue.[90] Within a month of the bishop's death, 15 May 1491, Thomas had sold Bray the manors of Great Stambridge (Essex) and Marylebone (Middx.) at approximately two-thirds of the market value. Stambridge was subsequently alienated, but in 1496 Marylebone was leased to Thomas Hobson, Lady Margaret's auditor, for 20 marks p.a., and sold to him in 1499.[91] In 1492 Stillington sold Bray yet other lands, in Paddington and elsewhere in Middlesex, at a still more favourable rate. It may have been an arbitration award by Chief Justice Hussey and others that prompted Stillington and another claimant Robert Cotton to make over their title to Bray, who alienated the lands to Margaret Beaufort as part of her intended endowment to the King's chantry at Westminster. The degree of compulsion emerges in 1493, when Bray pursued Stillington to the point of outlawry on a debt of 515 marks.[92]

After 1494 the simple correlation between office, profit and wealth *and* opportunity, investment and land breaks down. Bray's income now came from many sources other than office. Estate expansion acquired its own momentum, as he bought or sold lands, or added small parcels to manors retained in hand. He bought where he could, from those in debt or without heirs, as well as the politically indigent. Bray's own focus shifted towards Windsor: he clearly welcomed the chance to buy and consolidate the fractured manor of Clewer (within the modern boundary of the town) in a series of conveyances that may have been in the interests of all the parties concerned.[93]

Bray's acquisitions read like a sonorous roll call of the English countryside. Most were 'made sure' by concords reached in the court of common pleas. By 1499 Reynold Bray stood at the height of his powers. He remained exceptionally close to the King, particularly as a president of the nascent council learned in the law, an intimate and increasingly influential manifestation of the King's council. The political element remained and indeed the council learned gave Bray a further power base for his own enrichment, available for use without derogation to the interests of the King.[94]

In 1494 Bray purchased from the childless Henry Lord Grey of Codnor the Northamptonshire manors of Newbottle and Charlton, in a complex series of conveyances intended to secure his title without further interruption.[95] Drayton (Middx) required concords with various parties over three years to secure Bray's title; and the conveyance of Irchester (Northants) was probably to Bray's immediate use.[96] In 1495 Bray assured his title to Eaton; obtained from Robert Wright, the manor of Erdington (Warw.), and, from the King, Steane and Hinton; although the preservation at Westminster of an account for Erdington 1492–3 with liveries to an unnamed lord may indicate an earlier transfer of title.[97] In 1496, besides Ilmington, he bought lands in Medmenham (Bucks.) and the small manor of Knyll in Tarring (Sussex); secured from the senior branch of the Hussey family recognition of his title to Standen Hussey and lands in Harting; and exchanged lands with Thomas Oxenbridge, thereby acquiring Battlesden (Beds.), a useful staging post between the Eaton manors and those lands centred on the town of Bedford. The exchange appears to revise an indenture of the previous year and may thus be connected with the heavy recognizance for allegiance in which Oxenbridge was bound in 1495. It hints at continuing legal difficulties over parcels of the Hussey inheritance. Later additions to Battlesden enable us to see Bray's own estate council at work and to see how his privileged position enabled him to employ duchy officers in his own private service.[98]

In 1498 he bought Cottesbrooke manor (Northants.) and lands in Bedfordshire from John Markham, taking collateral security on two Lincolnshire manors; at the same time Markham was also selling land to Lord Daubeney, and Humphrey Banaster. Is this the same Markham who, little more than a year later, was indicted for murder in the King's books, 'which is of greate substans as Sir R. Bray can tell'?[99] As lord of Cottesbrooke, Bray became founder of Pipewell Abbey and he sought from King Henry the franchises of free warren and frankpledge within the manor.[100] 1499 was his annus mirabilis. His most important purchase was a valuable group of lands centred on Windsor, which brought him the manors of Clewer, Brocas, Buntingbury, Dedworth Maunsell and Foxley rated, in 1546, at over £85 p.a. The purchase was exceptionally complex. In November 1499 Bray brought from the childless William Brocas the manors and lands of which Brocas was the *caput* and gained immediate possession by buying out the life tenants. Clewer and Foxley were a tangle of legal rights, complicated by the involvement of Charles Rippon, a household man whose political future was now uncertain. The taint of treason and a riot involving him and John Preston (vendor of Remenham) suggests he was not a willing partner. His interests were protected in the short term and Rippon was allowed a lease in the small manor of Foxley, an inducement to sell used by Bray on at least one other occasion. Suits against William Skulle and John Rykes can be explained as buying out co-parcenors, although Rykes, like Rippon, was involved in the miasma of treason around Edmund de la Pole, for which both were indicted in 1502 and for which Rippon suffered the ultimate penalty. For the aged and childless Thomas Danvers sale of his rights may have been a part of the pre-testamentary division of his estates.[101] Deeper undercurrents run also beneath the re-purchase of Mawneys.[102]

Edgcote (Northants.) is superficially uncontroversial, although the names John and James Clarell suggest a link with Margaret Beaufort and of Thomas Hasilwood with Richard Empson. Combined with the alleged earlier exclusion of a rightful heir, it may be that Bray bought out a disputed title as part of a generally acceptable settlement. In May 1498 Henry VII himself advanced Bray money for building works there.[103] This payment and Henry VII's visit of 16 September 1498 point up a problem that we meet writ large with both Great Milton (Oxon.) and Broadwater (Sussex). In all three the formal legal process post-dates Bray's occupation. Great Milton and Broadwater were purchased from Sir William Radmyld, who retained a life interest by a prior agreement in 1497 with John Shaw, to whom the manors were to revert. Yet even the final concord of 1503 fails to give unambiguous evidence that Great Milton belonged to Bray and a deed acknowledged in 1499 in king's bench by Radmyld's widow (daughter of Elizabeth Duchess of Norfolk) suggests a joint use, whereas a court roll shows Bray's tenure dating from at least April 1499 and the rental was renewed at his first court. Broadwater, where he first bought land in 1496, followed a similar descent, but may not have come to Bray until late 1501 or early 1502.[104] Hinton Pipard (Wilts. and Berks.) reasserts the Windsor connection. It cost Bray four days meat and drink to the vendor and the mayor of Windsor besides the purchase price.[105] The conveyance of Great Rissington (Glos.) and the purchase of the advowson of St Leonard's Hospital in Bedford (to which Bray immediately presented Hugh Oldham) complete a frenetic year.[106]

In 1500 Bray acquired a manor in Weston Turville (Bucks.), part of the Cokesay inheritance; another part, Coldicote in Gloucestershire, was simultaneously purchased from the same parties by Richard Empson.[107] Westhay (Beds.) came, like Bedford Hospital, ultimately from the impecunious Thomas Bassingbourn. In Husborne Crawley we again encounter an uncertain use. A feoffment of 1499 was said to be to the use of Humphrey Coningsby, a senior lawyer who was a Bray feoffee; yet charters of 1500 and 1501 specifically name Bray and it was certainly he whom the Exchequer sued for distraint of homage. The manor was assigned in 1510 to Edmund Bray.[108]

Two purchases show more clearly the darker side of office-holding. Late in 1500 Bray purchased the Somerset manor of Eastham. But after his death one of his feoffees, William Cope, King's cofferer, claimed it, alleging that Bray had bought only an annuity and that he, Cope, had purchased the manor itself from John Hayes, when Hayes, suspected of treason, was in his custody and for whom he had sued to the King for pardon. Eastham, by this account, fell to Cope as part payment of the 500 marks required by the King to buy his grace. Although Hayes's title may itself have been doubtful, there are other parallels to Cope's story, and the inquisition *post mortem* returned after Cope's death agrees with his version of events. The wrangle over title survived both Cope and Bray, and was unresolved more than thirty years into the sixteenth century.[109] Even more explicit is the background to Bray's acquisition in 1502 of the small manor of East Haddon in Northamptonshire by processes which reflect credit on none of the parties concerned. When Edmund Bray was sued for it in the court of requests, the father of the original vendor alleged the false augmentation of the terms of the deed of sale and that the style of manor was 'colorably' put into the fine. The depositions further charge that Reynold obtained the manor only by virtue of 'hys myte, power and grette extorte'. The council found against Edmund Bray in 1521.[110]

In 1501–2 minor parcels of land were added to the house of Bray's birth. Bray never lost interest in his Worcestershire lands, infinitesimally small in value though they were. His sister Lucy had oversight of the lands and literary evidence shows how far his might eased his purchase and deterred possible rivals.[111]

His last two years show no let up in his expansionist mood. New acquisitions include the eponymous manor of Bernersbury (Barnsbury, Middx.) acquired from Lord Berners, a Stafford client, and Kempston Daubeney, acquired in a tripartite exchange shortly after the return of a commission of concealments relating to the manor.[112] Boveney and Dorney (Bucks.) and Cruchfield (Berks.) were acquired from John Wayte, a surety with Charles Rippon in 1498 for further conveyance of Remen-ham.[113] If the evidence of stained glass no longer extant be allowed, Burnham and West Town (Bucks.) were more than a passing fancy, and in Pavenham he bought out both the reversioner and the tenant in possession.[114] Thirteen other conveyances transferred title to Bray for lands in five counties, in addition to the indenture concerning Wandsworth and a process involving Thomas Lucy, of which the details are now lost.[115] Again, we may speculate, was the purchase of Charlton in

Hopgras dependent on the purchase by the vendor, John Isbury, of a licence for alienation in mortmain from Henry VII?

The most important acquisition cannot be dated with precision. Broadwater and its attendant manors may have yielded £90 p.a. It came, like Great Milton, from William Radmyld. Albourne, Beverington and Lancing were exchanged, with other lands, for Kempston Daubeney. In Broadwater itself we have a glimpse of Bray as parochial seigneur, giving rabbits for the patronal feast of the parish church, engaging in remedial building works, looking for the best tenants; and, most interestingly, though we cannot be certain whether Bray or Shaw was the moving spirit, searching in public and private records for evidence of ancient rights.[116] It may also instance a rare clash of interests with Henry VII. Rather than alienate his own estates to Westminster, Henry assigned over £30,000 to buy land. Bray's exchange with Bergavenny was certainly a hollow sham, for Bergavenny was required to assign his share to Westminster. Only two weeks before his death, Bray and his feoffees obtained a mortmain licence including Broadwater and, more obviously, Remenham: yet his will specifically devised the Radmyld lands to his nephews, rather than to the corporate good of the Tudor soul.[117]

In this hurricane of activity, much of it in the last four years of Bray's life, it is understandably difficult to draw up a definitive list of his estates. Both the manner and the rapidity of their accumulation left tensions unresolved at his death. Although lacking heirs of his own body, he clearly felt a strong sense of dynasty. Not only did he will the bulk of his estates to the sons of his brother John, but he also provided for their marriages. The eldest, Edmund, may have married in Bray's lifetime according to the terms of an agreement made in 1497 with Sir John Norbury. Edmund was to take the lion's share (or so Bray intended) of the purchased lands. More interestingly, Edmund's younger brothers were to marry the heirs general of his wife: the daughters and heirs of Katherine's sister Constance and her husband Henry Lovell. They were given a remainder right in the purchased lands, but were to take all the Hussey inheritance, plus the valuable manors of Chelsea and Broadwater, with remainder each to each 'as long as any of the same heirs males of my name and bloode shall endure'. To this end Reynold purchased from Henry VII the far from valuable wardship of Agnes and Elizabeth Lovell. But although Bray paid Henry at least £140 as the whole, or the final portion, of the purchase price, and the warrant was duly signed by the King and delivered into the Chancery, death intervened before the fees of the hanaper were paid, or the patent enrolled.[118]

Death broke the bonds of office and obligation and Henry VII proved ruthless in the aftermath. He resumed the wardship, selling it to Edmund Dudley on the excuse that Bray's grant had been found 'insufficient and voide in the lawe' and then recommended disingenuously to Dudley that he should resell the wardship to Bray's executors 'to thentent that the said mynde and last will of the said Sir Reynold may be performed and take effect aftre his said entent'. Although Bray's feoffees indeed repurchased the wardship, transferring to Dudley the manors of Newbottle and Charlton at a loss to fund the 1,000 marks purchase price, Bray's mind was never fully performed. By 1509 Agnes was married to John, son of Richard Empson, one of the feoffees, and Elizabeth to Anthony, son of Andrew Windsor, Dudley's first brother-in-law.[119] William Sandys may have taken advantage of the minority of John Bray's sons to press for a share of Reynold's estate rather than the reversionary interest allowed him by the will. Edmund lost part of his portion to Sandys, but, in 1510, divided with him those lands destined for his brothers.[120] The King himself, in Dudley's words, so managed matters that 'the executors of Mr Bray were hardlie dealt with at dyvers tymes'.[121] They not only lost the wardship, but were fined £800 for alleged commercial misdealing by Bray and paid an even larger fine, of 5,000 marks, for a general pardon.[122]

Reynold's death at a time of royal celebration leaves no immediate trace in the records. But although the bond of office was now broken, and Henry VII in his turn creamed off the profits, the King did not quite forget his deeper obligation. It is there in general terms in his will, when he acknowledged his gratitude to all those who had made him King. More profoundly and more personally and after any direct obligation had ceased, he expressed it in 1507 in a payment for a trental of masses for Katherine Bray's soul.[123]

Just how rich was Reynold Bray, and how much profit did he derive from office? The question is not one which can be satisfactorily answered, primarily for the reasons outlined in the introduction to this paper. We cannot even place a value on the wages of office. Fees for major offices are generally specified in the patent, but for lesser grants the patent often refers only to the accustomed wages. We are thus dependent on the uncertain survival of detailed evidence, complicated in the case of Bray by the numerous occasions on which the patent incorporated a joint grant. We cannot hope to quantify the hidden benefits, or trace the full extent of the commonwealth of interest which lead others to follow Henry VII's example and retain Bray by office or by fee. *The Great Chronicle* offers a revealing backhanded compliment in its epitaph of Bray:

> which by his lyfe lyvid not withowth much haterede and many an unkeynd and untrewe report of many of the kyngys subgectys . . . [but he] . . . dyd bettyr than he wold make countenaunce ffor, and

therewith reffucid gyfftys of valu and took oonly mete or drynk, and where he took, the gyver was suyr of a ffreend and a speciall solicytour of theyr matyer.[124]

Fear and detestation is no less a measure of influence.[125]

When we look at Bray's lands we cannot apply a simple multiplier to their purchase price (even where known) to derive an annual value. Dugdale, who cites no evidence, asserts that the post-1497 purchases alone were worth more than 1,000 marks a year; McFarlane, with typical thoroughness, totalled more than £5,400 for bargains whose entry on the close rolls (to 1500) made mention also of the purchase price.[126] Between 1485 and 1503 Bray spent over £10,000 on buying land. Over this, other lands, acquired by inheritance, purchase or gift, were worth in excess of £420 p.a. Of others again (although much the lesser part) we know neither the value nor the purchase price. Nor can a multiplier be applied to Katherine Bray's dowerlands, for they were considerably less than a one-third share. There may be good reason for this. Reynold and Katherine had an equal interest in seeing the conditions of his will fulfilled. His nephews were to be married to her nieces, and, in name at least, unite the Hussey lands. Both took an interest in Jesus College, where Katherine's munificence outstripped his, and, in their prestigious building works at Windsor. If Bray willed lands worth 40 marks for the maintenance of perpetual alms in the chapel, Katherine matched this interest with equal pragmatism, leaving goods 'as nede shall requyre' primarily to the repair of the highway at Eton and 'the ordynaunce of house of eseament' for the canons: a bequest founded, no doubt, on Bray's assignment to her of half his plate.[127] There are more precise pointers. Bray customarily paid the whole purchase price of land within a very short period of the signing of indentures for its sale. He offered the greatest contribution of any layman other than Margaret Beaufort herself to the benevolence of 1491. Although Bray's £500 is nearly matched by £400 from Thomas Lovell (treasurer of the chamber and chancellor of the Exchequer), and a similar amount from Lord Treasurer Dynham, such offerings contrast with £68 paid at days by Lord Willoughby de Broke, the king's steward of household, or the £40 proffered by Richard Empson, attorney of the duchy.[128] Besides Eaton, Bray was building at Newbottle and Edgcote, and our evidence is woefully incomplete. His public benefactions, too, were munificent. He funded works on a massive scale at Windsor, and seems to have shared in the costs of building at Malvern, Bath and Jesus College, besides lesser works.[129] After Bray's death Henry VII demanded the enormous sum of 5,000 marks for a pardon. What is immediately significant is that the executors called the King's bluff, and more than half this fine had been paid by February 1505. A further 1,200 marks obtained their discharge from prosecution for alleged customs offences: Henry required collateral security of lands worth £290 p.a. for the payment, but forgave them 400 marks of the principal.[130] Office, we may reasonably conclude, brought Bray wealth as its most visible outward profit.

Despite this undoubted success story, we are, perhaps, left to wonder why the rewards were not even greater. Bray had built up a landed estate easily sufficient to support a title, yet remained a commoner. In 1501 he was admitted into the exclusive ranks of the knights of the Garter, though we may speculate on the pedigree of his election.[131] He kept estate in London, and peers paid him court, but he did not join their ranks. The answer may not lie simply in Henry's parsimony with honour and the *Great Chronicle* may offer us a clue. For all Henry VII's chequered upbringing and colourless reputation, he was sensitive to occasion and to the nuances of the cursus of honour. Bray, we are told, was 'playn and rowth in spech'.[132] The inventory of his goods (although too defective to be good evidence) gives no hint of cultured or chivalric interests, but he was not untouched by learning. If a chantry priest was recommended to him primarily for his ability to cast accounts, Bray patronized both Pembroke and Jesus colleges; Hugh Oldham and William Smith were among his friends; John Colet, son of his old friend Henry, was to be his wife's executor; and Thomas Linacre attended his deathbed.[133] There is a similar ambiguity in his war record. Despite the large contingent he took to France, his indenture deleted the duty of personal service, and Bray travelled there in a primarily civilian capacity; he went to Exeter in 1497 as much a councillor as man of war; but the bloody battle of Blackheath saw him win his banner and augmentation of his arms.[134] Treasurers of England in general commanded a peerage, spiritual or lay, but Bray held office for less than five months. It was he and the King who enhanced the always prestigious chancellorship of the duchy. Bray's younger and more martial heirs met a youthful and more warlike King. William Sandys was raised to the peerage in 1523; Edmund Bray, a younger man, in 1529. But Henry VIII was yet his father's son. When William Sandys expended his wealth in the King's service (and in speculation in ex-monastic property) and died in debt to the crown, Henry VIII prised the Clewer complex, inherited from Bray, from Thomas Lord Sandys in part settlement of the debt.[135]

But for Reynold Bray himself, the profits of office have their lasting monument. He lies beneath his chantry at Windsor. Above him, his badge of the hemp brake, carved in stone, and round about the heavy symbolism of the monarchy and house of Beaufort, whom he had served so well. Thus ossified and in sculpted form, Bray's profits of office are remembered into the twentieth century.[136]

The Lands of Reynold Bray

	COUNTY	ACQUIRED	BRAY/ SANDYS	SOLD
Haynes	Beds	1487	B	1564/80
Eaton Bray		1488/90	B	1623
Totternhoe		1488/90	B	
Houghton Regis		1488/90	B	1566
Bromham		1488	B	1565
Bedford		1490	B	1569
Stotfold		1490	B	1547
Battlesden		1496	B	1556
Hinwick		1498	B	1566
Husborne Crawley		1499	B	1566
Westhey (in Higham Gobion)		1500	B	by 1559
St Leonards, Bedford (advowson)		1499	B	
Pavenham		1502–3	B	by 1594
Kempston Daubeney		1503	B	1569
North Standen (Standen House)	Berks	1478	B	1533
South Moreton		1488	B	c. 1556
Brocas (in Clewer)		1499	S	1546
Buntingbury (in Winkfield)		1499	S	1546
Dedworth Maunsell		1499	S	1546
Clewer		1499	S	1546
Foxley (in Bray)		1499	S	1639
Cruchfield (in Bray)		1502	S	1577
Haywards (in Sonning)		1502	S	1609
Remenham		1503	S	1612
Buckhurst				1577–8
Ledburn	Bucks	1488/90	B	
Mentmore		1488/90	B	1563
Great Marlowe (land)		1494	B	
Medmenham		1496	B	1537
Weston Turville		1500	B	1529
Boveney		1502	B	1529
Dorney		1502	B	by 1529
Burnham		1502	B	1529
West Town in Burnham		1502	B	1529

	COUNTY	ACQUIRED	BRAY/ SANDYS	SOLD
Boxworth *alias* Overhall	Cambs	1496	–	by 1501
Great Stambridge	Essex	1491	–	by 1503
Mawneys (in Romford)		1489	–	1490
		1499	B	by 1523
Great Rissington	Glos	1498	S	1571
Queen Hoo (in Tewin)	Herts	1502	S	1536
Chelsea	Middx	1486	S	1535
Kensington *alias* Nottingbarons		1488	B	1519
Shepperton		1490	–	by 1503
Marylebone		1491	–	1499
Paddington, etc. (land)		1492	–	1501
West Drayton		1494–6	–	1501
Barnsbury		1502	S	1540
Tyburn		1503	–	1503
Newbottle	Nhants	1494	–	1505
Charlton		1494	–	1505
Irchester		1494	–	by 1511
Steane		1495	S	1551
Hinton		1495	S	1551
Edgcote		c. 1498		1535
Cottesbrooke		1498		1549
East Haddon		1502	B	1521?
Horley	Oxon	?		life tenancy
Great Milton		1499	B	1539
Kidlington (land)		1497–99		
Eastham (in Crewkerne)	Som	1500	B	1532
Flood	Suth	1483	S	1612
Freefolk		1488	–	1503

	COUNTY	ACQUIRED	BRAY/ SANDYS	SOLD
Carisbrooke and Isle of Wight		1488		life tenancy
St Mary's, Bury (land)	Suff	1497	B	
Claygate	Surrey	1486		life tenancy
Shere		1486/95	B	–
Wandsworth		1502	S	disputed
Harting	Sussex	c. 1478	B	by 1520
'Derndale'		?1478	–	1496
West Tarring		1496		
Broadwater		1501/2	S	1605?
Albourne		1501/2	–	1503/4
Beverington		1501/2	–	1503/4
Lancing		1501/2		1503/4
Erdington	Warw	1495	B	1530
Ilmington		1496	S	1550
Hinton Pipard	Wilts	1499	S	1606
Hopgras (in Hungerford)	Wilts (now Berks)	1501	S	1606
St John in Bedwardine (land)	Worcs	?	B	1501–2

Some small parcels of land have been omitted.

Notes

1. This article has incurred many debts: to the staffs of the archives cited, but particularly to Christine Reynolds and the late Nicholas McMichael of the Westminster Abbey Muniment Room; to those of the Public Record Office; to the late Prof. Charles Ross; to Dr Carole Rawcliffe, Dr Rowena Archer and Dr Michael Hicks who read, criticized, and supplied additional material for earlier versions. Without the unflagging encouragement of Dr Hicks it would not have seen the light of day, and I owe him especial thanks.
2. WAM 5472 ff.20v, 29, 31 et seq; WAM 12181 f.28v.
3. O. Barron, 'The Brays of Shere', *The Ancestor*, vi (1903), pp. 2–3; T. Habington, *Survey of Worcestershire*, J. Amphlett (ed.), (Worcs. Hist. Soc. 2 vols 1895–9), ii. p. 130.
4. A.F. Pollard, *The Reign of Henry VII from Contemporary Sources* (3 vols, 1913–14), i. p. 153; *The Anglica Historia of Polydore Vergil*, D. Hay (ed.), (CS 3rd ser. 1950), p. 133.

5. W. Dugdale, *The Baronage of England* (2 vols 1676), ii. pp. 303–4, 311; GEC ii. pp. 287–9; BL MS Add 32482 A 24 (brass of Jane Halliwell).
6. *CFR 1485–1509*, No. 755.
7. Below, pp. 156–7; for the later history of the title, see Barron, 'Brays of Shere', pp. 6, 8–9; GEC ii. p. 286.
8. WAM 5472, WAM 12181–12190, passim; WAM 5479**; WAM 5472* f.2.
9. 'Brays of Shere', pp. 2–3; *Leland's Itinerary in England and Wales*, L. Toulmin-Smith (ed.), (5 vols 1964), v. 229; given circumstantial support by WAM 5472 f.41v, WAM 16026, 16051; SC 6/Hen VII/1843. Bray's father leased the manor of Laughern, within the parish: information which I owe to Mr. G. Baugh.
10. WAM 5472 f.27; SC 6/Hen VII/1843; CP 25(1)/207/35 No. 1.
11. GEC vii. p. 11. The outside dates are provided by Bray's account books, which record in 1475 receipts from Harting and a loan to his then or future brother in-law, and by the 1478 division of the estates: WAM 5479**B; below, n. 13.
12. E 101/414/14 f.8; below p. 142.
13. WAM 5479** B; C 237/53/168; C 1/84/20.
14. PROB 11/5 ff.34–34v; SJC D56.186.
15. The portrait, *c.* 1500, is little more than a clothes hanger for his arms; and is in the *Magnificat* window of Great Malvern Priory; see also *Two Tudor Books of Arms*, J. Foster (ed.), (1914), pp. 226, 237. BL MS Add 5833 f.67v reports 'somewhat different' arms from Great Milton and Burnham, without further description: they are likely to be the arms in the post-1497 version. For 1485, see *A Book of Knights Banneret, etc.*, W.C. Metcalfe (ed.), (1885), p. 12.
16. M.M. Condon, 'Bosworth Field: a Footnote to a Controversy', *The Ricardian*, vii (1987), p. 364; Metcalfe, *Knights*, pp. 9–12; goods at Blackfriars and Coldharbour in 1503, E 154/2/10 ff.4–6.
17. R. Somerville, *History of the Duchy of Lancaster*, i (1953), p. 392; DL 28/6/1A f.7; J.C. Sainty, *Officers of the Exchequer* (List and Index Society suppl.ser. 1983), p. 199; E 36/125 f.7; M.M. Condon, 'An Anachronism with Intent? Henry VII's Council Ordinance of 1491/2', *Kings and Nobles in the Later Middle Ages*, R.A. Griffiths and J.W.Sherborne (eds), (Gloucester 1986), p. 234. Despite Sainty loc.cit., the *Handbook of British Chronology*, E.B. Fryde and others (eds), (1986), p. 107, is incorrect, and omits also Henry VII's first treasurer Archbishop Rotheram, E 405/75 mm. 1–3.
18. E 401/955, 959; GC 240; cf. *Materials* ii. pp. 158–9.
19. *The Letters of Sir Reynold Bray*, M.M. Condon and D.J. Guth (eds), (in preparation).
20. See *CPR 1485–94*, pp. 54, 59, 64, 114, 127, 139, 145; Somerville, i. p. 593; E 159/265 recorda Mich rot.23. Not all fees have been traced and summed and Eaton, where Bray's actual income may have been out of all proportion to his fees, is a particular problem, see below, p. 144.
21. SC 6/Hen VII/1843.
22. *Survey of London: The Parish of Chelsea*, W.H. Godfrey (ed.), i. p. 72; T. Faulkner, *Historical and Topographical Description of Chelsea and its Environs* (2 vols 1829), i. pp. 308–11.
23. CP 40/897 rot.355, 359; ibid. rot.cart. rot.1–1d; BL Add Ch 70849.
24. E 368/259 recorda Trin.rot.9–9d, citing pardon of 7 March.
25. CP 40/897 rot.cart. rot.1d; SC 6/Hen VII/1843; CP 25(1)/152/100 Nos. 17, 48, 51.
26. CP 40/897 rot.cart. rot.1d.
27. WAM 16355; CP 40/897 rot.359.
28. Below, p. 155; G. Baker, *History and Antiquities of the County of Northampton* (2 vols 1822–30), ii. p. 162; J. Bridges, *History and Antiquities of Northamptonshire* (2 vols Oxford, 1791), i. p. 504; *Feudal Aids* iv. p. 8 (from E 164/17); Metcalfe, *Knights*, p. 27; BL Seal CLXVIII.106 : cf. DL 25/2288; BL MS Harl 6157 f.4; WAM MS 43, an antiphoner associated with Reynold, also shows both quarterings of Bray. For Bray's 'historical' searches, see below, p. 155.

29. CP 25(1)79/97, Nos. 41, 42; E 136/79/12; GEC vii. pp. 4–11; VCH Gloucestershire vi. p. 100.
30. Below, p. 156.
31. C 137/71/17; E 383/395 Oxon and Berks; CP 40/903 rot.360d, ibid. rot.cart. rot. 1; E 210/5967–70, 5529, 5593; CP 40/773 rot.415; ibid. rot.cart. rot.1; see also below, p. 000.
32. CP 40/902 rot.154–154d; CP 40/906 rot.454; E 199/17/1; E 383/380 Suth; E 383/386 Suth; PROB 11/13 f.219v; CIPM Henry VII, iii. No. 626.
33. Barron, 'Brays of Shere', p. 2; Visitation of Bedfordshire, F.A. Blaydon (ed.), (Harleian Soc. xix, 1884), p. 162; BL MS Add 5833 f.67v; BL MS Harl 6157 f.4.
34. WAM 5472, 12181–90, passim; C 237/53/168; M.M. Condon, Itinerary of Henry VII (in preparation); History of the King's Works, H. Colvin and others, (eds), iv (1982), pp. 344–5.
35. WAM 12190 f.76; WAM 16056; PROB 11/14 f.134; CPR 1485–94, p. 128; E 159/265, recorda Mich. rot.23; WAM 32350; PROB 11/13 f.219.
36. CPR 1485–1494, pp. 139, 145; Materials for a History of the Reign of Henry VII, W.Campbell (ed.), (2 vols RS 1877), i. p. 61; E 159/263 brevia directa Mich. rot.11; GMR 85/6/40 m.1d. In the confusion of 1485 a patent of 5 September is not impossible, if unlikely; that of 25 September 1485 is not enrolled.
37. GMR 85/22/4; GMR 85/13/96; CAD iii. C 3273; CPR 1467–77, pp. 22, 68; RP vi. pp. 296–7; E 136/214/1; Materials, i. pp. 229, 295; Calendar of Ormond Deeds, E. Curtis (ed.), (6 vols Dublin 1932), iii. pp. 279–80, 285–7, 319.
38. CIPM Henry VII, ii, No. 434. The date of the grant is unknown.
39. CP 40/933 rot.262–262d; CP 25(1)/232/78, Nos. 44–46; cf VCH Surrey iii. p. 114.
40. SC 11/828, 829, 832; SC 12/18/50; E 101/413/2/3, 56; GMR 85/6/1 m.1; GMR 85/6/40; GMR 85/13/99; CP 25(1)/232/78 No. 56.
41. GMR 85/13/146; CP 25(1)/232/78 No. 56.
42. GMR 85/6/1; GMR 85/6/18; GMR 85/6/40; CP 25(1)/232/78 Nos. 65, 73; above, n.36.
43. The Book of Reckonings and other Memoranda 1500–1612 of the Church of St James, Shere, E.R. Hougham (ed.), (1978), p. 1.
44. William Smith, William Hody, William Cope, and Hugh Oldham passed from Margaret's service to the King's; Nicholas Compton was one of Bray's deputies as receiver-general; Humphrey Coningsby her councillor; and John Shaw her favoured goldsmith; WAM 12190 ff.93v-98; WAM 32355; WAM 31795; WAM 32364; SC 6/Hen VII/1238; SJC MS D91.17, pp. 3, 9, 26–7, 65, 67; M.G. Underwood, 'Politics and Piety in the Household of Margaret Beaufort', JEH xxxviii (1987), pp. 43–5; and below, n.73.
45. WAM 32364, 32390, 32355; SJC MS D91.17 pp. 37–8, 61, 63; SJC MS D91.20 ff.17, 25; SJC MS D102.9. f.183; Privy Purse Expenses of Elizabeth of York, N.H. Nicolas (ed.), (1880), passim.
46. CPR 1485–94, pp. 114, 231, 315, 380; CIPM Henry VII iii, Nos. 871–2; RP vi. pp. 275–8; E 159/267, brevia directa Hil. rot.10; for a perceptive general comment, see M.A. Hicks, 'Attainder, Resumption and Coercion, 1461–1529', Parliamentary History iii (1984), p. 19.
47. PSO 2/3, 10, 12 July 1 Hen. VII; CPR 1485–1494, p. 230; Hicks, 'Attainder', pp. 19–25; J.R. Lander, 'Attainder and Forfeiture, 1453–1509', Crown and Nobility 1450–1509 (1976), p. 145; CP 40/935 rot.239–239d; C 54/356 m.13d; Bedfordshire CRO BS/1; above, n.45.
48. WAM 3387; WAM 9219 A-D; E 154/2/10, f.10; M. Howard, The Early Tudor Country House (1987), pp. 22, 213. See also M.K. Jones, 'Collyweston – An Early Tudor Palace', England in the Fifteenth Century, D. Williams (ed.), (Woodbridge 1987), pp. 130–132; below, n. 158.
49. Place Name Soc. Beds, p. 121.
50. CPR 1485–94, p. 307; CPR 1494–1509, pp. 57, 73; CCR 1485–1500, No. 993;

C 82/157, 1 Dec.; *RP* vi. pp. 503–6; *CIPM Henry VII*, iii, No. 993.

51. *CCR 1485–1500*, No. 912; *Warwickshire Feet of Fines, 1345–1509*, L. Drucker (ed.), (Dugdale Soc. xviii, 1943), pp. 207–8; surrender by copy of court roll: photograph in Warwicks CRO, for which I am indebted to M. Farr. See also M.A. Hicks, 'Descent, Partition and Extinction: The "Warwick Inheritance"', *BIHR* lii. pp. 125–6; 'The Beauchamp Trust 1439–87', *BIHR* liv. pp. 135–49; *Ministers' Accounts of the Warwickshire Estates of the Duke of Clarence 1479–80*, R.H. Hilton (ed.), (Dugdale Soc. xxi, 1952), pp. x–xi. I am indebted to Dr Hicks for help with this point.

52. M.M. Condon, 'Ruling Elites in the Reign of Henry VII', *Patronage, Pedigree and Power in Later Medieval England*, C.D. Ross (ed.), (Gloucester 1979), pp. 124–5, 131–2; E 314/49; E 36/130 f.134v; *CPR 1485–94*, *CPR 1494–1509*, passim.

53. *CPR 1485–94*, pp. 382, 450, 470; *CPR 1494–1509*, pp. 22, 39; Somerville, i. pp. 561, 631, 636–7.

54. Condon, 'Ruling Elites', p. 116; DL 37/62 m.37d, paraphrased in Somerville, i. p. 524.

55. Somerville, i. p. 541; M.K. Jones, 'Lady Margaret Beaufort, the Royal Council, and an Early Fenland Drainage Scheme', *Lincolnshire History and Archaeology* xxi (1986), p. 14; DL 29/264/4141; DL 29/404/6482; DL 29/404/6483; see also Somerville, i. p. 266: removal of an unsatisfactory deputy.

56. *CPR 1494–1509*, p. 22; *VCH Hampshire* v. p. 223; E 368/269 recorda Hil. rot.4–5; E 159/272 brevia directa Hil. rot.1; E 101/413/2/2, ff.14, 26, 36, 41v; SC 6/Hen VII/669; BL MS Harley Roll A 38 (I owe this reference to Dr M.A. Hicks); E 163/28/13.

57. DL 29/404/6483; DL 29/264/4141; DL 29/262/4142; DL 29/343/5567.

58. WAM 16031; perhaps the best and most relevant study of the variable equations between profit, influence and local office is *Letters and Accounts of William Brereton of Malpas*, E.W. Ives (ed.), (Lancs. and Chesh. Rec. Soc., cxvi, 1976), pp. 15–33; see also R.A. Griffiths, 'Public and Private Bureaucracies in England and Wales in the Fifteenth Century', *TRHS* 5th ser. (1980), pp. 109–30.

59. PROB 11/13 f.195.

60. *BROU* i. p. 251; SC 6/Hen VII/1373; WAM 9216; *The Manuscripts of St George's Chapel, Windsor Castle*, J.N. Dalton (ed.), (Windsor 1957), p. 95; H.E. Reynolds, *Wells Cathedral* (Leeds n.d.), pp. 203–4.

61. Condon, 'Ruling Elites', p. 123; C. Rawcliffe, 'Baronial Councils in the Later Middle Ages', *Patronage, Pedigree and Power*, pp. 101–2; C. Rawcliffe and S. Flower, 'English Noblemen and Their Advisers: Consultation and Collaboration in the Later Middle Ages', *Journal of British Studies* xxv (1986), p. 159.

62. PROB 11/12 ff.29, 75v, 114; PROB 11/9 f.100; PROB 11/13 f.181.

63. WAM 16080; WAM 16025; WAM 13119; PROB 11/14 f.134; PROB 11/20 f.88; J. Armitage Robinson, 'Correspondence of Bishop Oliver King and Sir Reginald Bray', *Proc. Som. Arch. & Nat. Hist. Soc.* lx (1914), pp. 1–4; E 210/9904; Condon and Guth, *Bray Letters*.

64. Condon, 'Anachronism', pp. 230, 242–3.

65. *CSPM* i. p. 335.

66. *CPR 1485–94*, p. 228; GMR 85/6/40; GMR 85/6/18; WAM 12190 ff.83v, 90.

67. *CPR 1485–94*, p. 98, 268; E 401/957, 18 Feb; PROB 11/14 f.99.

68. This is a theme which I hope to develop elsewhere.

69. *CPR 1494–1509*, p. 81; C 76/175 m.18; C 76/177 m.10; E 122/142/11 ff.27v–29; E 122/142/12 m.8; E 101/415/3 ff.6, 14v, 24v; E 101/690/4; Condon, 'Ruling Elites', p. 128.

70. Henry VII Close Roll Calendars need checking against the originals: cf. the trenchant and entirely justifiable criticisms of K.B. McFarlane in *EHR* lxxiv (1959), pp. 114–5. On the legal records, A.M.B. Simpson, *Introduction to the History of the Land Law* (Oxford 1961), pp. 112–31.

71. On which, J.M.W. Bean, *Decline of English Feudalism* (Manchester 1968), pp. 104–5; Simpson, *Land Law*, pp. 27–43.

72. CP 40/962 rot.414; CCR 1500–1509, No. 217; CP 25(1)/152/101 No. 83; C 1/257/ 42; above, n.39.

73. William Hody and Thomas Rogers, Margaret Beaufort's auditor, until c. 1488: above n.44 and WAM 12188 f.88v; to the names in n.44 add Richard Empson, attorney of the duchy, and John Cutte, duchy receiver-general and Bray's receiver at Eaton. The London merchant Henry Colet is the most frequent 'occasional' addition. The list is compiled from the plea roll refs. cited throughout this paper.

74. CP 25(1)294/83 Nos. 33–5, 39; CP 40/948 rot.381d; CP 40/962 rot.516; E 36/123 p. 93; E 210/5023; E 101/414/16 f.49; CCR 1485–1500, Nos. 577–8; CPR 1494–1509, pp. 304–5, 310.

75. E 40/3987; O. Manning and W. Bray, History and Antiquities of Surrey (3 vols 1804–14), iii. pp. 350–1; cf. a mortgage to Bray by Elizabeth Tanfield, CIPM Henry VII, iii, No. 1002.

76. C 1/279/45; CP 25(1)152/100 Nos. 42, 50; WAM 4695 ff.5–5v, 22–23, 24–25v; deed in the former Middlesex RO Acc. 446/ED1. Drayton was intended for Margaret's endowment to Westminster, Middx. RO Acc. 446/M.26.

77. CCR 1485–1500, No. 905; CP 40/937 rot.294d; CP 40/938 rot.cart. rot.2; CP 25(1)30/101 No. 30; PROB 11/13 f.116v; CCR 1500–1509, No. 147; below, p. 153.

78. CP 40/928 rot.349; cf. CP 25(2)/31/211 No. 13; CP 40/913 rot.150d, 356d; ibid, rot. cart. rot.1–1d; CP 25(1)294/79 Nos. 22, 49; CCR 1485–1500, No. 85; PROB 11/14 f.322v : the account in VCH Middlesex iii. p. 5 is oversimplified. An indenture of 1495 transfers seisin to feoffees undoubtedly his.

79. C 54/378 No. 30; see also GMR 85/13/149.

80. C 1/279/45; C 54/378 No. 30.

81. WAM 16077; SC 2/212/15.

82. C 1/187/88; cf. CP 25(1)/72/293 No. 54; CP 40/939 rot.cart. rot.2; C 54/378 No. 30; CPR 1494–1509, p. 84.

83. GMR 85/6/1; GMR 85/6/18; GMR 85/6/40; WAM 3387; WAM 9219; cf. CP 40/940 rot.113, recorded by way of a plea of debt.

84. GEC ii. pp. 133–135; below, p. 152; Lives of the Berkeleys, by John Smythe, J. Maclean (ed.), (2 vols 1883), ii. pp. 128–32, 136, 148–9; M.K. Jones, 'Sir William Stanley of Holt: Politics and Family Allegiance in the Late Fifteenth Century', Welsh History Review xiv (1988), p. 12. On the bishop, see R.J. Knecht, 'The Episcopate and the Wars of the Roses', University of Birmingham Historical Journal vi (1957–8), pp. 128–9; Epistolae Acadamiae Oxonienses, H. Anstey (ed.), (2 vols Oxford Hist. Soc. 1898), ii. pp. 513–22; CCR 1485–1500 No. 123.

85. CP 40/905 rot.450; CP 40/914 rot.cart. rot.1.

86. CCR 1485–1500 Nos. 552, 567, 758 (originals in E 326/12179, E 328/111); CIPM Henry VII ii. No. 679; CP 25(1)/72/293 No. 60; SC 6/Hen VIII/6878; E 111/1; E 159/284 recorda Trin. rot.39; C 1/76/33, 124.

87. CCR 1485–1500 Nos. 293, 294; CPR 1485–94, p. 200; CP 40/903 rot.352; CP 40/904 rot.356d; CP 40/905 rot.450; CP 40/910 rot.549; CP 40/914 rot.81, 151d; CP 40/915 rot.cart. rot.2.

88. CP 40/905 rot.cart. rot.1; above, n.84.

89. CP 25(1)/6/83 Nos. 13, 14; CP 25(1)/72/294 No. 123; GEC ii, p. 135; CP 40/962 rot.cart. rot.5; E 101/414/16 ff.110v, 256; WAM 9194; WAM 9195; for Berkeley's law suits, Lives of the Berkeleys, ii. pp. 154–72.

90. E 202/183, 187, 192, London & Middx, Som & Dors; E 159/274 recorda Easter rot.4d; WAM 16067. Fox and Sherborne, however, required the King's pardon before they, in turn, could be discharged: CPR 1494–1509, pp. 309, 366; E 159/280 recorda Trin. rot.14.

91. Above, n.86; E 326/12163; Formulare Anglicanum, T. Madox (ed.), (1702), pp. 213–4, 287–8 (from originals E 327/358, E 328/111); see also C 1/108/51.

92. CP 25(1)152/100 No. 40; WAM 4695 ff. 10–16, 22–27; WAM 4700; WAM 16181–2; Middx. RO Acc 446/ED1; SJC MS D91.20 f.30; plea in Middlesex against Thomas Stillington of Acaster Selby, CP 40/925 rot.168: the plea may, of course, be directly related to the land sales.
93. Below, pp. 153–4.
94. Condon, 'Ruling Elites', pp. 131–4; on the crucial importance of 1497, I. Arthurson, *1497: The Fulcrum of a Reign* (forthcoming); see also McFarlane, loc.cit., p. 114; G.R. Elton, 'Henry VII, Rapacity and Remorse', *Studies in Tudor and Stuart Politics and Government* (2 vols Cambridge 1974), i. pp. 58–61.
95. C 54/355 m.19A dorse; the abstract in *CCR 1485–1500* No. 842 is misleading; CP 40/929 rot.356.
96. CP 40/928 rot.349, 350; WAM 4695 ff.1–4.
97. Above, n.51; WAM 622; cf. WAM 655.
98. Above, pp. 145–6; A.H. Plaisted, *The Manor and Parish Records of Medmenham* (1925), pp. 73, 370–6; CP 40/935 rot.301d, 306; CP 40/936 rot.cart. rot.1–1d; CP 25(1)/6/83 No. 30; CP 25(1)/6/84 No. 40; WAM 16035; CP 40/939 rot.306; CP 40/946 rot.cart. rot.1; C 255/8/4 Nos. 15, 22.
99. *CCR 1485–1500* Nos. 1101, 1117; CP 40/946 rot.494d (bowdlerized at rot.491); CP 40/947 rot.310, 347, 349d, 378d; ibid. rot.cart. rot.2d, 3; CP 25(1)/294/80/76; other parcels were later added, CP25(1)/179/98 No. 74; E 101/415/3 f.288.
100. WAM 16041; *CPR 1494–1509*, p. 214.
101. *CCR 1485–1500* Nos. 1094, 1119, 1195; E 326/12184–5; CP 40/949 rot.114d, 364, 402; ibid. rot.cart. rot.3; CP 40/950, rot.315d, 316d; ibid. rot.cart. rot.4; CP 40/951 rot.cart. rot.3; CP 25(1)/13/88 Nos. 31, 33–6; PROB 11/13 f.93v; Bodl. MS DD Brocas Ci/21; SC 11/63; LR 2/187 ff.33–49; BL Add Ch 6272; KB 27/969 rex rot.5; KB 29/134 rot.5; W.E. Hampton, 'The White Rose under the First Tudors', *The Ricardian* vii (1987), pp. 464–6.
102. Above, p. 151.
103. CP 25(1)/179/98 No. 58; CP 40/947 rot.cart. rot.1d; E 101/414/16 f.28; cf. E 154/2/10 f.10; Condon, *Itinerary*; C 1/110/138; Baker, *Northampton* i. pp. 492–3; *CCR 1485–1500* No. 611.
104. *CCR 1485–1500*, No. 994; *Abstract of Feet of Fines relating to the County of Sussex from 1 Edward II to 24 Henry VII*, L.F. Salzman (ed.), (Sussex Rec. Soc. xxiii 1916), pp. 293, 299; WAM 1631; WAM 1596; WAM 9217; KB 27/958 rot.39d; CP 40/946 rot.cart.rot.1; below, p. 156; see also CP 40/921 rot.cart. rot.1–1d.
105. CP 40/950 rot.317; CP 25(1)294/80 No. 80; CP 25(1)257/66 No. 36; WAM 16078.
106. Above, p. 141; CP 40/948, rot.384; rot.cart. rot.1; CP 40/947 rot.315d; rot.cart. rot.1; Lincolnshire Archive Office Episcopal Reg. XXIII ff.389–389v.
107. CP 25(1)22/128 Nos. 51, 65; CP 40/952 rot.115, 107d; *VCH Buckinghamshire* ii. p. 368; *CCR 1500–1509* No. 60; E 101/415/3 f.186.
108. CP 40/953 rot.230; CP 40/954 rot.cart. rot.1; CP 40/956, rot.cart. rot.1; C 54/378 No. 30; E 368/277 brevia directa Hil. rot.1.; CP 25(1)/6/83 No. 29; *CCR 1500–1509* No. 75.
109. *CAD* vi, C 5745, C 4651; C 146/10846; CP 25(1)/202/42 no.29; STAC 2/6/34–45; C 1/279/46–9; C 1/391/57; C 1/612/22–23; C 142/28/29; the deeds are likely to have been exhibits in court. Cf. *VCH Somerset* iv. pp. 12–13.
110. CP 40/962 rot.313; REQ 1/104 ff.130–132v; REQ 2/13/51; REQ 2/12/178; cf. Baker, *Northampton*, i. pp. 162–3 and above, p. 141.
111. CP 40/957 rot.104d; CP 40/958 rot.518; CP 40/956 rot.311d; CP 25(1)260/29 No. 18; CP 25(1)/260/29 No. 20; CP 26(1)/30 Trin.16 Hen VII; WAM 16026.
112. CP 40/961 rot.360; *CCR 1500–1509* No. 201; E 101/546/18; E 159/280 recorda Mich rot.4; KB 27/963 rex rot.10.
113. CP 40/959 rot.116, 106d; CP 25(1)/22/128 No. 70; E 210/5023; above, p. 154.

114. CP 40/960 rot.304, 252d; CP 25(1)/128/60–62, 64, 67; BL MS Add 5833 f.67v; CP 25(1)/294/83 No. 42; CP 25(1)6/84 No. 45; CCR 1500–1509, No. 165.
115. CP 40/959 rot.110, 120 (bowdlerized 113d); CP 40/960 rot.253d, 278d; CP 40/961 rot.415; CP 40/962 rot.517d; CP 40/963 rot.456d; CP 40/964 rot.263d, 305, 412; CP 40/965 rot.107d, 410; CCR 1500–1509 Nos. 100, 144, 166, 233, 278; E 101/415/3 f.285v.
116. Above, p. 141; WAM 4023; WAM 4029; WAM 5469; WAM 16033–4; PROB 11/11 f.258v; CCR 1500–1509 No. 201.
117. BL MS Add 59899 ff.7v, 28; CPR 1494–1509, pp. 304, 350–1, 374–9; WAM 4551, 4019, 4046.
118. E 101/413/2/3, p. 63; C 82/245, 28 June; E 101/219/4 (no entry); CIPM Henry VII ii, No. 645, iii, No. 1141; PROB 11/13 ff.219–20; CCR 1500–1509 No. 196; cf. CCR 1485–1500 No. 1017; E 326/8096–8105.
119. Kent Archives Office MS U455/T138; E 383/485, Surrey & Sussex; CPR 1494–1509, p. 612; BL Add MS 38133 ff.95–95v; cf. CIPM Henry VII iii, No. 1141. Dudley resold the manors almost immediately at a profit.
120. PROB 11/13 ff.219–220; C 54/378 No. 30.
121. C.J. Harrison, 'The Petition of Edmund Dudley', EHR lxxxvii (1972), p. 88.
122. BL Add MS 59899 ff.157, 182; Condon, 'Ruling Elites', p. 128.
123. E 36/214 p. 230; Stoneyhurst College MS 60 f.1v.
124. GC pp. 325–6.
125. Elton, 'Rapacity and Remorse', pp. 60–1; Plumpton Correspondence, T. Stapleton (ed.), (CS iv, 1839), pp. 177–8.
126. Dugdale, Baronage ii. p. 303; McFarlane, EHR lxxiv. p. 114.
127. PROB 11/13 ff.219–20; PROB 11/15 ff.256v-257; SC 6/Hen VII/1843; A. Gray and F. Brittain, A History of Jesus College, Cambridge (2nd edn 1979), pp. 27–32; W. St John Hope, Windsor Castle: An Architectural History (2 vols 1913), ii. pp. 450–58.
128. E 36/285, ff.8–9.
129. Above, n.127; WAM 12175; WAM 4023; WAM 16069; WAM 16077; E 154/2/10 ff.8–10.
130. BL Add MS 59899 ff.157, 182; E 36/214 pp. 441, 474–5; Condon 'Ruling Elites', p. 128.
131. The evidence is deficient: but only Gilbert Talbot spoke for Bray in 1499. Yet two years later, this 'principal benefactor' of the college was a gartered knight; and by his death had even obtained papal confirmation of the college's privileges: Register of the Order of the Garter (2 vols 1724), i. pp. 239–43; entry of obit in August calendar, 'Notice of a Sarum Breviary in the possession of John Eliot Hodgkin', Miscellanea of the Philobiblon Society ix (1865–6): I owe this to Dr N. Ramsay.
132. GC p. 325.
133. Above, p. 158; BROU i. pp. 462–4; ii. pp. 1147–9. 1396–7; iii. 1721–2; WAM 16035; E 154/2/10; Stoneyhurst MS 60 f.104v.
134. Condon, 'Anachronism', p. 230; Condon and Guth, Bray Letters; Metcalfe, Knights, p. 27; BL Add MS 46354 f.98v.
135. SC 11/63.
136. St John Hope, Windsor Castle, ii. pp. 450–8; S. Anglo, 'Henry VII's Dynastic Hieroglyphs', The Historian x (1986), pp. 3–8. The precise location of Bray's tomb is unknown; and his badges are found in both aisles and transepts, as well as his chantry – 175 times, by one count: M. Bond, The Romance of St George's Chapel, Windsor Castle (14th edn Windsor 1987), 22. He would, however, perhaps have appreciated the irony by which his chantry has been appropriated for the chapel shop, the profits of which contribute to the fabric fund : a truly 'perpetual alms'.

Select Personal Name Index